Oklahoma's Indian New Deal

Oklahoma's Indian New Deal

Jon S. Blackman

University of Oklahoma Press : Norman

Library of Congress Cataloging-in-Publication Data

Blackman, Jon S., 1946–
  Oklahoma's Indian new deal / Jon S. Blackman. — First edition.
      pages cm
  Includes bibliographical references and index.
  ISBN 978-0-8061-4351-4 (paperback)
  1. United States. Oklahoma Welfare Act 2. Indians of North America—Legal status, laws, etc.—History—20th century. 3. Indians of North America—Legal status, laws, etc.—Oklahoma—History—20th century. I. Title.
  KF8205.B58 2013
  342.7308'72—dc23
                    2012042872

The paper in this book meets the guidelines for permanence and durability of the Committee on Production Guidelines for Book Longevity of the Council on Library Resources, Inc. ∞

Copyright © 2013 by the University of Oklahoma Press, Norman, Publishing Division of the University. Manufactured in the U.S.A.

All rights reserved. No part of this publication may be reproduced, stored in a retrieval system, or transmitted, in any form or by any means, electronic, mechanical, photocopying, recording, or otherwise—except as permitted under Section 107 or 108 of the United States Copyright Act—without the prior written permission of the University of Oklahoma Press. To request permission to reproduce selections from this book, write to Permissions, University of Oklahoma Press, 2800 Venture Drive, Norman OK 73069, or email rights.oupress@ou.edu.

Contents

List of Illustrations	vii
Acknowledgments	ix
Introduction	3
1. Removal to Indian Territory	12
2. The Winds of Change	33
3. The Indian New Deal	54
4. Oklahoma's Newer New Deal	78
5. Revival	117
Conclusion	147
Appendices	
A. The Indian Reorganization Act	159
B. The Thomas-Rogers Bill (First Draft Introduced in Congress)	167
C. The Oklahoma Indian Welfare Act	181
D. Oklahoma Tribes Organized under the OIWA by 1950	189
Notes	193
Bibliography	213
Index	221

Illustrations

FIGURES

John Collier	104
A. C. Monahan	105
William Zimmerman	106
William A. Durant	107
A. M. Landman and Roly Canard	108
John Collier in Zion National Park	109
Delos Lone Wolf at meeting of Kiowas, Comanches, and Apaches	110
Theodore Haas	111
John Collier, M. L. Hannifan, and J. E. White	112
Phillips-Skelly No. 1 oil well	113
U.S. Senator Thomas with U.S. Representatives Cartwright and Rogers	114
"Backward March Commands John Collier" (political cartoon)	115
Indian agricultural laborer's house	116

MAPS

Tribal locations in Oklahoma	14
Oklahoma and Indian Territories, 1900	25

Acknowledgments

While it is impossible to mention and thank all who contributed in one way or another to this book, there are some who went the extra mile in helping me. I would be remiss if I did not publicly state my deep appreciation for the efforts of Dr. Thomas Pearcy and Dr. Brian Q. Cannon at Brigham Young University; Dr. Warren Metcalf, Dr. Albert Hurtado, Dr. Lindsey Robertson, and Dr. Terry Rugeley at the University of Oklahoma (OU); Bill Welge at the Oklahoma Historical Society; Carolyn Hanneman at OU's Carl Albert Center; and John Lovett at OU's Western History Collection. All guided, suggested, and encouraged me along the way, and without their help this book would never have materialized.

Oklahoma's Indian New Deal

Introduction

In 1836, during the Mashpee Revolt in Massachusetts, William Apes, a Pequot religious figure, published his famous "Eulogy on King Philip." The year 1836 also witnessed implementation of Andrew Jackson's removal policy. Apes wrote a speech that Metacom, war chief for the Wampanoags, might have given in the 1670s during King Philip's War. To rally his people, Apes stated,

> Brothers—you see this vast country before us the Great Spirit gave to our fathers . . . and you now see the foe before you, that they have grown insolent and bold; that all our ancient customs are disregarded; that treaties made by our fathers and us are broken. . . . Brothers these people from the unknown world will cut down our groves, spoil our hunting and planting grounds, and drive us and our children from the graves of our fathers, and our council fires, and enslave our women and children.[1]

Almost a century later, in 1934, President Franklin Roosevelt sent a message to Congress in an effort to build congressional support for the Wheeler-Howard Bill, which proposed a transforming overhaul of federal Indian policy. His words seemed to call for a restructuring of the world forced upon Native Americans by white Americans during the previous three hundred years. Roosevelt stated, in part: "It is in the main a measure of justice that is long overdue. We can and should, without further delay, extend to the Indian the fundamental rights of political liberty and local self-government and the opportunities of education and economic assistance that they require in order to attain a wholesome American life."[2]

The Indian Reorganization Act (IRA) became law in June of 1934 and marked a major shift in federal Indian policy. With its passage, the disastrous allotment policy instituted in 1887 ended. The policy had divided Indian lands into small parcels of individually owned property while opening millions of acres of Indian land to non-Indian settlement. U.S. Indian policy now focused on consolidation of Indian land, organization of tribal government, and economic development. The architect of the IRA, FDR's commissioner of Indian affairs from 1933 to 1945, John Collier, was an aggressive reformer. His many efforts and successes with the Indian New Deal are still legendary. Collier was the most influential person in federal "Indian affairs" in the twentieth century. Many scholars consider the IRA to have been the most important piece of twentieth-century federal legislation dealing with Indian affairs. Closely tied to the IRA was another piece of legislation enacted in 1936. The Oklahoma Indian Welfare Act (OIWA) brought the benefits of the IRA—the end of the allotment policy, the formation of tribal governments, and economic programs—to Oklahoma Indians along with other significant gains. While the IRA continues to receive a great deal of attention by scholars, the OIWA has been virtually ignored. This book focuses on the Oklahoma Indian Welfare Act—its origins, enactment, implementation, impact, and—most important—its unique significance as part of the Indian New Deal.

Politicking of the Oklahoma congressional delegation exempted Oklahoma Indians from six significant provisions of the Indian Reorganization Act in 1934. U.S. senator Elmer Thomas (D-Okla.) had this exemption incorporated into the bill as section 13. It was overwhelmingly approved by both houses since few members represented significant Indian populations (most generally deferred to legislators who had significant Indian populations in their districts). Yet just two years later, the Oklahoma Indian Welfare Act was enacted, providing virtually all the benefits contained in the IRA and then some. In 1935, Senator Thomas became chair of the Senate Committee on Indian Affairs, while fellow Oklahoma congressman Will Rogers (not the humorist or his son but the one who represented

Oklahoma's at-large district from 1933–1943) served as chair of the House Committee on Indian Affairs. Senator Thomas had proved instrumental in blocking application of the IRA to Oklahoma Indians in June 1934. Ironically, just eighteen months later Thomas and Rogers cosponsored a "Newer New Deal" for Oklahoma Indians in the form of the Thomas-Rogers Bill, known after its enactment in 1936 as the Oklahoma Indian Welfare Act (OIWA).

The OIWA was one of several significant pieces of Indian legislation enacted during the 1930s that are known collectively as the Indian New Deal. Besides the IRA, other acts included the Pueblo Relief Act (1933), the Johnson O'Malley Act (1934), the Indian Arts and Crafts Act (1935), and the Alaska Reorganization Act (1936). Except for an article, "John Collier and the Oklahoma Indian Welfare Act," written by Peter M. Wright more than thirty years ago, and a book chapter, "The New Deal for Indians" by Carter Blue Clark, little scholarly interest has focused directly on the OIWA. Wright confined himself to a brief legislative history of the OIWA. With the passage of almost four decades, it now seems incomplete and offers little of substance from the Indian perspective. Clark's chapter is a useful but partial exploration of both the IRA and the OIWA.[3]

The Oklahoma Indian Welfare Act of 1936, a New Deal measure aimed specifically at Oklahoma Indians, provides an important chapter in understanding the reform efforts of John Collier in the Sooner State. This book explores the OIWA from several perspectives, and focuses specifically on Oklahoma Indian views and involvement. Oklahoma Indians remained divided over the act, with some supporting and others opposing it, and they were involved in the political process in different ways, attempting to promote their particular interests and viewpoints. The vast majority probably demonstrated little concern with the OIWA, perhaps for reasons of daily survival exacerbated by the drudgery and hardship of the Great Depression. This book contends that, involved or not, Oklahoma Indians and their descendants felt the impact of the OIWA in a number of ways. Over several decades, federal allotment was formally ended, tribes were encouraged to organize for political and economic purposes, and economic development for both tribal groups and individuals was encouraged and fostered by funding available through credit associations. In short, the OIWA allowed Oklahoma tribes and individuals to improve their lot.

This book begins with a brief examination of the conditions Oklahoma Indians faced before the New Deal, and it concludes with an analysis of the impact of the OIWA up to the beginning of the termination era in Indian affairs when House Concurrent Resolution 108 was passed in 1953. (HCR 108 proposed that federal supervision of Indian tribes be ended and that American Indians become subject to the same laws and responsibilities as non-Indian citizens.) In many ways, the situation of Oklahoma Indians was unique. While tribes in western Oklahoma were segregated from much of non-Indian society through confinement to remote reservations, the landholdings of many eastern Oklahoma tribes became inundated with non-Indian farmers, miners, and oil people, and flourishing non-Indian communities. The exploitation of Indian land and resources took place with an intensity seen nowhere else in the country. Non-Indian leaders considered Oklahoma Indians further along the road to assimilation than Indians in other parts of the country. Many Oklahoma Indians, ones sometimes labeled "progressives," shared the belief that the IRA and then its stepchild, the OIWA, were steps in the wrong direction, keeping them bound to reservations and segregated from non-Indian society. At the time of the New Deal in the 1930s, a large percentage of the country's Indian population resided in Oklahoma. Nowhere else in the United States could a wider concentration of tribal affiliations and cultural perspectives be found. Understanding the background of Oklahoma Indians at the time of the New Deal is critical in considering questions that arise. Why (and how) were Oklahoma Indians initially exempted from six of nineteen provisions of the Indian Reorganization Act of 1934? Why just two years later was the Oklahoma Indian Welfare Act passed, giving Oklahoma Indians virtually everything contained in the IRA and then some?

Nationally, the Indian New Deal helped open the door to the self-determination movement that flourished in the 1960s and 1970s, and the OIWA, in many respects an arm of the IRA, was as important for Oklahoma Indians as the IRA was for American Indians elsewhere.

In Oklahoma, vocal non-Indian opposition to the Indian New Deal was concentrated in the eastern half of the state, and it represented a variety of interests, including oil, timber, mining, farming, and ranching. Most of these people, who masked their intentions by professing belief in Indian assimilation and participation into non-Indian society, had long participated in what historian Angie Debo termed "an orgy of graft and corruption" with respect to Indian land and resources.[4] The Thomas-Rogers Bill introduced to Congress in February 1935 threatened the status quo and they reacted vigorously. Farmers, ranchers, miners, oil magnates, lawyers, judges, and state legislators coalesced around Oklahoma congressman Wesley Disney. Disney's dogged opposition to the Thomas-Rogers Bill throughout the legislative process resulted in a large number of amendments and several sections being dropped completely. Most significant of these was a proposal to remove control over Indian probate matters, involving the restricted allotments of the "Five Civilized Tribes" in eastern Oklahoma (Cherokees, Chickasaws, Choctaws, Seminoles, and Creeks) from the jurisdiction of the Oklahoma county court system and place these allotments under the control of the Interior Department. If this particular proposal had been enacted, the "orgy" of exploitation that characterized Indian affairs in Oklahoma before the Indian New Deal might have ended abruptly.

John Collier, chief architect for both the IRA and the OIWA, fought tenaciously to secure passage of both legislative proposals. His legacy with respect to enactment and implementation of the IRA is well known and continues to be explored by scholars. His involvement with the OIWA, though, is an important factor in this book. Just days before congressional approval of the IRA in June of 1934, Senator Thomas had thwarted Collier's efforts, securing exemption for Oklahoma Indians from six important provisions of act. Thomas was an assimilationist and fervently opposed the efforts of Indian policy reformers such as John Collier. Thomas also clearly knew what side his political bread was buttered on—Oklahoma whites, not Oklahoma Indians, kept returning him to Washington. So why did Thomas, who was, with Disney and Rogers, responsible for blocking passage of the IRA until it was tailored to exempting Oklahoma Indians from it, do an about-face in a short period of time and support Collier and others in their attempts to bring the New Deal to Oklahoma Indians?

Shortly after enactment of the revised IRA, Collier visited Oklahoma at the invitation of Thomas to develop a legislative proposal tailored for Oklahoma Indians, one that would bring them the benefits of the Indian New Deal. Collier and Thomas held seven Indian congresses across the state addressing the fears and misconceptions held by many Oklahoma Indians concerning individual allotments, the removal of restrictions on the sale of land, programs for long-term economic development, and the renewal of tribal governments. The relationship between Collier and Thomas is a classic American political battle, pitting Thomas's assimilationist ideology against John Collier's reform agenda, referred to by some as the "tribal alternative," and this is part of the story that develops as this book progresses.

Collier's shadow continued to loom over both the IRA and the OIWA—and over all federal Indian policy. For two decades following the New Deal years, he provided the widely accepted interpretation of the Indian New Deal, with a definition of assimilation that proved at odds with the traditional viewpoint of the Indian being incorporated into American society. Collier asserted, "Assimilation, not into our culture but into modern life, and preservation and intensification of heritage are not hostile choices, excluding one another, but are interdependent through and through."[5] In his words, "The New Deal told the Indians: you are of the world and the world is of you. Draw now on your own deep powers; come out of your silence; choose your own way, but let your way lead to the present and future world. The huge past in you has a huge future—a world future—now."[6] Collier structured his writing to throw favorable light on himself and his administration, but nevertheless it contains valuable insights found nowhere else. He envisioned a future with Indians participating in American economic, political, and social institutions as equal partners, while at the same time maintaining their cultural heritage.

Collier believed, according to historian E. A. Schwartz, that the "Indian New Deal was not as effective as it could have been, because of 'the institutional structure of the government's Indian Service. That service was no-wise [sic] autonomous; but was geared to the Government's budget-making and congressional appropriations, and the Government's all-embracing system of civil service and job classification.'"⁷ The careers of many Indian Affairs employees had been flavored by assimilationist ideology that was deeply ingrained in their psyches. Collier's policies represented change they did not understand and could not accept, and many fought doggedly to maintain the status quo.

Besides investigating why Senator Thomas came to support the OIWA, there are other good questions. Congressman Disney, from the First Congressional District in eastern Oklahoma, was the political figure that many groups and interests in Oklahoma coalesced around to focus opposition to the OIWA. What provoked his vehement and sustained opposition? Finally, why would Senator Thomas, along with other New Deal legislators such as Montana senator Burton K. Wheeler, cosponsor of the Indian Reorganization Act, later join together in the early 1940s and push for repeal of both the IRA and OIWA?

An important but almost totally unexplored chapter of the OIWA story is that of its impact. What effect did the act have on Oklahoma Indians? Did it solve or create problems for them, or both? Historian Angie Debo and Interior Department solicitor Theodore Haas both examined the impact of Indian New Deal legislation. Their work spanned the late 1940s and 1950s and continues to stand alone. No one has followed them to further explore the impact of the OIWA. Debo's research provided case studies of a number of Indian families, but for the most part remains unpublished. Haas published a sterile statistical report pertaining to the IRA, a study with a nationwide perspective that included figures for Oklahoma and the OIWA. At best, both studies relate only a small, incomplete history of the OIWA and its effect on the Indian people of Oklahoma.

Perhaps of greater importance to me researching this history are abstract influences, factors difficult to quantify. Oklahoma tribal governments were impeded by legislative enactments, judicial reorganization, and executive policy during the 1890s and early twentieth century. The OIWA offered a mechanism whereby Oklahoma Indians could organize or reorganize their tribal governments. While eighteen out of twenty-nine tribal groups in the state would organize tribal governments under the OIWA up to the 1950s, they represented only about 10 percent of the Oklahoma Indian population. With respect to the Five Tribes, only three Creek towns would organize under the OIWA during the time period of this study, 1936–1953. The rest would organize later, in the 1980s, either under the OIWA or under their tribal sovereignty. In spite of these statistics, the Indian New Deal affected most Oklahoma Indians significantly. Indian law scholar Carter Blue Clark believes the IRA and the OIWA "rekindled a tribal fire of survival that had been all but completely extinguished" among Oklahoma Indians and contributed later to "Indian nationalism that erupted in the militancy of the 1960s."[8] Historian Donald Parman contends the Indian New Deal "planted the seeds of Indian tribal autonomy" that emerged during the last three decades of the twentieth century."[9] This book agrees with these conjectures and explores them more fully.

Most of the limited research directed toward uncovering the story of the OIWA is confined to the legislative struggle to secure its passage, waged by non-Indian legislators and bureaucrats. Since Indian participation was included in the record only when it showed support of non-Indian perspective and interests, but was otherwise relegated to the shadows, the inclusion of the Indian voice here is integral in telling the complete story. According to Richard Greene, the tribal historian for the Chickasaws, the amount of written source material created by tribal members declined dramatically after the Curtis Act of 1898 brought about the dissolution of tribal governments.[10] However, detective work can bring to light an understanding of Indian involvement and opinion. Historian Donald Parman believes that many "scholars present strong prefatory promises that their [studies] will reveal the Indian perspective, disclose the Indian voice, and portray Indians as active participants in the story, but the [studies] deal almost entirely with non-Indian actions and policy matters."[11] While the involvement of non-Indians is certainly a part of the story, this book includes Indian perspective and covers Indian involvement in the enactment and implementation of the OIWA. As Erik M. Zissu, author of *Blood Matters*, writes, Oklahoma "tribal members did not relinquish the political initiative; they were not reduced to helplessness. Instead, they undertook political activity and fashioned a renewal of their collective identity."[12] Historian William

Cronan has written, "Being overpowered is not a sign of passivity."¹³ Oklahoma Indians may have lacked political sophistication, but they were not passive. Though limited in their access to power in non-Indian society, and often blocked from diverting non-Indian encroachment, Oklahoma Indians struggled against the tide of change in a variety of manners, and this book explores that struggle.

The OIWA can be located under the broad umbrella of the Indian New Deal. Oklahoma Indians exempted from the most significant provisions of the IRA in 1934 became the focus of the OIWA, a broader reform measure, in 1936. Oklahoma Indians demonstrated divisions over their support for a "Newer New Deal," divisions that certainly affected the development and implementation of the act. Oklahoma Indians were not exempt from the Great Depression, World War II, industrialization, and urban growth, and these forces too are a vital part of the story. Finally, there is the most important issue of the impact of the OIWA on Oklahoma Indians. While most scholars recognize the IRA as a watershed event in twentieth-century Indian affairs, can the same be said for the OIWA and Oklahoma Indians? This book focuses on examining these issues and underscore the Indian story behind the act. The OIWA was indeed "Oklahoma's Newer New Deal" for its Indian citizens and it was an important chapter in the Indian New Deal.

CHAPTER 1

Removal to Indian Territory

> For what crime then was this whole nation doomed to this perpetual death? Simply because they would not agree to a principle which would be at once death to their national existence... [would] set aside the authority of the national council & principal chief... and [would] dispose of the whole public domain, as well as the private property of individuals, and render the whole nation houseless & homeless at pleasure.
> —Reverend Daniel Butrick, December 31, 1838[1]

Daniel Butrick served as a Methodist missionary among the Cherokees in Georgia for twenty years prior to their forced removal during the winter of 1837. He accompanied the Cherokees on their journey to Indian Country and penned the above words on New Year's Eve, while the group hunkered down, waiting for a raging snow and ice storm to dissipate. Butrick reflected on events among the Cherokees over the year that was ending. As we look back now, much of what Butrick wrote seems prophetic. All Oklahoma Indians—not just the Cherokees, not just the Five Tribes, but also tribal groups from the Great Plains that were removed to Indian Territory over the balance of the nineteenth century—would suffer the fate predicted by Butrick.[2]

To understand the Oklahoma Indian Welfare Act and its impact on Oklahoma Indians requires a brief overview of significant events and forces occurring between the 1830s and the 1930s. This first chapter is not designed as a comprehensive history of Oklahoma tribal groups but instead provides a selective overview of their experiences, showing a people uniquely forged by removal, the Civil War, Reconstruction, rapid westward expansion of non-Indians into Indian Territory, and industrialization and commercialization during the late nineteenth and early twentieth centuries. These broad themes of the era's American history channeled the course of Native American history. However, Oklahoma Indians stood apart from other Native Americans. Historical events and circumstances molded them in unique ways, and the OIWA was birthed and implemented with that uniqueness in mind.

A portion of the expansive Louisiana Purchase designated as the Indian Territory became the state of Oklahoma in 1907. Tribal groups including the Osages, Quapaws, Wichitas, Caddos, Comanches, and Kiowas inhabited this area for generations. Several tribes from the East—bands of Choctaws, Chickasaws, and Cherokees—seasonally undertook hunting expeditions into what is now eastern Oklahoma. During the first two decades of the nineteenth century, a number of Kickapoos, Delawares, Shawnees, Sauks, and Foxes, all from north of the Ohio River, voluntarily removed themselves to lands west of the Mississippi in the face of white westward expansion. With rapid expansion of the cotton culture, the "Indian problem" (as the federal government termed the perceived need for removal) became particularly acute across the Deep South, involving those Indians designated the Five Civilized Tribes.[3]

Andrew Jackson's exploits as an Indian fighter partly created his national image. A southerner and a strong nationalist, he lived also as a disciple of Jefferson's dream of the American nation firmly resting on the backs of self-sufficient, prosperous white yeoman farmers. Indians represented loathed obstacles in the path toward that dream. As president, Jackson was instrumental in influencing the course of federal Indian policy, pushing the Indian Removal Act through Congress in 1830. This legislation provided the mechanism by which the federal government accomplished removal and opened former Indian lands to non-Indian settlement. The Five Tribes endured a dramatic removal from the Old Southeast to Indian Territory during the 1830s. In a number of contrived agreements and treaties, these tribes ceded their valuable eastern lands for huge tracks of land in Indian Territory few had seen. The treaties promised the lands would remain theirs as long "as the grass grows and the rivers run."[4]

Removal, forced upon the Five Tribes in the Southeast, proved a divisive factor. A deep division occurred among the Cherokees in late 1835 when a minority faction signed the Treaty of New Echota,

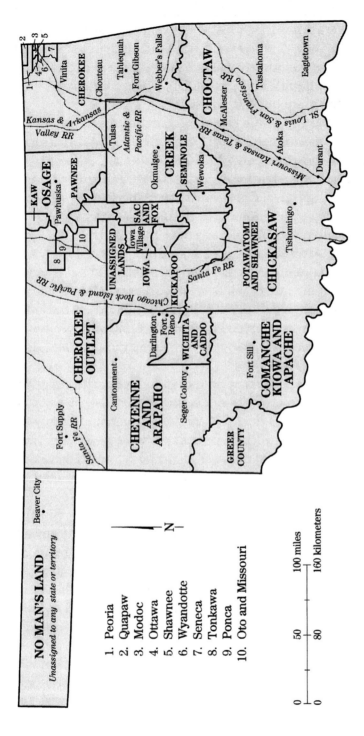

Tribal locations in Oklahoma. From John W. Morris, Charles Robert Goines, and Edwin C. McReynolds, *Historical Atlas of Oklahoma* (Norman: University of Oklahoma Press, 1987). Reprinted by permission from the University of Oklahoma Press.

thereby relinquishing their homeland in the southeast for $5 million and accepting removal west of the Mississippi River. This group, known as the Treaty Party, was led by John Ridge, Major Ridge (John's father), Elias Boudinot, and Stand Watie. The group was vehemently opposed by John Ross, principal chief of the Cherokee nation, and Cherokees known as the National Party, who lobbied hard, attempting to have the U.S. Senate not ratify the treaty, which they believed was a sellout of not only their lands, but their tribal history and culture as well. Ross's attempts proved unsuccessful when the Senate approved the treaty by one vote in May of 1836. The stage was now set for removal to Indian Territory. Relinquishing property and possessions, thousands were forcibly marched to Indian Territory over what the Cherokees called the Trail of Tears. Most experienced horrendous physical and psychological suffering. At the end of 1838, the Reverend Daniel Butrick lamented the Indian experience, "O what a year it has been! O what a sweeping wind has gone over, and carried its thousands into the grave, while thousands of others have been tortured and scarcely survive, and the whole nation comparatively thrown out of house & home during this most dreary winter."[5] Thousands died along the way from disease, starvation, or exposure.

Disgruntled tribal members assassinated several leaders of the Treaty Party, including Major Ridge, John Ridge, and Elias Boudinot, shortly after their arrival in Indian Territory in 1839.[6] By the 1930s, few if any of the Indian participants in the removal of the 1830s were alive. However, the legacy of their hardships, losses, and sufferings were passed down from generation to generation. The experience of forced removal became a bitter part of the collective tribal memory, continuing to flavor Indian-white relations as well as Indian-Indian relations for generations.

During the interlude between removal and the Civil War, the Five Tribes flourished in Indian Territory, isolated from the influences of non-Indian civilization to the east. These groups proved resilient and in a little over a generation rebuilt a lifestyle in Indian Territory rivaling that which they had enjoyed in the East. However, the Civil War was a watershed event in Indian Territory. Native Americans found themselves caught in the middle of a confrontation that tore the nation into warring factions, with each side fighting for dominance and survival. Some members of the Five Tribes were prosperous slave owners and felt closely linked to the cotton culture of the South. Other groups within the Five Tribes directed their loyalty to the North. The Civil War became a divisive and emotional issue. The war affected no Indian groups across the nation as strongly and in such a manner as it did those in Indian Territory.

During the Civil War, both the South and the North placed a strategic value on Indian Territory for several reasons. In order to help sustain their war effort, the South obtained much-needed agricultural products, including wheat and corn, as well as beef, horses, and minerals such as salt and lead for ammunition from Indian Territory. Southerners also viewed Indian Territory as part of the gateway for expansionist plans into the American West. Indian Territory served as a buffer between Texas and Union Kansas and provided a base of Confederate operations for launching invasions into the southwestern territories. The North took a decidedly opposite viewpoint on these issues, which resulted in Indian Territory becoming a battleground during the war.

Among the tribes, factionalism existed between Union and Confederate sympathizers. While the Choctaws and Chickasaws remained fairly united in their support of the Confederacy, several hundred "Unionists" fled to Kansas and Union security. "Although their national [tribal] governments signed treaties with the Confederacy, the majority of [individual] Cherokee, Creek, and Seminoles seem to have favored the Union cause," writes Circe Sturm, author of *Blood Politics*, a book about the Cherokee nation of Oklahoma.[7]

The Civil War in Indian Territory seriously impaired much of the Indian population. By 1865, widows constituted one-third of the population in Indian Territory. Sixteen percent of the children were fatherless, with 14 percent orphaned.[8] Farm buildings, crops, and livestock were destroyed. Nearly one thousand members of the Five Tribes displaced by the war died in refugee camps. Marauding troops from both sides drove off an estimated three hundred thousand head of cattle. Many farms remained idle or even vacant during the war years and suffered physical deterioration.[9] With the weakening of tribal governments, disorder and lawlessness infiltrated

Indian Territory. Tribal governments lost annuities from the federal government and being cash-strapped they weakened and could not function effectively.

As the war ended, Reconstruction treaties were negotiated with each of the Five Tribes. These treaties continued protections from previous treaties, including express protections of tribal government. However, these treaties also would be the forerunner of dire consequences for all tribal groups. James Harlan, secretary of the interior and chief architect of the Reconstruction policy for Indian Territory, claimed his policy aimed at "territorialization: tribal unification under federal direction and with such a degree of subordination to Washington that white settlement of the Indian Territory, reallocation of tribal lands, and Statehood must soon follow."[10] Forced to cede varying amounts of land that collectively totaled over five million acres, the Five Tribes forfeited lands originally granted to the Indians by treaties for "as long the grass grows and the rivers run." The government asserted its authority to settle tribal groups from other parts of the country in west-central Indian Territory on lands ceded by the Cherokees. For example, the Lane-Pomeroy Plan obligated the Five Tribes to surrender part of their landholdings to Indians removed from lands in southern Kansas coveted by non-Indians. Federal officials viewed "Indian Territory [as] a conquered province" where the people had to "submit to the terms set by the conqueror," writes Oklahoma historian Arrell M. Gibson.[11]

Reconstruction treaties dealt a blow to tribal courts by allowing for "a court of courts [federal] to be established in said Territory with such jurisdiction and organization as Congress may prescribe."[12] Supplanting tribal courts inaugurated an important first step in preparation for statehood. Judicial reform served as a tool of the federal government to bring Indian Territory under its full authority, and "by the late 1890s, all the real authority in Indian territory lay with the federal courts," writes historian Jeffrey Burton.[13]

Finally, with the abolition of slavery, legally effected with the Thirteenth Amendment to the Constitution in December of 1865, another dynamic was introduced into Indian Territory. The Reconstruction treaties forced Indian slave owners to free their slaves. The Five Tribes handled this requirement in different ways, but the results were the same. Former slaves added to the mix of people within Indian Territory after the war. The freedmen and racially mixed black Indians offered opportunities for commerce, trade, exploitation, as well as serving as bridges between Indians and mainstream cultures. Freedmen formed another avenue for change within the region.[14]

Railroads proved a key ingredient in fulfilling the concept of Manifest Destiny across the North American continent. Congress aided the railroads with the Act of July 4, 1884, which approved railroad rights of way through Indian Territory. Many Indians discerned a pending threat to their way of life and survival. Cyrus Harris, Choctaw governor, stated: "But we, with any degree of certainty, continue with the hope of holding lands in common, when railroad agitators and land speculators are using all available means to open our country to the settlement of the whites."[15] Demonstrating an understanding and trust in the federal court system, the Five Tribes struggled aggressively and tenaciously during this time to maintain their land and way of life. The Cherokees attempted to fight the railroads through the judicial system, but saw their efforts thwarted with the decision in *Cherokee Nation v. Southern Kansas RR* (1889), which upheld the Act of July 4, 1884. By 1890, nine different railroads operated on one thousand miles of track in the territory.[16] Railroads were active in boosterism and drew more non-Indians into Indian Territory. Railroad companies joined other business groups in exerting pressure on the government to break up Indian communal landholdings and open these areas for settlement, development, and exploitation by non-Indian settlers. With statehood in 1907, operating rail track in Indian Territory had increased by more than 500 percent to almost 5,500 miles.[17] Railroad construction in turn fostered the growth of commercial farming and ranching, logging, mining, and manufacturing, which helped to open the floodgates of non-Indian settlement in Indian Territory even wider.

Divisions or factions within tribal groups proved an ongoing disruptive factor. Many scholars have categorized these factions as "traditionals," those resisting change and desiring to maintain their Native cultural heritage by eschewing assimilation into non-Indian society, and "progressives," those favoring a closer relationship with white society by incorporating non-Indian language, dress, technology, and business practices into their lifestyle. Though the traditional-progressive dichotomy facilitates scholars in explaining much of the divisiveness within tribal groups, the tags become misnomers. They lump tribal members into one of two groups, but the truth was often much more complex. This book will shun the use of that type of labeling.[18]

Jim Padgett, a Chickasaw, in speaking of the influx of non-Indians, the railroads, and commercialization said, "One side was in favor of progress, of accepting the white man's ways and opening up the country. What if Statehood came, they argued, wouldn't it be a good thing? The other side wanted this country for the Indian way, the land held in common by the tribes."[19] Edmund McCurtain, a Choctaw chief, attempted to bridge the separation between tribal groups. He recognized the dangers of factionalism, proclaiming, "Union is strength."[20] Over time, these divisions inhibited "tribal members from effectively confronting non-Indian settlement and federal authority," Erik Zissu writes.[21]

Following the war, westward expansion resumed with a frenzy. Veterans, freed slaves, immigrants, speculators, cattlemen, miners, farmers, and entrepreneurs descended on Indian Territory over the next several decades seeking opportunity. By 1890, 110,000 non-Indians, including 19,000 former slaves, outnumbered 50,000 Indian inhabitants, now representing only 39 percent of the population. By 1907 statehood, Indians comprised only 9 percent of Oklahoma's population.[22] With Indians a small minority in their own territory, non-Indian political, economic, and social institutions defined and controlled all facets of life. The experience of Oklahoma Indians remained unique. Indian Territory became a dumping ground for tribal groups from the Great Plains relocated to make room for non-Indian expansion, groups with differing histories, languages, and cultures gathered nowhere else in such close proximity.

A wide gulf existed between tribal groups removed from the Southeast and Plains Indians relocated to reservations in the western half of present-day Oklahoma, which became known as the Oklahoma Territory during the last half of the nineteenth century. The Five Tribes and other smaller tribes from east of the Mississippi occupied the eastern half of present-day Oklahoma, which became known as Indian Territory. The Five Tribes had experienced decades of partial assimilation of Euro-American thinking and practices and based their economy in agriculture. In the west, Cheyennes, Arapahos, Apaches, Kiowas, and Comanches rooted their lifestyle in traditional hunting and gathering. Even many former hunters maintained their other traditional cultural practices and shunned most contact with non-Indians as well as the Five Tribes to the east. These groups "existed as two wholly different peoples . . . [and] instead of creating a middle ground of cooperation and unity, they remained different, suspicious, and separated," writes historian David La Vere.[23] Creek chief Roley McIntosh expressed the general perspective of the Five Tribes toward the Plains Indians, stating, "These wild Indians depend almost altogether upon the chase for support, and their glory is war. We are anxious to pursue a different course. Our object is to cultivate the land, to support our families . . . and to preserve the peace not only with our white, but with our red brothers."[24] On the other hand, the Plains Indians looked upon the southeastern tribes as Indians but not as "brothers." They viewed them as weak—and as invaders of their lands. Avoidance of one another characterized the relationship of the two groups during this period. This gulf between began to be healed only in the years following World War II.

Unlike in many other places of the West, non-Indians in Indian Territory gradually mingled with the Indians rather than following a policy of removing or exterminating them. Even though non-Indians dominated Indians in sheer numbers, most tribal governments enforced a variety of restrictions. Communally held Indian land thwarted non-Indian ownership of the land they farmed. Non-Indians paid for work permits, fees, and taxes, with most Indians exempt from such charges. The annual permit fees, $2.50 for laborers and $5.00 for mechanics and farmers, became important sources of revenue for the Five Tribes. With no vote and almost no political voice in the territory, non-Indians often found it virtually impossible to collect debts or settle most types of civil disputes. Lawlessness escalated as criminals used Indian Territory as a hideout from formal law exercised in the neighboring states of Kansas, Missouri, Arkansas, and Texas.[25]

As the non-Indian population increased, disgruntled non-Indians, experiencing backseat citizenship, sought relief from the federal government. Federal administrators and Congress recognized the problems in Indian Territory as an impediment in the path of non-Indian progress and domination. Many of the non-Indians echoed the sentiments of Commissioner of Indian Affairs J. D. Atkins, who in 1886 addressed the situation concerning the Five Tribes in Indian Territory, saying, "These Indians have no right to obstruct civilization and commerce and then set up an exclusive claim to self-government, establishing a government within a government."[26] As the number of non-Indians increased, so too did their cries for abolishing communally held tribal lands and tribal governments.[27]

The struggle for control of the land and its resources was at the core of the conflict between Indians and the burgeoning non-Indian population. Settlers wanted to realize their dreams by developing farms on Indian land they viewed as not being utilized by tribes. Ranchers wanted grazing lands free from Indian leasing fees and taxes. The timber industry hoped to exploit rich stands of pine, hickory, and oak located in the southeastern area of the territory, which could satisfy any number of needs in the developing territory, including the increasing demand for railroad ties. Mining interests sought the opportunity to exploit coal and oil reserves, as well as minerals such as lead and zinc. The non-Indian call for "individual land ownership and political reorganization of the territory into a state" was directed toward Washington.[28]

By the 1880s, land-hungry westering settlers joined forces with white eastern reformers often termed "friends of the Indians" to promote privatizing Indian lands. This struggle would continue over the next fifty years and involve federal legislation, court decisions, and administrative policies aimed at Indian landholdings and tribal government. Allotment became a cornerstone of federal Indian policy in 1887, and the government attempted to instill the concept of private property in the minds of Indians. As land began to be held individually, individualism replaced communalism, providing a path for assimilation into the dominant society. Allotment devastated tribal landholdings while assimilation destroyed tribal cultures.[29]

Congress enacted the Dawes Act on February 8, 1887. This legislation distributed plots of land to individual Indians to farm and opened up millions of acres of "excess" tribal land to non-Indian settlement. Allotment proceeded quickly among tribes in the western half of Indian Territory. Although exempted from the Dawes Act, the Five Tribes in the eastern half voiced opposition to the idea of allotment. The Choctaws registered a formal response opposing allotment, stating, "The history of every Indian tribe that has allotted their lands has been the same: The Indian got the allotment and deed and the white man got the land."[30] The *Cherokee Advocate*, a newspaper published by the Cherokee Nation from 1844 to 1906, counseled its readers, "Not just because we so vehemently oppose and dread allotment, but because it now seems so imminent we should put greater and more serious attention [to the issue] and if there is any possible way for us to escape such an event, let us discover wherein it is."[31] The Five Tribes remained strongly opposed to any plans to cede or open any of their lands to white settlement, one of the primary objectives of the allotment policy.

For a time, the Five Tribes effectively maneuvered in non-Indian legal institutions to fight against and delay the allotment process they feared. A Cherokee leader counseled his tribe, "It is by conventions, speech making, passing resolutions, and running newspapers that the whites control everything, and I think the Indians should adapt the same methods."[32] The Five Tribes showed themselves capable of using the non-Indian legal system to delay allotment, but incapable of stopping the tide from eventually sweeping over Indian Territory. Other efforts were expended by non-Indians to wrest land away from the eastern Oklahoma Indians. In 1889, the Unassigned Lands, a tract of approximately two million acres purchased from the Creeks, opened for non-Indian settlement with a land run in which over one hundred thousand settlers participated. Other areas of Indian land opened to non-Indian settlement by land runs and lotteries.[33]

In 1893, Congress established the Dawes Commission "to work for the allotment of Indian lands and the dissolution of tribal governments" in Indian Territory.[34] In giving Dawes Commission members their instructions prior to being sent west to Indian Territory in early

1894, President Grover Cleveland uttered a prophetic statement: "Be careful, gentlemen, lest in elevating the Indians to a higher civilization you do not pauperize them."[35] The chair of the commission, former senator Henry L. Dawes (R-Mass.), who considered himself a "friend of the Indian," stood as a strong proponent of assimilation. He claimed that to be civilized was to "wear civilized clothes . . . cultivate the ground, live in houses, ride in Studebaker wagons, send children to school, drink whiskey, [and] own property."[36] Almost immediately, the commission met an unqualified negative response from the Five Tribes during initial discussions.

After five years of continual negotiations, only one agreement was reached with the Five Tribes. In 1896, the Choctaw and Chickasaw Nations signed the Atoka Agreement, which was subsequently "decisively defeated in a referendum by Chickasaw voters."[37] However, the handwriting was on the wall, concerning the inevitability of allotment of the Five Tribe's lands, as early as 1894. In early March, the St. Louis *Globe-Democrat* reported that in response to the legal foot-dragging of the Five Tribes, "Sentiment in both the House and Senate is ripe for the dissolving of tribal relations."[38] As Indian landholdings shrank, so too did tribal sovereignty. Indian legal scholar F. Browning Pipestem asserts that "the real loss was evidenced by a congressional restriction of tribal powers."[39]

Between 1885 and 1907, over a dozen pieces of federal legislation, coupled with a number of federal court decisions, systematically whittled away at tribal sovereignty in Indian Territory. In 1885, Congress enacted the Major Crimes Act in response to the 1883 court decision, *Ex Parte Crow Dog*, which blocked federal court jurisdiction over crimes committed on Indian land by one Indian against another. The Major Crimes Act granted federal jurisdiction over seven major offenses, striking a blow at tribal court systems.[40] The following year, in *U.S. v. Kagama*, the Supreme Court validated the congressional authority outlined in the Major Crimes Act. The Organic Act of 1890 established government and courts for non-Indians in the western half of Indian Territory, another blow to the effectiveness of tribal court systems. In March of 1893, legislation created the Dawes Commission to prepare the Five Tribes for allotment. The Act of March 1, 1895, while strengthening federal court authority over

Indian Territory, did exempt the Five Tribes from the Major Crimes Act. Powerful economic interests pursuing economic development in Indian Territory continually pressured Congress during this time for favorable legislation. The Appropriations Act of 1897 subjected tribal laws to the approval of the president. Federal as well as Arkansas state legal codes became the law in Indian Territory. Since Arkansas was adjacent and served as the major portal from the east, Indian Territory often served as a sanctuary for criminals escaping arrest or prosecution by Arkansas authorities.

In 1898, Congress, frustrated with the slow pace toward allotment among the Five Tribes, passed the Curtis Act, which gave teeth to the Dawes Commission. The act abolished tribal legislatures and rendered tribal courts impotent. It ended "tribal [common] tenure without the Indian's consent," writes lawyer and scholar Felix S. Cohen.[41] Contractors surveyed and incorporated towns within Indian Territory. Non-Indian townspeople acquired voting rights. Communities provided public schools for both Indian and white children. All residents of Indian Territory, white, black, and Indian, became subject to federal law and the laws of the state of Arkansas. The president approved appointments to tribal governments, with tribal affairs now orchestrated and approved by the secretary of the interior. The Curtis Act also empowered the Dawes Commission to prepare tribal membership rolls in preparation for allotment of Indian lands. By 1907, the tribal rolls of the Five Tribes enumerated a little over 101,000 people. Allotment reduced the 19,525,966-acre land base of the Five Tribes by 15,794,000 acres.[42] Reluctantly, the Indians realized they could not fight the inevitable and chose to obtain the best deal possible. The Creeks signed an agreement in May of 1901 that eased, though it did not change, the application of the Curtis Act to their nation. Their chief, Pleasant Porter, later recounted, "I was conscious that I was compelled under the advance of civilization to sign the paper that I now know took the lifeblood of my people."[43]

The Curtis Act accomplished two objectives. First it established a timetable for dismantling the functioning governments of the Five Tribes, a direct blow to tribal sovereignty. Second, it provided the mechanism needed for allotment of Indian land. The provisions of the act led to a gut-wrenching transformation of the Indian lifestyle.

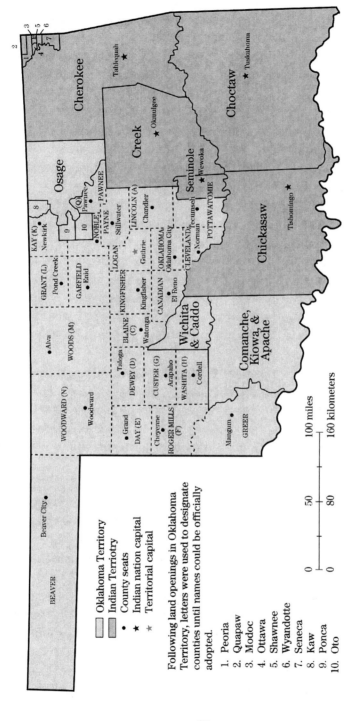

Oklahoma Territory and Indian Territory, 1900. From John W. Morris, Charles Robert Goines, and Edwin C. McReynolds, *Historical Atlas of Oklahoma* (Norman: University of Oklahoma Press, 1987). Reprinted by permission from the University of Oklahoma Press.

Rolly McIntosh, Creek chief, referred to the Curtis Act as "a law repugnant to our people, and in which they have had not hand or work in the making."[44] The act closed the door to Indian legal resistance and dampened the Indian voice as the territory prepared for statehood.

Finally, in 1901, the federal government declared all Indians in the territory to be U.S. citizens, and the Five Tribes Act of 1906 allowed the president to remove tribal chiefs. Chiefs would now serve at the president's pleasure. Indian court systems were dismantled, with federal and state laws imposed over all Indian Territory.

Indian legal scholar Rennard Strickland contends that these laws and governmental actions constituted "legal genocide."[45] Indian political institutions were not just weakened by these governmental actions; they were for all practical purposes destroyed.

However, not all members of the Five Tribes accepted this as their fate. A number of "full-bloods" from each tribe refused to be enrolled or accept their allotments, and they formed a variety of separatist groups, unifying their protest against tribal groups more accepting of allotment.

A pan-tribal group, the Four Mothers Society, organized in 1895, embraced members from the Choctaw, Chickasaw, Creek, and Cherokee Nations. They wanted to return to the old life that existed before the Dawes Commission and the Curtis Act. This society operated for well over ten years, claiming almost twenty-four thousand members at its zenith.

Among the Cherokees, the Keetoowah, a secret society, refused to accept their allotments. By 1901, an estimated fourteen hundred fullblood Keetoowah members refused to enroll with the Dawes Commission. They did not move, even after "the threat of U.S. troops from Ft. Gibson was threatened."[46] The Keetoowah remains today a force in the Cherokee political structure.

Chitto Harjo, a Creek and Four Mothers Society leader also known as Crazy Snake, led the Snake band of Creeks, who boldly defied the changes forced upon their tribe. The Snakes adamantly demanded that removal treaties signed during the 1830s be honored. Harjo told Alex Posey, the Creek writer and poet, "The agreement between the white man and the Indian gave the Indian the right of undisturbed possession and enjoyment of this country as long as the grass grows and the rivers run. I notice the grass is still growing and the water in the North Canadian is still flowing.... I see no reason why that treaty should be abrogated."[47] The Snakes formed an ad hoc government based on the old tribal models of communal life, passing laws that forbade the acceptance of allotments, rental of land to non-Indians, and the use of white labor. They organized light horsemen, a quasi-police force, to enforce their laws. They arrested and whipped several Creeks who accepted allotments. In recounting their dedication, Posey stated, "I met one old Snake Indian who said he would rather see his children dead than enrolled and their land parceled out to them."[48] Local sheriffs and deputies arrived to put down this uprising (subsequently called the Crazy Snake Rebellion) and arrested almost one hundred Crazy Snake followers. After sixty were tried and convicted and facing prison sentences, the Snakes reluctantly disbanded and accepted their allotments.[49] Although Indian resistance to allotment eventually failed, the turmoil exacerbated longstanding fissures within tribal groups, and had a detrimental effect on inter-tribal and intra-tribal relationships that lingers to the present.[50]

By 1905, with the breakup of communal tribal lands through allotment and the hamstringing of tribal governments, the stage for statehood was set. Non-Indians favored a plan that would unite Indian Territory with the Oklahoma Territory, producing a unified state. Five Tribes leaders believed Indian interests would be better served by forming a separate Indian state they would call Sequoyah.

On August 21, 1905, almost two hundred elected delegates from the Five Tribes gathered in Muskogee to draft a constitution for a new Indian state. This convention accomplished its objective within three weeks, producing a document similar to the U.S. Constitution. Charles Haskell, a non-Indian delegate and Oklahoma's first governor, claimed, "It [the Sequoyah Convention] was largely a struggle for political power and supremacy . . . by those who were seeking political position in the new state."[51] While Congress rejected the constitution, it did make legislators aware of the need to speed up the statehood process for the territory.

On June 16, 1906, Congress adopted the Hamilton Statehood Bill, now commonly referred to as the Oklahoma Enabling Act, which called for delegates from both the Oklahoma and Indian Territories to meet and draft a constitution for one state. The project took almost eight months to complete. On November 16, 1907, President Theodore Roosevelt signed the proclamation that admitted Oklahoma as the forty-sixth state. With statehood, old institutions vanished. Non-Indian agricultural and commercial development dominated in Oklahoma.

As the allotment process ended, most of the Five Tribes land base had either been allotted to tribal members or—in the case of lands possessing timber, coal, or other valuable minerals—put into reserve and held in trust by the Department of the Interior. "There were no surplus lands within the Five Civilized Tribes to be returned to the public domain and opened to homesteading," writes historian Francis Paul Prucha.[52] This lack of surplus land presented an obstacle for land-hungry settlers and commercial interests. However, the grafter, a new class of entrepreneur, soon realized a new way around that obstacle. Grafting became an insidious method used by non-Indians to separate Five Tribes people from their land and its resources, initiating an "orgy of plunder and exploitation probably unparalleled in American history," asserts Angie Debo.[53] Specifically, grafting was "the name given to [the] business of locating non-Indians on Indian allotments," writes historian Danney Goble, and it quickly became "the chief and most thriving industry in the whole community."[54] This involved the leasing and selling of Indian land in order to spur economic development, while clearing a profit for the grafter. Grafters took advantage of Indians' ignorance of property rights and values, real estate contracts, deeds, leasing arrangements, and probate.

Guy Cobb, a grafter from Ardmore testifying before a congressional hearing in 1906, described his view of the Indian allottee in the following way: "He is an ignorant man. He does not know anything. He is poor, ignorant, and illiterate, and does not know one single step of the process. He does not know how to act for himself, to say nothing of his children."[55] Many non-Indians accepted grafters as people helping white Oklahomans realize goals of acquiring personal wealth while also promoting commercial development. Oklahoma grafters came to occupy almost the same societal position as slave traders in the antebellum South, a necessary evil tolerated to achieve desired ends. No other area in the country experienced such an intense and sustained unscrupulous effort by non-Indians to obtain control of Indian land and its resources by whatever means necessary, from legal maneuvering to systematic murder. This situation continued for the next twenty-five years.[56]

In May of 1908, Congress enacted a law nicknamed "the Crime of 1908." The Act of May 27, 1908, applied only to the Five Tribes and introduced the concept of "blood quantum" to ascertain whether an Indian's allotment should have restrictions placed upon it. In short, those promoting the blood quantum idea argued that the higher percentage of Indian blood, the "more prone [an individual] was to the negative aspects of the typical Indian character, characterized by ignorance, laziness, and thriftlessness," writes Erik Zissu.[57] Those with 50 percent or more Indian blood were determined "incompetent" to handle their own legal affairs and had restrictions placed on their allotments, preventing their sale for twenty-five years. However, in most instances, allotted land could be leased with the approval of the secretary of the interior. Leasing opened a door for grafters to acquire the land and resources of Five Tribe Indians. This law also transferred jurisdiction of restricted Indian children and minors from federal to Oklahoma probate courts, separating Indian children from the protection of the federal government and exposing them to the will of county and state courts, courts often friendly to grafters and non-Indian guardians.[58]

Local courts appointed a guardian, usually a non-Indian lawyer or real estate person, to administer allottees' landholdings and their resources. With little oversight from the federal government, this local arrangement opened the door to systematic looting of Indian allotments and their resources. Historian John H. Moore describes this time as "a dark and terror-filled period in Oklahoma history, a period in which those who merely stole from Indians were regarded as upright citizens." Moore asserts that "from about 1887 to 1920 the employees of the Bureau of Indian Affairs (BIA) [then known as the Office of Indian Affairs] in Oklahoma, the politicians of the state, and the non-Indians who lusted after Indian land and minerals were not three different and discrete self-interested groups; they were largely the same people."[59]

In 1902, Pleasant Porter, the Creek chief, "estimated that [grafters] had acquired control of almost one million acres . . . under leases that virtually amounted to deeds."[60] With only eight judges, and inundated with criminal and civil cases, the courts found neither the time nor the resources to monitor the activities of almost twelve thousand court-appointed guardians. Periodic reports required by the court verified the existence of proper lease or rental contracts by guardians. However, guardians were not required to submit any type of record as to how rental and lease fees were distributed, and to whom. Twenty years later, the Meriam Report characterized the Oklahoma probate system as "a flagrant example of the white man's brutal and unscrupulous domination over a weaker race."[61]

A circuit court decision in 1903 made it even easier for grafters to exploit Indian landholdings. The decision led to new procedures whereby individuals were appointed by the court as legal guardians to Indian children. Full-bloods labeled incompetent with respect to their own allotments also lost control of their children's allotments. In one situation a grafter appointed as a legal guardian charged a $1,200 annual fee against his ward's estate valued at $4,000.[62] Another grafter filed with the court and received "at one time the custody or guardianship of 161 children."[63] Some of these individuals ended up controlling thousands of acres of allotted land. In one case, a grafter controlled between 75,000 and 100,000 acres of allotted Indian land.[64] The grafter leased out most of the land, with the Indian allottees often receiving none of the income.

Congress gnawed away at remaining restrictions, allowing loopholes that grafters used to gain control of individual allotments. On April 21, 1904, Congress passed a measure allowing an allottee to bypass the twenty-five-year period with approval from the secretary of the interior by way of a competency certificate. This effectively removed all restrictions against allotments held by whites and freedmen, with the exception of "homesteads" and the allotments of minors. More than 1.5 million allotted acres became available to land-hungry whites.[65] Federal legislation passed in 1905, the Act of March 3, 1905, authorized the Department of the Interior to investigate cases of reported fraud. Ironically, the same act neglected to cover the investigation of leases and rental agreements of court-ordered guardians.

Almost two decades later, in 1923, S. E. Wallen, the Office of Indian Affairs superintendent at Muskogee, stated in a letter that "within less than ten years 75 or 80 per cent of the race [Indian] of land lords, through their own inexperience and lack of appreciation of thrift . . . have been transformed into a race of tenants."[66] While the complexities and legalities of the allotment process, including rentals, leasing, mineral rights, sales, and inheritance issues typically confounded the inexperienced Indians, non-Indian speculators and grafters easily navigated these.

During the first quarter of the twentieth century, an oil boom in northeastern Oklahoma fueled a particularly insidious chapter in the exploitation of Oklahoma Indians' resources. The discovery of oil under the surface of primarily allotted Osage lands resulted in a new effort by speculators and grafters to gain control. The power of these interests would extend into congressional hearings for the Thomas-Rogers Bill in the spring of 1936. Then a last-minute political compromise exempted Osage County from the Oklahoma Indian Welfare Act, breaking a deadlock that otherwise would have spelled death for the bill. The Osages were permitted to maintain a tribal governmental structure with at least a degree of voice in their affairs and resources.[67]

In 1906, the year before Oklahoma statehood, the Osage Reservation underwent allotment. Each of the 2,229 Osage received 658 acres of land broken down into 160 acres for a homestead and 498 acres held as surplus. Unlike for other tribes, only the surface land was allotted. The Osages maintained control over subsurface mineral rights.

Almost simultaneously, large deposits of oil were discovered beneath Osage land. A production boom quickly followed to meet the growing demand for oil, not only from expanding American industries but also the advancement of the automobile. From then until the mid 1920s, Osage fortunes burgeoned due to oil royalty checks. With the discovery of the Burbank oil field in 1920, royalty payments increased substantially. In 1923, the Osages were paid $27 million all told for mineral rights. During the first three decades of the twentieth century, northeastern Oklahoma became the scene of unparalleled efforts by grafters to cash in on the Osages' good fortune. The Osages, possessing neither experience nor understanding of the non-Indian economic system, became easy targets for schemers attempting to cheat them out of their royalties.

In 1929, Osage chief Fred Lookout, a full-blood, lamented, "My people are not happy. Some day this oil will give out and there will be no fat checks every few months from the great white father. There will be no more fine motorcars and new clothes. Then, I know, my people will be happier."[68] By the early 1930s oil production plummeted as wells ran dry. The bubble burst and for most Osage their wealth disappeared almost as quickly as it had come.

Over the almost forty-year period from the creation of the Dawes Commission in 1893 to the Indian New Deal in the mid 1930s, Oklahoma Indians experienced a level of exploitation by whites unmatched by any other tribal group in the nation. During this time, Indian landholdings shrank by 90 percent, from 15,000,000 acres to 1,500,000. By 1920, of the original 102,209 enrolled members of the Five Tribes whose allotments were classified as restricted by the Dawes Commission in the 1890s, only 21,000 remained in that category.[69]

In addition to the loss of tribal lands, Indian sovereignty experienced an ongoing and almost systematic attack during this time as well. As mentioned above, tribal courts and councils were rendered virtually powerless through congressional legislation, federal court decisions, and administrative policies. While tribes fought doggedly to maintain their lands, resources, and sovereignty, in the end they proved unable to withstand the onslaught of determined non-Indian settlement and development in Indian Territory.

CHAPTER 2

The Winds of Change

During the 1920s an era of reform began in Indian affairs. Social scientists, politicians, bureaucrats, business and commercial leaders, idealists, reformers often known as "friends of the Indians," and Indians themselves would explore, discuss, and debate the continuing deteriorating situation of Native Americans. A wide variety of approaches and proposals would be offered as solutions to the "Indian problem." Oklahoma, due to its large Indian population and the number of tribal groups, came to garner significant attention from these reformers.

Familiarity with this era of reform-related debate is key to understanding the origins and legacy of both the Indian Reorganization Act of 1934 and the Oklahoma Indian Welfare Act of 1936. It was during the 1920s that the seeds were planted for the Indian New Deal of the 1930s. This chapter examines the reform movement in Indian affairs during the 1920s, with an emphasis on Oklahoma.

The Indian affairs reform movement comprised a disparate group of individuals and organizations with no overarching national organization or leadership. Many in this movement focused only on a specific issue affecting a local tribe or band. Some had deep religious roots. Women were actively engaged in the reform movement, primarily through the Central Federation of Women's Clubs. Native Americans involved themselves in organizations including the Indian Rights Association, the American Indian Association, and the Association of Oklahoma Indians. One individual, John Collier, increasingly dominated the Indian reform movement in the 1920s and early 1930s. In 1923, Collier founded the American Indian Defense Association, one of the most vocal groups that began lobbying on a wide variety of Indian-related issues across the nation and specifically in Oklahoma.

In 1923 as Indian reformers lengthened their stride, Charles H. Burke, then the commissioner of Indian affairs, assigned the superintendent of the Five Tribes, S. E. Wallen, to the job of investigating Indian probate affairs in Oklahoma. Wallen submitted his findings to Commissioner Burke on December 31, 1923, concluding that "bad management and great waste of the estates have been the rule; . . . guardians' and attorneys' fees are excessive, and in many cases unconscionable."[1] Wallen believed that "the care and protection of the interests of the Indians [was] a national duty," and he recommended that legislation be passed that would give "exclusive supervision and control over the estates and funds of . . . restricted Indians of the Five Civilized Tribes" of Oklahoma to the secretary of the interior.[2] In effect, this was a call to reverse policies and court decisions dating back to the "Crime of 1908," the Act of May 27, 1908. Just days before Wallen's report was submitted to Commissioner Burke, the Oklahoma Bar Association published a statement in which the bar, "noted for its many able and outstanding members," took great steps to distance itself from probate practice, which they viewed as "essentially political" and something with which "the better class of lawyers are seldom found connected."[3] Perhaps they sensed a coming storm in Oklahoma Indian affairs.

Following on the heels of the Wallen investigation, in 1924 a scathing report was published concerning the results of another investigation into Oklahoma's county probate system, with respect to Indian allotments and resources: "Oklahoma's Poor Rich Indians: An Orgy of Graft and Exploitation of the Five Civilized Tribes—Legalized Robbery." The report, published by the Indian Rights Association (IRA), represented a joint venture involving Gertrude Bonnin of the General Federation of Women's Clubs, Charles H. Fabens of the American Indian Defense Association (AIDA), and Matthew K. Sniffen of the AIDA. All three were recognized leaders in the Indian affairs reform movement of the 1920s.

The report was clear and brazen in its accusations. Focusing on six counties in eastern Oklahoma with significant Indian populations, the investigators examined 14,229 probate cases. The report charged "the average cost of administration [of an Indian probate case] to be twenty percent and in some instances [as] high as seventy percent [of the total value of the estate]." In other areas of the United States, the costs for probating Indian estates "cannot exceed a total of $75. In most cases the cost is not over $20."[4] One eastern Oklahoma attorney, who never once appeared in court, absconded with $35,000 for handling a single Indian probate case. The report continues for almost forty pages, citing example after example of Oklahoma Indians blatantly defrauded of their income from allotments and their natural resources. It revealed how land speculators, grafters, court-appointed guardians, lawyers, and judges had taken advantage of Indians time and time again. For example, in 1918, a Creek, Sina Battiest, died. She miraculously appeared four years later in the Stephens County courthouse as a man, and in front of two witnesses affixed a signature to a lease for her allotment. The report concluded, "Thus, it will be seen that the grafters can bring the dead to life, and even change her sex!"[5] It blamed the fact that Oklahoma county courts had jurisdiction over Indian probate matters with the Five Tribes in eastern Oklahoma. Since statehood, Congress, through several pieces of legislation, beginning with the Act of May 27, 1908, the "Crime of 1908," and continuing on into the 1920s, "vested exclusive jurisdiction over probate matters in the county courts of Oklahoma."[6] This left the Interior Department "powerless . . . to protect these Indians from . . . wholesale plundering."[7] Some likened the situation in Oklahoma Indian affairs to giving the fox the key to the henhouse door.

The report contended that the only hope for the remaining twenty-one thousand restricted Oklahoma Indians did not lie in reforming the existing system, with probate affairs controlled solely by county courts, but in restructuring the entire system. The report concluded that "legislation should be enacted at once giving the Department of the Interior complete control of all Indian property and Indian minors and incompetents as constitutional limitations will permit, and this should apply to all Indians of Oklahoma."[8] The report urged all "friends of the Indians" to pressure their legislators to secure passage of such a bill. However, a decade passed before Congress considered the type of overhaul the report recommended.

Several circumstances fed the deteriorating situation of Oklahoma Indians that the 1924 report exposed. The prevailing assimilationist ideology of non-Indians was paternalistic, envisioning Native Americans incorporated into mass society at a position somewhat below non-Indians.[9] Compounding the situation was the inability of Native Americans to operate from a position of unity—there were not yet any viable pan-Indian organizations. Most tribal groups were decentralized and factionalized into a number of strongly held viewpoints, and seemed to defy attempts at forming workable coalitions that would permit a stronger influence in government policy concerning their economic and other affairs. Without unity these factions found it difficult to challenge political interests united under the banner of assimilation. Non-Indians owned and controlled the playing field and continued to successfully promote their interests and dominate Indians. Many Indians did not possess the skills or experience to maneuver in non-Indian social and political structures, and the gap between traditionals and progressives remained almost universal.

The charges outlined in the Indian Rights Association report produced an angry storm of protest and accusations from all sides involved in the issue. The loudest voices came from the Oklahoma congressional delegation. In late 1924 and early 1925, the House Committee on Indian Affairs held hearings in Oklahoma to investigate the charges made by the report. The committee, which included Oklahoma Democrat William Hastings, remained united in its defense of the Oklahoma probate system, and the hearings challenged the various charges. The following congressional report accused the Indian Rights Association of "sensationalizing" a problem involving just a handful of county attorneys and court-appointed guardians.[10] The committee stated that "the principle author [of the Indian Rights Association report, Matthew K. Sniffen] has evidently acted on the belief that it was necessary for him to make sensational statements about the wrongs suffered by Indians in order to justify his position which he holds in that association."[11] Finally, the committee concluded, "the wholesale charges made against the judges, attorneys, business and professional men of Oklahoma are not sustained by any evidence, and are libelous in their character."[12]

The committee did condemn "unconscionable attorneys and persons who make it a profession to obtain appointments as guardian."[13] It also recognized deficiencies within the Burke Act of 1906 (which was itself designed to correct deficiencies in the General Allotment Act of 1887) and subsequent legislation, stating that there existed "much uncertainty in the law relative to the jurisdiction of the administration of the affairs of the Five Civilized Tribes" and proposing legislation to correct these deficiencies.[14] In effect, the committee found problems with the administrative system as it was structured, but not with the individuals at federal and state levels who operated the system.

This caustic refutation of the accusations of the Indian Rights Association brought about an equally vehement rebuttal by the association. In a pamphlet titled *Out of Thine Own Mouth*, the association called the congressional investigation a "whitewash." It further stated that the committee had published its report before "all the available evidence had been heard and considered."[15] Finally the report laid a large portion of the blame on Congress, decrying, "THIS IS AS SEVERE AN INDICTMENT OF CONGRESS BY THE COMMITTEE AS ANYTHING SAID IN OUR REPORT [sic], for that authority [probate matters in the hands of county courts] was granted by Congress."[16] Several Oklahoma newspapers jumped on board. The *Tulsa World* boldly stated, "The Committee all but called liars of everyone who intimated that conditions in some Probate Courts have been bad. It gave the courts a clean bill of health and departed."[17] The *Bartlesville Examiner* declared, "Indian affairs are in the limelight, and no amount of whitewashing will end the persistent charges made against certain Oklahomans."[18] Finally, the *Muskogee News* exclaimed, "Is it not to be wondered at that citizens of other States express doubt that Oklahomans have any sense of justice."[19] This intense public furor proved short-lived, but reformers maintained continued agitation for change. The battle, a sustained effort to remove restrictions from full-blood Indians and those declared legally incompetent, continued through the 1920s and up to 1933 with the appointment of John Collier as commissioner of Indian affairs. By the late 1920s, the amount of allotted land in Oklahoma diminished considerably, yet a sizeable number of Indians and non-Indians continued to push for an easing of restrictions so more Indian land and resources could be sold and exploited.

The passing of a measure tied to an appropriation bill in 1928 marked the beginning of a turning point in Indian–federal government relations in Oklahoma. This provision changed the superintendency of the Five Tribes based in Muskogee from a political appointment to a merit position, falling under the civil service. This removed the position from influence of the spoils system and at the same time placed more direct control with the commissioner and the secretary of the interior.

In 1928, President Herbert Hoover appointed Charles J. Rhoads as commissioner of Indian affairs and Joseph Scattergood as his assistant. These wealthy philanthropists were expected to usher in an era of reform of the federal government's handling of Indian affairs. Many believed that if anyone could bring significant reform, it would be Rhoads—who had served as president of the Indian Rights Association—and Scattergood. However, their effectiveness proved limited. Indian scholar Benay Blend characterizes the commissionership of Rhoads and Henry Scattergood as "committed to humanitarian programs, but incapable of altering Indian affairs," writing that "they lacked the political muscle to push legislation through Congress."[20] Conservative, hard-line assimilationists and proponents of the allotment of Indian lands, both in Congress and in the Office of Indian Affairs, blocked the way to substantive change. Appropriations for Indian affairs administration increased during the Hoover administration, but the onset of the Great Depression and its impact on Native Americans and the rest of the country soon negated much of the effect of increased spending. Rhoads and Scattergood were successful in bringing a greater degree of professionalism to the Office of Indian Affairs, as well increased diplomatic relations with the Indians themselves.[21] Other factors, however, mitigated their effectiveness in substantially altering the path of Indian-government relations.

During the 1920s, the most notable event in Indian-government relations was the publishing of the Meriam Report in 1928. Hubert Work, the secretary of the interior under Calvin Coolidge, commissioned the Institute for Government Research (later the Brookings Institution) to perform an independent investigation of the conduct of federal Indian affairs. The findings, formally published as *The Problem of Indian Administration* in February of 1928, examined eight areas, including "policy; health; education; economic conditions; family and community life; the activities of women; migration; legal aspects; and missionary activities."[22] The Meriam Report revealed that the allotment policy had failed and that the Office of Indian Affairs had beneficially addressed virtually no areas of the lives of Native Americans.

The Meriam Report devoted considerable attention to Oklahoma Indians. "The exploitation of Indians in Oklahoma has been notorious," the report declared. "In some instances acts of Congress have resulted in the wholesale exploitation of the Indians."[23] The latter assertion was a direct reference to "the Crime of 1908," which, among other things, transferred jurisdiction for probate matters involving Indian lands in Oklahoma from the Department of the Interior to Oklahoma county courts. Continuing to chastise state politicians, the report stated, "Oklahoma, which has evidenced a great desire to get control or possession of Indian property, has evidenced little tendency to protect the Indians or provide requisite developmental work."[24] The report asserted, "The present 'guardian system' in operation among the Five Civilized Tribes has caused much well founded complaint . . . effort should be made to abolish the guardian system and place the administration of Indian property and income in the hands of thoroughly competent national government officers."[25] Finally, the Meriam Report referenced the deteriorating condition of many of the Five Tribes members who had become impoverished since Oklahoma statehood through the loss of their land and resources: "They are in a forlorn condition, neglected both by the national government and by the state."[26] The report asserted, "The national government should oppose the removal of restrictions until the state of Oklahoma has shown as much interest in the social welfare of its Indians as it has shown in securing control of their property."[27]

The Meriam Report sparked ongoing congressional hearings in the late 1920s and early 1930s. These hearings, conducted by both the House and Senate Committees on Indian Affairs, investigated the conditions of Indians by geographical area. Considerable time was spent in looking into the situation of Oklahoma Indians, the Five Tribes in eastern Oklahoma as well as the Plains Indians in the western part of the state. The results sustained much of the Meriam Report by bringing to light depressed and deplorable circumstances in a number of areas, including general living conditions, health, education, and the administration of Indian policy. Many Oklahoma Indians found themselves in dire straits as the Depression set in during the early 1930s.

General living conditions seemed to be poor and declining in the 1930s. V. M. Locke, a former principal chief of the Choctaws, stated, "Their [Choctaws'] living conditions are the worst I ever saw. No colored persons of the most poverty stricken type could be in worse condition."[28] For three years, Oklahoma experienced a severe drought. Speaking of the financial condition of many Indian farmers, Jim McCurtain, a Chickasaw testified, "We full-bloods . . . have had several years of crop failure, and especially this year [1930] it has all been burned up and nothing made."[29] Conditions for many Indians for the coming winter [1930–1931] looked bleak as well. A. L. Irvine, an Office of Indian Affairs field clerk from Idabel, in southeastern Oklahoma, stated, "It looks to me about 400 [Indian families]; pretty nearly all of them are going to have a pretty hard time to get through the winter."[30] Speaking of the desperate conditions many Indians faced, one witness testified, "Many of your Choctaws over there don't eat but once or twice [a day] and the meal is corn bread and water."[31] Their situation had been deteriorating for decades, as they had lost their allotments and resources through all manner of swindle and graft, and with a government unresponsive to their interests. The Great Depression and the Dust Bowl exacerbated matters.

During these hearings, several Indian leaders made recommendations that tribal monies being held by the Department of the Interior be released in the form of per capita payments as a form of immediate relief. William A. Durant, a Choctaw from Oklahoma City, advocated that 306,230 acres of un-leased coal and asphalt deposits be sold at the appraised value [determined by the Interior Department] of $9,578,629.[32] The funds received by the tribe would be distributed to its members on a per capita basis. Durant also suggested that the tribes be allowed to borrow from the federal government using their landholdings as collateral for an amount that would allow an immediate relief payment of $200 per person. This amounted to a little over $5 million against holdings valued at over $23 million. These recommendations to the investigating committees were never carried out. However, they demonstrated the extreme measures tribal leaders sometimes advocated in order to receive some form of aid for their suffering tribal members.[33] The condition of Oklahoma Indians had become desperate.

Poor health conditions among Oklahoma Indians prevailed, the rule rather than the exception. A Creek, Nellie Laphan, stated, "The health conditions have been poor for 20 years. . . . There is tuberculosis," and when asked if it was increasing, responded, "Yes, sir."[34] About 50 percent of the children were afflicted with trachoma. In addition, Laphan stated that 11 out of 123 students at the Indian school near Eufaula, Oklahoma, had confirmed cases of contagious (and usually fatal) tuberculosis.[35] Most Oklahoma Indians could not afford even minimal medical care, and many lived in remote areas far from the few doctors, clinics, or hospitals.

The Senate investigation closely examined Indian education. William Tidwell, a county judge from Idabel, testifying before the subcommittee, estimated that between 25 and 50 percent of Indian children did not attend school, compared to only about "10 percent" of white children who did not attend.[36] D. H. Johnston, governor of the Chickasaw Nation, attributed the high dropout rate among Indians to the fact that Indian children represented a minority: "Everything is for the majority. Consequently the Indian children get dissatisfied and they quit after they get up to 12 or 13 years old."[37] Many of these Indian children spoke little if any English, most having only a minimal understanding of non-Indian society and culture. Some adults referred to more practical reasons for Indian children not attending school, including living too far from school, undernourishment, and parents "so poor they cannot provide clothing and necessaries with which to attend school."[38] Johnston confirmed what many other Oklahoma Indians knew and had experienced: "financial difficulty [of parents] bars most of [their children] from an education."[39]

While Oklahoma Indian children benefited little from formal education, almost all Indian leaders recognized the need for education efforts to continue. William Durant said, "We recognize our tribal schools as having been the most beneficial influence in our tribal life.... We favor and recommend the policy of placing our children in the public schools, where they will mingle with and become accustomed to the ways of other children."[40] Another Choctaw, A. P. Matthews, saw that "the greater portion of the full blood Indians are clearly at a disadvantage when dealing with the white people. Time, experience, and education will finally remove this disadvantage."[41] Forbes Cravat, a Chickasaw leader from Pontotoc County, pleaded with the subcommittee, stating, "If you want to save us, take our children and try to educate them better."[42] The Choctaw principal chief, Ben Dwight, strongly urged governmental assistance so children could be equipped with "suitable and sufficient clothes and books and such other school supplies as are useful to enable them to attend the school and feel themselves [equal] with other children attending the school."[43]

Many criticized the administration of federal Indian policy. Durant believed that while the "majority of the acts of Congress have been favorable to the Indians ... it is the execution of the policies of the Government I object to."[44] Grady Lewis, a Choctaw tribal attorney, singled out a particular field agent as representative of many, saying of him, "He does not have any sympathetic understanding of the [Indian] people. He deals with them in terms of 320 acres of land and $500 in cash rather than with human beings."[45] A table of delinquent royalty payments by the Department of the Interior for Choctaw and Chickasaw coal leases totaled $20,748.28 and represented delinquent payments from as far back as 1921.[46] Because of poor interoffice communication, an agent from the Indian Affairs office in Muskogee was often unable to tell how much money the government was holding in trust for a specific Indian. A medical field agent at Muskogee, when asked whether tubercular cases in the preceding three years had increased or decreased, stated, "It is mighty hard for me to say. It would not be anything but a guess."[47] William Tidwell testified that the system for sending royalty checks for Indians to their guardians should be stopped: "If you let an Indian guardian get hold of the money, they spend it."[48] These testimonies point to an unresponsive Office of Indian Affairs in which the head often did not know what the tail was doing.

Oklahoma Indian historian Muriel Wright, Choctaw, a contemporary of Angie Debo, examined the conduct of Indian affairs administration in eastern Oklahoma in the late 1920s. She characterized the Office of Indian Affairs in Oklahoma as led by a political appointee in Muskogee, and staffed by civil service employees who, "whether they be white men or Indians, when they take a position in the bureau, they [lose] their identity as individuals and become a part of the great machine."[49] The Office of Indian Affairs had the power to "make arbitrary rulings for the administration of law passed by Congress" and "its present policies are in many instances obsolete." Wright spoke of tribal leaders holding "their positions through the patronage system of the party in power in Washington, largely in the hands of the senators from Oklahoma, approved by the bureau, and appointed by the president."[50] Wright alluded strongly to a bureaucratic monolith greased by politics and responsive to bureaucrats who maintained it but not to the Indians it was created to serve.

The intermingling of Indians and non-Indians contributed another factor affecting the conditions of Oklahoma Indians during the tough years of the late 1920s and early 1930s. The Indians were far from assimilated and their landholdings lay checkerboarded with non-Indian holdings. Restricted Indian landholdings were exempt from state and local taxes. Government-funded roads passed over both Indian and non-Indian land, though only the latter was taxed to support such a service. Public schools provided another government service that included many Indian children. While the federal government paid the state twelve cents per day for each Indian public school student, non-Indian educational administrators complained that this in no way covered the complete cost, and non-Indian taxpayers were forced to make up the difference. In 1933, Oklahoma county administrators estimated that "the tax loss to the Oklahoma counties, plus expenditures on behalf of the Indians, is more than $2,280,000."[51] As the Depression worsened, Oklahoma became more and more strapped for cash. Local leaders viewed Indians as wards of the federal government and not the responsibility of state or local governments, a view that contributed to an already acute situation for most Oklahoma Indians. Virtually no state social welfare services were available to them. As it became increasingly difficult for local governments to function as the Depression wore on, they resorted to using the long-accepted policy of giving up on the administration of Indian affairs, viewing this as entirely the domain of the federal government, thereby saving their limited resources for taxpaying non-Indian citizens.

In the 1920s the Office of Indian Affairs proved unable to administer effectively and in the best interests of Oklahoma Indians. The allotment policy failed, destructive to the Indians, who lost 90 percent of their landholdings. With tribal governments ostensibly abolished, Indian culture was endangered, and the overall conditions for Indians deteriorated to dangerously low levels. An assimilationist perspective fused with condescending paternalism pervaded non-Indian relations with their Indian neighbors. The Oklahoma congressional delegation, Office of Indian Affairs administrators, and state and local officials were all steeped in this paternalistic outlook. These attitudes helped to promote an open season on Indian land and resources, which remained relatively unchecked, particularly in the Five Tribes area. Oklahoma Indians were not in a position to bargain from a position of strength. Ongoing congressional investigations, the reports of reform organizations such as the Indian Rights Association, and the Meriam Report presented a clear picture of the plight of Oklahoma Indians during the 1920s, but fell short of effecting legislation or substantive change to remedy problems. As the decade ended, the Depression rendered an already desperate situation among Oklahoma Indians even more critical.

The Depression made poverty and food shortages a constant companion for many Indians. By 1933, the annual per capita income of members of the Five Tribes was $47. Most Oklahoma Indians had lost their allotments and were left landless. Members of the Five Tribes had originally received 110,000 allotments. However, by 1933, 72,000 members owned no land at all. With the easing of restrictions, many Indians already struggling to hold on to their land now became subject to state taxes, including property taxes, that most could ill afford. Some landless Indians squatted on public land while many others crowded onto small allotments of relatives, rendering them incapable of supporting even basic subsistence. With hunger and even starvation not far from the door, many depended on meager handouts from kin or other tribal members.[52] Many Oklahoma Indians mirrored the feelings of Curt Holtin, Creek, who stated to Senator Elmer Thomas in a letter in late 1931, "Personally I have very little confidence in Mr. Hoover as far as the common people are concerned."[53]

Senator Thomas seems to have been a conservative Oklahoma Democrat intent on retaining his role and life in Washington, where he eventually retired and died. Thomas was often at the forefront of debates and legislative struggles involving federal assistance for Oklahoma. He had become involved in politics during the 1896 election when he had stumped for William Jennings Bryan during Bryan's first presidential bid. During the Depression years, Thomas grounded himself in populism, and promoted raising commodity prices for agricultural products and an inflated money supply as the answers to the economic woes of Oklahoma farmers. During his years in the Senate, 1927–1951, Thomas spent considerable time and effort in educating himself on the money issue. Many in government and in banking circles considered him somewhat of an authority, and Thomas apparently took great pride in this recognition. During his senatorial career Thomas served on agricultural, Indian affairs, and banking committees. He was also a key player in the course of both the IRA and the OIWA, but you would not know that from his writings. At the end of his career Thomas wrote two books, an autobiography (*Forty Years a Legislator*, recently published) and one titled *Financial Engineering*. Outside of one bill Thomas introduced in 1923, there is no mention in either book of his role in Indian affairs administration. Perhaps this omission reflects Thomas's view of its importance.

Assimilationist thinking underpinned Thomas's views on Indian affairs administration and legislative proposals such as the IRA and the OIWA. Emulating the nineteenth-century role of "friend of the Indian," he viewed Oklahoma Indians as unique, believing that they were further along the road to civilization than Indians elsewhere. Thomas often made statements to the effect that Oklahoma Indians were not reservation Indians and that they should not be thought of along with tribes in the West and Southwest. Thomas's actions with respect to the legislative battles surrounding both the IRA and the OIWA often reflected this viewpoint.

Early in his congressional career, Thomas honed skills required to push legislation through Congress. Fighting a seemingly uphill battle against a Republican-controlled Congress, he was able to obtain appropriations to build two fish hatcheries in Medicine Park, a community he had established in 1904 as a planned tourist resort, along with approval for two retention ponds to provide water to a growing and thirsty nearby Lawton. Thomas was even able to obtain labor from federal prisons in McAlester and Anadarko to build needed roads and dams in the area. Like many politicians, he was not opposed to pork barrel projects to keep his constituents happy and supportive.

From 1929 to Roosevelt's inauguration as president in 1933, Senator Thomas, like many other legislators, found it difficult to secure relief for constituents from a laissez-faire executive administration. Herbert Hoover, a fiscal conservative, appears to have been almost totally unprepared for the severity of the economic crisis that commenced in 1929. Hoover believed that economic recovery was dependent on an uninhibited business and manufacturing community. In 1931 he stated, "Nothing can be gained in the recovery of employment by detouring capital away from industry and commerce into the treasury of the United States, either by taxes or loans."[54] With respect to aid to individual citizens during this time, he found the idea of government aid abhorrent. Hoover believed the role of providing aid to those in need belonged with churches and private charities, not the government. Unable to provide assistance early in 1931, the Office of Indian Affairs appealed to the Red Cross for aid (food, shelter, clothing, and medical care) for almost ten thousand Indians in eastern Oklahoma who did not own land and were therefore not considered the responsibility of the federal government.[55] In August of 1931, Senator Thomas complained that although Oklahoma contained over one-third of the Indian population in the United States, only $3 million of the $28 million appropriated for Indian affairs was earmarked for the state.[56] By 1932, Senator Thomas was discouraged by the lack of response from the Hoover administration, which was clearly demonstrated when he told Frank Davis, a Creek, "It is impossible to get much help under the present administration. . . . I am in hopes that March, 1933 will see a change in administration and . . . then we can look forward to helping the Indians."[57] Between 1929 and 1933, the federal government allocated only $817,968 for emergency relief measures across the state of Oklahoma, with the vast majority going to whites.[58] Frank Mauhuchu, a Choctaw, wrote Elmer Thomas and spoke of Oklahoma Indians being in a "suffering condition." He stated, "We have been to the county and elsewhere for help and they refuse to help us because we are Indians; they told us to go to the [federal] govt. for support."[59]

Oklahoma Indians directed much of their frustration and anger toward the federal government, the Office of Indian Affairs in particular. The presidential election of 1932 marked a turning point for them, however. Many Oklahoma Indians, feeling that the Office of Indian Affairs had abandoned them, "convinced that politics was the source of their problems, decided that political action was the only way to solve them," writes Indian historian B. T. Quinton.[60] Quinton quotes an Oklahoma Pottawatomie who captured the feeling of Oklahoma Indians on the eve of the 1932 election when he said, "Because Republicans believe in depression, the Indians are praying for a Democratic administration."[61] Over 90 percent of the state's Indians who voted cast their ballot for Roosevelt.[62] With their overwhelming electoral victory, FDR and the Democrat majority in Congress held center stage, commissioned to prove themselves to the economically depressed, socially marginalized, and highly skeptical Oklahoma Indians. Like most Native Americans, the latter needed relief not only from the effects of the Depression but also from their position at the bottom rung of American society.

Following Roosevelt's victory, many Oklahoma Indians took a keen interest in his selection of the next commissioner of Indian affairs. The Choctaw-Chickasaw Protective League endorsed Gabe Parker, a Choctaw and former superintendent of the Five Tribes. In response to the endorsement, Parker stated, "I will not seek the appointment unless the Indians of Oklahoma are united behind me."[63] With this statement, Parker touched on an ongoing obstacle Oklahoma Indians faced as they attempted to make their presence felt at all levels of the political system. A strong, effective Indian voice in politics was often inaudible, due to factionalism within and among tribal units. In this situation, a small group of Indians promoting their favorite son operated at a disadvantage, with little political strength.

Oklahoma Indians supported a wide variety of candidates for the commissionership. In February, fifty Ottawas met in Miami, Oklahoma, to form a tribal government that represented viewpoints and desires of all Ottawas. This group endorsed former Oklahoma congressman, E. B. Howard, a non-Indian, for Indian commissioner. The Osage tribal council endorsed Thomas J. Leahy. The Creek Nation waffled between Gabe Parker and Edgar B. Merritt, a non-Indian congressman from Missouri. A mixed group of over four hundred Indians meeting in Oklahoma City split over support for A. F. Snyder, a Pawnee, and E. B. Howard. Several members of the Oklahoma congressional delegation, including William Hastings, Choctaw, and Wesley Disney, kept their fingers on the pulse of Indian support for the commissioner's appointment, but argued that, "Oklahoma [remains] too divided over a group of favorite sons and cannot rally enough support for any one individual."[64]

On February 8, 1933, Utah senator William H. King delivered a speech on the Senate floor in support of John Collier's nomination as the new commissioner of Indian affairs. Directing his comments to President-elect Roosevelt, King counseled, "We suggest that your administration represents almost a last chance for the Indians."[65] Senator King also referenced a petition, signed by over six hundred prominent educators, social workers, and reform-minded citizens, sent to Roosevelt. This petition begged FDR to employ careful consideration in his choice for commissioner, stating, "If there are any appointments in the Government service which deserve to be lifted above the political considerations, the appointments to the Indian Bureau are such.[66]

Members of the Oklahoma and Missouri congressional delegations wrangled and maneuvered in promoting their favorites for the position. Senator Thomas opposed Collier's nomination as commissioner in favor of one of his own political allies, Edgar B. Merritt of Missouri. The Senate majority leader, Joseph T. Robertson of

Arkansas, also pushed Merritt's name to President-elect Roosevelt. However, Harold Ickes, the new secretary of the interior, sold Roosevelt on Collier. Ickes said, "John Collier, with whatever faults of temperament he may have, has to a higher degree than anyone available for that office, the point of view towards the Indian that I want in the Commissioner of Indian Affairs."[67] Thomas vowed to do all in his power to block Collier's appointment to the post and promised to "oppose his confirmation" in the Senate.[68] Roosevelt told Senator Robertson, "Well, you see, Joe, every highbrow [reform] organization in the country is opposed to Merritt, and Secretary Ickes, under whom he would have to work, doesn't want him.[69] Disappointing many politicians, Roosevelt chose Collier, the most vociferous critic of past Indian policy and the Office of Indian Affairs bureaucracy. Thomas, a consummate politician, apparently tested the political winds and grudgingly swung his support to Collier during the confirmation vote. He later explained that he felt "continued opposition was futile and that he had to work with the new commissioner in the future."[70]

John Collier, the product of a genteel Georgia family, was raised in "a constant atmosphere of 'public work,' underpinned by the social pressure of noblesse oblige."[71] His father had served as mayor of Atlanta, and both his parents had died tragically in Collier's youth, his mother from addiction to a painkiller and his grieving father from suicide three years later in 1900. Collier entered Columbia University in 1902 and soon became an idealist exploring socialism, social Darwinism, and psychology. Collier met Lucy Crozier, an instructor at Columbia, who introduced him to New York City's salon life and ultimately social reformation through social work.

In 1908, Collier became associated with the People's Institute, a progressive organization dedicated to helping immigrants build a sense of community in Manhattan neighborhoods. Over the next eleven years, Collier converted to the principles of social engineering by exploring and testing a wide variety of progressive, utopian, and sometimes socialistic ideals in the community laboratory of cosmopolitan New York City. During these years, Collier threw himself wholeheartedly into his endeavors, growing in knowledge and experience, which aided him in later years.

Collier left New York in late 1919, moving to the Los Angeles area where he accepted a position with California's adult education commission. There he focused his attention on immigrant groups. However, Collier soon found himself under investigation by the Justice Department over comments he had made in several classes concerning the Russian Revolution. The Red Scare was intensifying in 1920 and Collier's salary was cut from the state budget. He resigned his position and left California with his family for an extended trip into the Mexican wilderness to reorient himself.[72]

At this time, Providence took a hand in Collier's life as he and his family diverted from their Mexican destination to Taos, New Mexico, instead. In December of 1921, Mabel Dodge, a wealthy New Yorker and former Collier associate, invited him to Taos. Through letters and telegrams, Dodge lured Collier, as he later wrote, "repeating her stories of the magical habitation there of six hundred magical Indians."[73] In Taos Collier quickly immersed himself in the cultural and religious life of the Pueblos. He believed the Pueblos "were still the possessors and users of the fundamental secret of human life—the secret of building great personality through the instrumentality of social institutions."[74] Collier's faith in the principle of community as a building block to effect positive social change germinated in New York and evolved in Taos. Over the next nine months, Collier and his family stayed in Taos with Dodge—and the Pueblos. Collier and Dodge believed that the cultural survival of the Pueblos was key, but they also believed that Euro-American civilization spelled their eventual doom. Indian culture had much to offer modern white civilization, in Collier's judgment, but at the same time needed protection from the danger of being sacrificed in the path of white progress. Collier wrote, "These tiny communities [pueblos] of the red men, archaic, steeped in a not-rational world view of magic and animism ... might live on, ... might use the devices of modern economic life, and pragmatically take over the concepts of modern science, and yet might keep their strange past.... And if the Pueblos lived on, could white civilization acquire anything from them?"[75]

It was during this period that Collier formulated basic understandings and beliefs about American Indians that shaped his thinking over the remainder of his life. Indian historian E. A. Schwartz argued, however, that "Collier's depiction of his Taos experience was more drama than fact."[76] Granted, Collier was dramatic. This is demonstrated in much of his writings throughout his career. However, Collier's article "The Red Atlantis," published in 1922, contains embryonic thoughts that become important planks in the Indian New Deal over the next decade. Collier focused on the failure of allotment and the dissolution of tribal governments, stating, "Today the non-citizen Indians are 'wards' of Congress and the Bureau of Indian Affairs. . . . The guiding policy down to the present has been to deprive the Indian of his land and trample out his community [tribal] life." Secondly, "the dwindled reservations . . . must be conserved," and "some form of cooperative land holding" must be established. Finally, Collier explained, "the Pueblos as agricultural and industrial communities must be given advantages equal to . . . those claimed by white farming communities all over the country."[77] These proposals evolved into the push for tribal organization, the end of allotment, the consolidation and enhancement of tribal landholdings, and economic programs and cooperatives.

Collier left Taos in the early fall of 1921 to accept a teaching position at San Francisco State College. He spent considerable time talking with anthropologists and Office of Indian Affairs officials, and reading "every report by each successive Indian Commissioner since 1852."[78] Collier taught one year before being drawn fully into the Indian reform movement. He quickly became allied with Stella Atwood, president of the General Federation of Women's Clubs.

Their first battle focused on the Bursom Bill, introduced in July of 1922. Aimed at settling the ongoing feud over land claims between the Pueblos and white squatters, the bill, favoring the latter, was supported by Warren Harding's secretary of the interior, Albert B. Fall, and influential Arizona senator Dennis Chavez. By August, Collier, Atwood, and the General Federation of Women's Clubs were waging a sophisticated media campaign against the bill. Collier was soon thrust to the head of this complex faction of reformers. He published an article in *Sunset Magazine* in November 1922 and became a regular contributor over the next year. A letter-to-the-editor campaign was directed at newspapers across the nation, and Collier and Atwood both testified before congressional hearings. Their efforts were successful, and in the spring of 1923 the Bursom Bill died in committee, much to the chagrin of Secretary Fall and the commissioner of Indian affairs, Charles Burke.

In 1923, Collier formed the American Indian Defense Association (AIDA), and he served as its executive secretary for the next decade, moving to Washington to act as a lobbyist for Indian reform. During these years, the underlying ideology of the Indian New Deal evolved. The basic tenets included preservation of Indian civilization and culture, promotion of Indian arts and crafts, opposition to the government's long-practiced allotment policy, freedom for American Indians to practice indigenous religious beliefs, self-government, and a type of credit system to provide capital for economic development. Years later, writing his memoirs, Collier claimed that by 1922 he had "formulated ideas to end allotment and . . . by 1924, what was to become the Indian New Deal had become rather thoroughly formulated."[79] Some accused Collier of promoting a form of assimilation wrapped in another package. However, Collier asserted, "Assimilation, not into our culture but into modern life, and preservation and intensification of heritage are not hostile choices, excluding one another, but are interdependent through and through."[80] Collier developed a line of thinking that can be traced back to progressivism and that was dubbed "the tribal alternative" by historian Graham Taylor.[81] This multicultural approach would bring American Indians into full political and economic participation in white society while maintaining their cultural heritage.

Historians Lawrence Kelly and Kenneth Philp extensively studied the pre–New Deal era of John Collier's life and present an extremely complex individual in their respective books, *The Assault on Assimilation: John Collier and the Origins of Indian Policy* and *John Collier's Crusade for Indian Reform, 1920–1934*. First there is Collier the idealistic reformer, motivated by a belief in the goodness and purity of Indian culture, religion, and philosophy. The public person, the John Collier most people knew, confronted the status quo and initiated fundamental changes in Indian-government affairs. Many became inspired by his unwavering zeal. However, Collier, a private man, sometimes was troubled with doubt and often needed to escape the pressure of public life with retreats into the solitude of nature, from which he emerged refreshed, determined, and ready to resume battle. Both Kelly and Philp breathe life into this important figure in Indian affairs policy.

The 1920s produced an important antecedent for the Indian New Deal of the 1930s. Historian Randolph C. Downes characterized much of the Indian policy reform efforts of the 1920s as "muckraking journalism, pressure group politics, and governmental investigations," which served both as a means of education and as the "impetus for change" in Indian affairs in the 1930s with the New Deal.[82] With Collier's confirmation as commissioner of Indian affairs, the stage was set for the ideas of reformers to come into play. What resulted was a fascinating struggle of reformist ideas in conflict with political reality, frequently resulting in unexpected outcomes. This book now turns to examine many of those outcomes as they influenced Oklahoma Indians through the Oklahoma Indian Welfare Act of 1936.

CHAPTER 3

The Indian New Deal

John Collier was sworn in as commissioner of Indian affairs on April 21, 1933. On that date, he issued a press release giving a glimpse of the new philosophy that would now guide the Indian Bureau. Collier spoke of the need not only for increased expenditures to enlarge a number of programs designed to aid impoverished Native Americans but also for a reorganization of the Office of Indian Affairs. "I strongly believe that the responsibility of the United States, as guardians of the Indians, ought to be continued," Collier wrote. Nevertheless, "in the long run, the Indians must be their own saviors and their own helpers." "It means decreasing the paternalism of the Government and extending civil rights and the facilities of modern business enterprise to the Indians."[1] Collier envisioned the day when "the Indian Bureau becomes a counselor rather than the responsible agent."[2]

Collier brought a new perspective on Indians and Indian affairs to the office along with four basic objectives he hoped to promote: rebuilding Indian tribal societies, enlarging and rehabilitating Indian landholdings, fostering Indian self-government, and preserving and promoting Indian culture.[3] The ideology of forced assimilation into white society had served as the bedrock of government Indian policy for two generations. Collier's Indian New Deal introduced a new ideology with progressive origins. As mentioned above, Graham Taylor termed this new set of ideas the "tribal alternative."[4] Political scientist Elmer Rusco contends that the tribal alternative "abandoned the goal of assimilation in favor of the belief that Native American societies had a right to exist on the basis of a culture different from the dominant one in the United States."[5] Much of Collier's reform program rested on this idea, including ending the allotment policy, preserving Indian culture, and promoting self-government and incorporation. The tension and conflict between this position and the entrenched ideology of assimilation underpin the many struggles Collier found himself in during the reform battles of the 1920s and during his tenure as commissioner of Indian affairs from 1933 to 1945.

Having been an outspoken critic of the office and its policies for over a decade, Collier had to "contend with the entrenched and selfish outside interests that have controlled and exploited the bureau for so many years at the expense of the Indians."[6] Over the years, Collier had irritated a number of people in Congress and in the Indian Bureau. This plagued his working relationship with Congress and the bureau throughout his commissionership. Assimilation had been the formal basis of federal Indian policy since 1887 with enactment of the Dawes Act. To Indian Bureau careerists it seemed obvious that Indians must give up their culture and fully Americanize by becoming landowners and embracing white culture and Christianity. Assimilationists viewed Collier and his proposals for revolutionizing Indian policy as a direct threat to all they had worked for over the years. Church missionaries who opposed Collier recommended, "The Indian must be saved by a process of Christian assimilation of American life, not by carefully guarded and subsidized segregation."[7] Senator Burton K. Wheeler, cosponsor of the Indian Reorganization Act, declared it was Congress's responsibility to "aid Indians as nearly as possible [to] adopt the white man's ways and laws."[8]

In addition, the American public accepted assimilation as the path Indians needed to follow. Indians needed to adapt and be incorporated into mass society, though their rights and position in that society remained unclear. Ingrained ideas of racial and cultural superiority leavened the assimilationist ideology. Frederick Hoxie captured the underlying sentiment of many whites when he wrote, "The white protestant majority continued to imagine that its values and the nation's were identical."[9] Traditional Indian non-Christian culture, with its emphasis on communalism and what seemed for many to be archaic cultural practices, was seen as standing in the path of America's destiny.

Within the Oklahoma Indian population were many who endorsed the idea of assimilation into white society. Often these people were referred to as "progressives." Many claimed mixed ancestry, had been educated at federal Indian schools, and also embraced Christianity. This group frequently interacted with whites as neighbors and through the white economic system. "Progressives" believed a promising future came with incorporation into white society. James Kawauypla, a Fort Sill Apache, stated, "Reservation life will retard and eventually prevent us from adjusting ourselves to fit in the white civilization in which we live." For whites and some Indians, assimilation by Native Americans into the dominant white society made sense and seemed the only path to follow.

In May of 1933, Collier, with the aid of Secretary Ickes, persuaded FDR to issue an executive order abolishing the Board of Indian Commissioners, which he viewed as a citadel of assimilationist thinking. This group had existed as an advisory board on Indian affairs since the days of Ulysses Grant's Peace Policy, advising the president and Congress. Several former commissioners, such as Flora Warren Seymour and Dr. C. C. Lindquist, continued to oppose Collier and his reform agenda.

On August 12, 1933, in a bureau order signed by Secretary Ickes that all but ended the allotment policy, Collier directed, "Due to existing economic conditions and the very poor market for Indian owned restricted lands, it is hereby ordered until further notice that no more trust or restricted Indian lands shall be offered for sale." Collier specifically mentioned the unique situation of Indians and their landholdings in Oklahoma when he said, "The foregoing shall apply to the Osages and the Five Tribes Indians insofar as the sale of their land is subject to control by this Department."[10]

Collier's appointment convinced numerous individuals that "for the first time in many years the Indians have a right to expect justice and sympathy from their guardians in Washington."[11] The evolution of the Indian New Deal mirrored the Roosevelt administration's New Deal as a whole: first came relief measures, then reform. Collier wasted little time in getting to work. He spent much of his first few months developing stopgap measures to provide immediate aid for economically depressed Indians, and he finagled with various agencies and departments to get Native Americans included in existing New Deal programs. This saved considerable time, prevented duplication of efforts, and conserved bureau appropriations for other programs. Collier worked to establish the Indian Division of the Civilian Conservation Corps, which eventually supplied thirty-two hundred jobs for Oklahoma Indians, and proved instrumental in helping Oklahoma Indians receive benefits from a variety of other early New Deal programs, including the Agricultural Adjustment Act, the Public Works Administration, the Federal Emergency Relief Administration, and the Works Progress Administration.[12] These would help mitigate some of the severe conditions experienced by Oklahoma Indians by providing income for basics such as food, clothing, seeds, and tools.

Collier also harbored the long-range objective of revamping the Indian Bureau to rectify the many wrongs he saw in federal Indian policy. It was obvious that his objectives extended much further than piecemeal patching. His policies sought to achieve "[e]conomic rehabilitation of the Indians, principally on the land; organization of the Indian tribes for managing their own affairs, and civil and cultural freedom and opportunity for the Indians."[13] Collier adamantly believed that the allotment policy of the federal government had for almost sixty years symbolized the main obstacle to Indian economic advancement and saw the bureau during this period as maintaining near despotic control over Indians. He viewed these as two evils needing to be destroyed.[14]

Collier realized that many of his proposals required Congress to pass reform legislation. After witnessing Roosevelt's legislative success during his first hundred days in office, he decided to incorporate his reform objectives, including overturning the allotment policy, into an omnibus piece of legislation. Throughout the summer and fall of 1933, Collier, Felix S. Cohen, Nathan Margold, and other legal staff members of the Interior Department hammered out a legislative proposal.[15] In September of 1933, Indians across the country, including those in Oklahoma, got to see the proposed legislation firsthand as the Office of Indian Affairs circulated drafts of the bill in order to obtain Indian opinion and support. These drafts were sent to tribal councils through the bureaucratic pipeline. It is questionable how many Indians actually saw these drafts and probable that few were able to wade through forty-eight pages of legal phraseology and arrive at a clear understanding of the proposed measure and its aims.

In early January of 1934, Collier held a conference at the Cosmos Club in Washington, D.C., seeking support for his legislative proposals from various reform groups, including the National Association on Indian Affairs, the American Indian Defense Association, the General Federation of Women's Clubs, and the Indian Rights Association (IRA), with which he had worked through most of the 1920s and early 1930s. At this conference, all the groups supported Collier and his proposals to one degree or another, and he left elated, feeling he had achieved a mandate.

Opposition to Collier's Indian New Deal rose almost immediately in Oklahoma, however, with most of it originating in the eastern half of the state. The *Muskogee Daily Phoenix* became the mouthpiece for Oklahoma opposition to Collier and his proposals, carrying on a verbal onslaught against Collier and the Indian New Deal. An abrasive editorial dated November 18, 1933, is characteristic in tone of many that followed: "Oklahoma's Indians, more than the entire number in the United States, want no tribal reservations, no communal fishing and hunting grounds. . . . Oklahoma will hope that Mr. Collier will not be permitted to erase all the great progress and void all the achievement of the last two decades in betterment of the American Indian in this state."[16]

Eastern Oklahoma remained the center for ongoing opposition to Collier, his legislative proposal (which would become the Wheeler-Howard Bill and then the Indian Reorganization Act), and later the Thomas-Rogers Bill, which would become the Oklahoma Indian Welfare Act in 1936. On February 9, 1934, Collier introduced his proposed legislation to Oklahoma, addressing three hundred Indian Bureau employees in Oklahoma City who represented almost every tribal group in the state. Collier outlined a two-step program. He proposed first that "the Indians must be organized and then given land that is fit to live on," and then that "the government must provide credit for [economic] rehabilitation." Collier cautioned his audience by saying, "We don't intend to drive the Indian back to the farm but if he wants to go, and most of them do, land must be provided for them and they must be taught modern farming methods." In concluding, Collier warned that his proposal offered no quick fix. He continued, "It will take years to bring the Indian[s] to their proper level. After ten years under our program we should begin to make a showing and it will take years more to bring it to a conclusion."[17]

Collier's proposals marked a radical change in federal Indian policy and fostered controversy in many quarters. Several former members of the Board of Indian Commissioners claimed the proposed legislation to be socialistic or communistic or both. Most vocal was Flora Warren Seymour, who, in a series of magazine and newspaper articles, described it as "the most extreme gesture yet made by the administration in this country toward a Communistic experiment."[18] C. C. Lindquist echoed, "Collier's plan is socialism and communism in the rankest sense."[19] The *Daily Oklahoman* picked up this charge and brazenly editorialized that "the similarity of what is proposed to the soviets of Russia is strong enough to be noticeable."[20] These charges that Collier's proposals were a "Communistic experiment," smacking of Soviet influence, continued over the time in which the IRA and the OIWA were debated, amended, and enacted. Originating from more cosmopolitan eastern Oklahoma, they often received national press coverage and proved an ongoing thorn for Collier.

Senator Wheeler of Montana and Representative Edgar Howard of Nebraska introduced the bulky bill into Congress in February 12, 1934. Collier dubbed it the "Bill of Indian Rights."[21] It contained most of his key objectives for Indian policy formulated during his involvement in the Indian reform movement during the previous decade. Title I established procedures for Indians "to organize for purposes of local self-government and economic enterprise ... [with] powers common to all municipal corporations." It authorized a $500,000 annual appropriation for organizing Indian tribal governments and a $10 million credit loan fund to aid tribes pursuing economic and agricultural development. Title I also eased civil service requirements so that the Office of Indian Affairs could employ more Indians. Title II concerned education and established, among other things, scholarships and loans for vocational training and college for Native Americans. Title III not only ended land allotment but also provided for the return of previously allotted lands to Indian tribes. Indian lands held in trust by the federal government were also to be returned to tribal control. Title III further established the policy of "a constructive program of Indian land use and economic development, in order to establish a permanent basis of self-support for Indians living under Federal tutelage [on reservations]." This title also authorized an annual $2 million appropriation for purchasing land to enlarge reservations. Title IV created a Court of Indian Affairs possessing original jurisdiction and to be conducted in accordance with Indian traditions for tribes who organized under Title I, thereby removing them from the jurisdiction of state and local courts.[22] This proposal represented not only "a new approach, [but] also an attempt to streamline the archaic and complicated system of Indian law."[23]

Collier felt that with this legislation a new foundation for Indian law would be established. However, strong opposition quickly arose within Congress to the Wheeler-Howard Bill, opposition centered among a handful of legislators knowledgeable about federal Indian policy, including many from states with significant Indian populations. Lack of knowledge of Indian affairs and plain indifference further hindered attempts to gain congressional support. American Indians contributed such a small percentage of votes that for most legislators Indian affairs policy took a backseat to more immediate challenges of the Great Depression. Passage of the bill was delayed for months.

Commissioner Collier fought hostility and apathy in Congress by embarking on a nationwide publicity campaign to promote Wheeler-Howard, hoping to develop public support that would pressure Congress to pass it. Mailings requesting support were sent to thousands of religious leaders, university presidents, newspaper editors, and celebrities such as Will Rogers. Magazines, scholarly journals, missionary groups, the Kiwanis Club, and the General Federation of Women's Clubs received the same. At the bottom of one page of a mailing list used by Collier and the bureau is the note, "I wonder if it would be possible for you to ask Father Coughlin to speak of [the] bill over radio. He has an immense audience. It would not do harm to try."[24] Clearly the bureau left no stone unturned in efforts to promote the Wheeler-Howard Bill.

Collier, a prolific writer, authored a number of articles promoting the bill that were published in popular American magazines, and women's magazine *Good Housekeeping* interviewed him in April of 1934 as the battle in Congress heated up. Collier elevated the struggle to a moral level when he compared his land restoration proposals, affecting "perhaps only 200,000 Indians," to those in Mexico, "a very poor country, [which] has assumed as a moral obligation the restoring of land to more than 2,000,000 Indians." Collier continued that "unless this is done more than two hundred thousand of our allotted Indians . . . are increasingly going to become tramps, as many of them are already." He warned, "That is a public menace a hundred times graver than investing some money now in colonizing these homeless Indians and putting them on their feet permanently."[25] Vera Connolly, the article's author, made an impassioned plea to American women, stating, "The Indians are doomed unless [Indian policy] is changed. Congress is the arbiter. Will you women of the United States help? . . . The outcome of that battle will depend—to an enormous degree—on you!" Connolly gave voice to Indian women who implored, "Help us! Help us! white women of America! . . . We starve. We shiver in rags. We drop with disease. We are being robbed, by our Federal guardians, of all we have left. Help us. Save us!"[26] The article concluded with an urgent request from the editor: "Readers of *Good Housekeeping*, help Commissioner Collier! Write your Senators and Representatives, urging them to sponsor this proposed Indian legislation."[27] The tone of many other magazine and newspaper articles and interviews published at the time was similar. Collier had demonstrated an ability to employ the media to gain public support.

Many Oklahoma Indians already felt assimilated into white society and resented the attempt to reinstitute tribal control over their property and lives. A second problem arose from a contradiction noted later by Lawrence Kelly: "despite the emphasis in the act on Indian self-determination, few Indians were consulted while the bill was being drafted."[28] This was noted by many Indians across the country and holds some validity. In drafting the legislation, Collier had relied heavily on legal experts such as Margold, Cohen, and other Interior Department lawyers. This would be rectified to some degree, as Indian input would be sought in congressional hearings and in the series of Indian congresses held for both the Wheeler-Howard Bill and the Thomas-Rogers Bill. This Indian involvement will be discussed later in this chapter as well as in chapter 5. In commenting on the proposed Wheeler-Howard Bill, Joseph Bruner, a Creek from Sapulpa, Oklahoma, and founder of the American Indian Federation, said, "As I see it, it would segregate us. We have taken our place with white people and helped build up this country. I'm against this bill."[29]

Many Oklahoma Indians believed that Collier based his views on his understanding of the Navajo and Pueblo Indians from the 1920s and early 1930s, and they felt that Collier had erroneously "concluded that Indians everywhere would wish to return to tribal communal life."[30] Collier, they believed, lumped together all Indians, as if they shared the same cultural heritage and faced identical challenges. Many Oklahoma Indians saw themselves as unique. Individual land ownership remained the rule, but most were landless and the tribes possessed little communally held land. With little land, many believed that Wheeler-Howard's proposed return to communal land ownership and the reservation system would not be best for them. Joseph Bruner, who besides founding the American Indian Federation was also president of the National Indian Confederacy, summed up his views in a letter addressed to both the Senate and the House: "We do not want—we will not voluntarily or cheerfully accept separate schools, separate communities, separate courts, or additional impeding obnoxious interference from Washington."[31]

Like Indians across the country, most Oklahoma Indians never read the bill and possessed little understanding of its proposals. This, coupled with the general mistrust of the actions of the federal government, led initially to cross-state opposition to the bill by many.

Eastern Oklahoma newspapers continued to attack Collier and his proposals. The *Tulsa Tribune* countered, "It [the Wheeler-Howard Bill] is not so attractive to Oklahoma Indians of the five Civilized Tribes, who are as competent for the duties of citizenship as the average white citizen of Oklahoma, and who lead the same kind of lives as their white neighbors."[32] The *Tribune* criticized Collier by saying, "It is doubtful if the commissioner himself quite understands that the Indian problem in Oklahoma is not the same as that of the Blackfoot or Apache reservation."[33] The *Bartlesville Examiner* suggested, "The secretary of the interior and the commissioner of Indian affairs should make an exhaustive first hand study of the Indian situation in Oklahoma. They should both spend considerable time in the state."[34]

After initially announcing support for Collier's legislative proposal during the Cosmos Club conference in January, the Indian Rights Association came out against the bill in March of 1934. In that month's issue of its *Indian Truth*, Matthew K. Sniffen decried what he and the IRA considered to be "revolutionary departures in Indian policy."[35] The IRA vehemently opposed the Wheeler-Howard proposal, claiming, "It perpetuates segregation under the guise of self-government. It jeopardizes individual Indian property rights, and shifts the incentive which the authors of the Allotment Act had in mind for individual ownership of property leading towards citizenship. The policy is a reversal of the past."[36] Though a well-respected, long-time advocate of reform in Indian policy, the IRA had an ideological framework rooted deeply in assimilationism. Vine Deloria, Jr., and Clifford M. Lytle, coauthors of *The Nations Within*, attribute the IRA's shift from support to opposition to an internal power struggle between conservative and moderate factions in the organization.[37]

Within the Office of Indian Affairs, there also arose pockets of resistance to the proposed Wheeler-Howard Bill. Many longtime employees feared Collier's new ideas and the prospect of change. Evidently this resistance reached a level where it caught the attention not only of John Collier but also Harold Ickes. Both men moved quickly to stifle internal opposition. Ickes issued a blunt memo to all Indian Bureau staff: "If any employee wishes to oppose the new policy, he should do so honestly and openly from outside the service. This would mean his resignation."[38] Collier and Ickes might have to deal with opposition from without, but it was not going to be tolerated from within.

Collier tied his success as Indian commissioner to enactment of Wheeler-Howard, and he believed that expressed Indian support would influence Congress positively. In order to garner Indian support, he visited ten reservations across the United States in the spring of 1934 to promote the bill. Possessing a large percentage of the country's Indian population, Oklahoma was considered key by Collier. In March 1934, he crisscrossed the state, conducting three congresses with representatives from more than thirty tribes. Several thousand Indians attended large, daylong meetings held in Anadarko, Muskogee, and Miami. A cross-section of tribal communities attended each congress, ranging from people who spoke English and had business savvy (usually young people) to those who maintained a traditional Indian lifestyle and often required interpreters.

Over two thousand Indians from the western plains tribes attended the first congress, held in Anadarko on October 15, 1934. Collier conducted this meeting in much the same fashion as he would the others. First he launched into a detailed explanation of the bill. He decried the allotment system, saying, "It is correct to say that the allotment system intends for all Indian allotted lands to pass to whites."[39] He mixed into his explanations a sales pitch designed to gain Indian approval for the bill. During the Anadarko congress, a member in the crowd asked Collier what would happen to Indians who "don't come in." Collier replied, "The tribe which does not want to come into this bill at all will go on just the way it is now until all of the land is lost and then I suppose it will come back and ask for a charter and some new land."[40] At all three congresses held in Oklahoma, most discussions and questions from the Native Americans centered on the issue of land. In Anadarko, Collier discussed the fact the "four out of every six Indians [in western Oklahoma] . . . are landless. . . . Seventy-two thousand of the Five Civilized Tribes are totally landless." Collier concluded, "The basic fact is that there is not enough land belonging to the Indians. We have got to get more land to supply the landless Indians."[41]

Questions ranged from specific inquiries to broad concerns. At Anadarko, Morris Bedoka, a Kiowa, asked, "Now to secure a charter, as I understand it, you would have to have the recommendation of the local agent with the approval of the Secretary of the Interior. Is that correct?" Jasper Saunkeah, chairman of the Kiowa-Comanche tribal council, wondered, "Would this bill take away the voting privilege we have in state and national affairs?"[42] Henry Roe Cloud, speaking for an Indian outside of the meeting, expressed the fear many Indians seemed to have that the bill would establish "colonies" [landholdings purchased by the federal government for the tribes and opened to group settlement by tribal members] which "would segregate the Indians—put them all by themselves."[43] At all three congresses, Collier communicated his belief that the allotment system was intended "for all Indian allotted lands to pass to whites."[44]

At the second Oklahoma congress, held in Muskogee on March 24, 1934, Collier spent considerable time talking about the need for the Five Tribes to organize. With tribal organizations abolished around the time of statehood in 1907, Collier found it "strange to find the biggest group of Indians in the country without organization to speak for it officially or authoritatively."[45] Collier believed that Oklahoma Indians, especially in the eastern part of the state, could wield considerable political power in the state by organizing, stating, "I think that their use of the franchise would in the long run be made ten-fold in effectiveness by this bill."[46] While Collier discussed most aspects of the bill at each congress, at Muskogee he attempted to sell members of the Five Tribes the idea that by working together as a group organized under provisions of the Wheeler-Howard Bill, the tribes would be able to enhance their political voice both with Congress and with the Indian Bureau.

The Miami congress, held on March 26, 1934, again focused on the issue of land. Collier discussed hidden costs of administering the allotment system. Using the Five Tribes as an example, Collier pointed out that the Five Tribes Agency in Muskogee was spending roughly 80 percent of its annual $300,000 appropriation, or $240,000, to cover administrative costs for Indian allotments. Collier spent time discussing and answering questions concerning Indian access to credit. "Indians are handicapped because they have no access to credit," he said.[47] Collier promoted the $10 million revolving credit system set up in the bill. The revolving credit fund allowed a tribal government, an economic development organization, or merely a group of independent tribal members who joined together under a charter to take out federal loans to finance a business venture.

An Osage at the Miami congress asked, "Could a tribe now rejecting the bill, now requesting to be excluded from it, ever get a chance to apply for a charter, that is, ever get a chance to be let into it again?"[48]

At each congress, the audience received time devoted to their questions. Collier responded to the bulk of the questions himself, only deferring to staff members for questions involving technical legal points or as his voice tired in the evening after a long day. At each congress, Collier emphasized the fact that he was there to explain the proposed bill and gain Indian input. Various Indian groups pressured Collier, resulting in over thirty amendments to the Wheeler-Howard Bill. Many of these amendments addressed Indian concerns over the possibility of individual allotments being returned to the tribe as communal property. Many Indians drew a line in the sand over this proposal. Historian Francis P. Prucha correctly contends that with these amendments, "Collier wisely retreated to what he thought he could get enacted."[49] Though Collier is considered by many to have been an idealist with his head in the clouds, he exercised a keen sense of knowing when to fight, when to compromise, and when to retreat in political battles. These amendments were important for two reasons. First of all, they demonstrated Collier's determination to see Wheeler-Howard passed, even if he had to compromise on some points. More important, Collier not only listened to input from Indians, he acted on it as well. Amendments to the bill reflected Collier's willingness to include Indians directly in the give-and-take of the legislative process. This was itself a radical departure from Indian policy of the previous fifty years.

Collier believed that American Indians should play a greater role in determining their own futures. The heart of Wheeler-Howard reflected his deeply held beliefs, with provisions for Indians to organize themselves for the purposes of self-government and economic development. However, Collier also represented the system in which he operated. During the previous fourteen years, Collier had been deeply involved in the Indian reform movement. Most of his colleagues were white. His dearth of direct contact with American Indians limited his influence among them. Few Indians were directly involved in the movement. Those involved had become acculturated to a large degree and often seemed distantly removed from their Indian brothers and sisters. Whites led the battle for changes in Indian policy and struggled with non-Indian legislators and bureaucrats to see their proposals enacted and implemented. Non-Indians might consult with Indians to determine their needs and desires, but non-Indians expressed those needs and targeted which ones to pursue and what courses of action to follow. Professionals such as anthropologists and sociologists helped provide understanding of Native American social and cultural nuances. Non-Indian reformers often seemed to believe they knew the needs and desires of Native Americans better than the Indians themselves did. Often reformers such as Collier appeared paternalistic and condescending to Native Americans.

All three of the Oklahoma congresses were daylong events that extended late into the evening. After each session was formally concluded, Collier and his staff held small-group meetings for those interested, to further explain topics and to respond to additional questions. For example, Collier himself might cover the subject of tribal organizations. Felix Cohen or Nathan Margold might conduct a session covering legal aspects of guardianships and heirships. Ward Shepherd, a bureau specialist in land policies, might cover the subject of land acquisition. Unfortunately no records were kept for most of these types of informal meetings as the bill was being drafted.

The charge that Indians were not included in the drafting of the Wheeler-Howard Bill remained one of its chief criticisms. Outside of the congresses, there are no records of Collier, his staff, or the congressional sponsors, Senator Wheeler and Representative Howard, contacting or being contacted by any Indian individual or group as the bill was being drafted. The congresses therefore proved beneficial to Collier and the Indian Bureau as well as to many of the Native Americans who attended.

Recognizing the absolute necessity of obtaining substantial Indian support for this proposal that originally contained such a large part of his overall vision for reforming federal Indian policy, Collier placed great emphasis on making the congresses successful. Many Indians, however, attended with only a sketchy idea of the legislative proposal. More than likely most never saw or read a draft of the bill, and many received misinformation about it, thinking, for example, that allotment holders might be forced to give their allotments to the tribe and resort to communal landholdings. All Indians held a degree of doubt and mistrust concerning the proposed Indian New Deal. Based on past dealings with whites and the Indian Bureau, most hesitated to accept Collier and his proposal as the answer to all their problems. Most Indians did not share his zeal in restructuring federal Indian policy.

Clearly Collier realized the situation he faced as he entered the congresses. Patiently and repeatedly he sought Indian input, gave full and clear explanations, and did not dodge tough questions or take offense at the abrasive or apprehensive attitudes of some Indian attendees. Collier gave the impression to many that he cared about the Indians. For the most part, these efforts paid off for him. Concerns were addressed and often eliminated. Doubts and mistrust were mitigated. While not all Indians left supporting the Wheeler-Howard Bill, Collier garnered a greater deal of support from these congresses. Perhaps most importantly, Collier planted seeds in the minds of many Indians that a new era with a brighter dawn in federal Indian affairs was now opening.

Nevertheless, the congresses obtained mixed results in the state. Indians remained divided on the Wheeler-Howard Bill, with neither an overwhelming acceptance nor rejection. Contained in the minutes of the three congresses held in Oklahoma were resolutions and verbal pronouncements introduced by twenty tribal groups from across the state. The tribal business committee for the Pawnees, Poncas, Kaws, Otoes, and Tonkawas brought a resolution to the Anadarko congress that simply stated that the "sentiment of the various tribes was opposed to the bill." Thomas W. Alford, a Shawnee registered his qualms, "We are willing to take anything that we believe to be for the best interest of our people. This is a program that is a puzzle to us." The Sacs and Foxes approved the bill, stating, "[We] believe that a long sought opportunity has come to the Indian people through this bill." The Cheyennes and Arapahos rejected the bill and appealed to John Collier "to retain the present status of rights and privileges given the Indians comprising the Cheyenne and Arapaho reservation." Three groups, the Quapaws, the Osages, and the Delawares, tabled any endorsement or rejection, opting to "think it over." The Muscogee Creeks tabled consideration because they felt they lacked an official organization to make such a decision. The Creek Emigrant Indian Committee sent a resolution "asking you [Collier] to get our Treaty [1835] back just like it was before and let us run it ourselves."[50] While it is impossible from this information to determine the number of individuals who either favored or disapproved of the proposed legislation, it is quite evident that a wide spectrum of support and opposition for the bill existed among Oklahoma Indians.

An Office of Indian Affairs document entitled "Analysis of Official Vote of Indian Tribes on Wheeler-Howard" tells a different story. It reports that nationwide 139,824 Indians from fifty-one tribes approved of the Wheeler-Howard Bill, while 12,364 Indians from eleven tribes opposed it. For Oklahoma, this report shows that a total of 29,925 Indians representing four nations of the Five Tribes voted (the Seminoles and the plains tribes of western Oklahoma are not included). A number of scholars have used the figures from this report in their studies, but their accuracy seems questionable at best.[51]

Almost immediately after Collier's return to Washington from the Oklahoma congresses, both the Senate and House Committees on Indian Affairs resumed hearings on Wheeler-Howard. With both committees, Collier faced a conservative group of legislators who remained rabid assimilationists and considered Collier's legislative proposal a return to communal property, with Indians segregated from mass society. In the Senate, Collier faced a troika of opposition from Senator Wheeler, who now waffled on the legislation he had sponsored, Senator Thomas, and Senator Henry Ashurst from Arizona.[52]

Wheeler, chairman of the Senate Committee on Indian Affairs and cosponsor of the bill, proved an ongoing antagonist for Collier throughout the Senate hearings. A diehard assimilationist who felt Indians were not capable of governing themselves, Wheeler questioned much about the original proposal. He viewed the section involving the proposed Indian Court of Affairs as a step backward for many Indians. Ashurst wanted to spar with Collier over his continued opposition to provisions included in the Pueblo Relief Act passed almost a year earlier, in May 1933.[53]

Thomas was enraged over comments Collier had made to the Indians at the Anadarko conference. Collier had stated, "You know that at the present time President Roosevelt controls both Houses of Congress. When President Roosevelt wants a piece of legislation, he gets it from Congress." Thomas acidly responded, "You told my Indians down at my home that it made no difference what Congress thought about it, that you would pass the bill if you wanted to, and would pass it quickly . . . you have the opinion then, that you [Collier] can pass this bill through quickly, whether or not the Congress wants the bill?"[54] This type of exchange was sprinkled throughout the hearings and demonstrates a gulf of enmity separating Commissioner Collier from many congressional leaders.

The minutes of both the House and the Senate hearings are readily available and have been examined by scholars in detail. Few, however, have offered much more than a cursory look at Indian testimony and viewpoints offered at these hearings. While attention to the hearings in their entirety is necessary to understand what groups and thinking molded the bill, my focus here is on Indian contributions to the hearings.

Both the House and Senate hearings began in late February 1934, just days after the bill was introduced on February 12. Both committees held several initial sessions and then adjourned until April when Commissioner Collier attended the ten Indian congresses across the country. During both sets of hearings, Collier or close aides such as Margold or his Margold's assistants, Charles Fahy or Felix Cohen, spent considerable time and effort explaining in detail the forty-eight page bill. Senators and representatives grilled them on any number of technical or legal points, wanting to know the specifics of Collier's proposals for land purchase, self-government, the revolving credit fund, the proposed Court of Indian Affairs, and educational benefits. Most of the legislators operated from a deeply ingrained assimilationist ideology. Collier's proposals seemed radical and threatened the status quo in federal Indian affairs. Many accused Collier of moving backward in Indian affairs administration. With the Wheeler-Howard Bill, they feared a return to the reservation system and segregation of the American Indian from white society. Two schools of thought—assimilation and a new ideology, "the tribal alternative"—battled for dominance through the course of these hearings.

Native Americans found themselves in the middle of this legislative struggle, most tribal people being well acquainted with congressional proceedings. During the 1920s, a number of congressional committees as well as private research foundations had examined Native Americans. This time, however, things seemed different. Instead of merely investigating the "conditions" of Native Americans, the government was now seeking their viewpoints and suggestions on a legislative proposal under consideration. This was unprecedented. In general many Indians were distrustful, and justifiably so. They had experienced a long history with whites of broken treaties, unfulfilled promises, and almost a complete disregard and respect for their interests and culture.

An examination of the minutes of both the Senate and House hearings makes it apparent that many Native Americans had little if any understanding of the proposed bill. They held misconceptions concerning its overall intentions. Vern E. Thompson, representing the Quapaws from Oklahoma, presented a resolution to the House Committee on Indian Affairs on March 13, 1934. Adopted by the Quapaw tribal council on March 10, it requested that the Quapaws be excluded from Wheeler-Howard. The council had first seen the forty-eight-page bill the day before, on March 9. It is difficult to understand how the Quapaw tribal council could digest and fully understand the complex bill in twenty-four hours and formulate a reasonable position on it.[55]

The Quapaws considered their situation unique among tribal groups. In 1895, the Quapaws, with congressional approval, had instituted their own allotment program, which granted each tribal member two hundred acres of prairie land, which was "practically all alike, there was no distinction in quality."[56] Each member received forty acres of timberland as well. Their resolution argued, "These Indian people have, in good faith, attempted to do what the Government is asking them to do, amalgamate with the white citizenship.... These Indians ... in good faith have attempted to adopt the laws and customs of the white men."[57] They expressed contentment with their situation and asked to be left alone.

Thompson appeared before the House committee again on April 9, after the congress held in Miami on March 24, 1934. Approximately two hundred Quapaws had attended the congress, including the tribal council. At the conclusion of the congress they submitted a second resolution and again requested exclusion of the Quapaws from Wheeler-Howard. They also submitted several questions to Commissioner Collier, which he answered to their satisfaction. They came to believe that the bill was a good measure and would prove "to be of great benefit and assistance to certain of our Indian brethren," but they "respectfully request[ed] that said bill be amended so as to exempt the Quapaw."[58]

James Saluskin, a full-blood Pawnee, expressed a fear in common with many tribal groups. Saluskin testified that "it is the landless Indian, the Indian that has sold his land; they are going to rule as a majority." Saluskin spoke of the division between full-bloods and mixed-bloods. He said that "it is the landless Indian, the half-breed and from there up, they take things upon themselves and exercise their rights, without the knowledge of the tribal council."[59]

Testimony from Oklahoma Indians during the congressional hearings demonstrated a wide divergence in viewpoint on Wheeler-Howard. The Fort Sill Apaches opposed passage of the bill. Taking what many would consider a pro-assimilationist viewpoint, they asserted, "It will check our economic and social advancement. Reservation life will retard and eventually prevent us from adjusting ourselves to fit in the white civilization."[60] On the other hand, the Comanches of Oklahoma opposed Wheeler-Howard, but from a more traditional perspective, stating, "We however would much prefer to have our affairs looked after in the manner they . . . always have." They opposed the idea of self-government and change in general. By contrast, the Cherokees, from eastern Oklahoma focused on the idea of obtaining land and seemed excited about the bill, believing "it gives the Indians a permanent home and stops the allotment system, gives the rising generation a home that they call their own."[61]

Ute Arapaho, of the Oklahoma Cheyenne and Arapaho Tribes, like many other Indians, was concerned about land issues. Speaking through an interpreter, Arapaho testified to the House committee that he was concerned that "the landowner would [be forced] to give his title and right to his allotments for the benefit of landless Indians."[62] Arapaho also wanted to see provisions in the bill concerning heirships amended so that rather than being placed in the tribe's communal land holdings, allottees could to pass their holdings on to their descendants.

Jesse Rowlodge, representing the Oklahoma Cheyenne and Arapaho Tribes before the Senate Committee on Indian Affairs, gave four disparate reasons why the Cheyennes and Arapahos remained reluctant to endorse the bill. First, "[i]t is so technical that no member of the tribe is able to interpret it." Second, with almost two-thirds of the twenty-eight hundred tribe members landless, there was concern as to where those members would go when the government provided land for them. Rowlodge mused, "Many of them [landless tribal members] seem to think that they are going to be drifted back to some arid land where no one else would be able to make a living."[63] Third, the tribes expressed concern over the continuity of the proposed legislation once enacted in the event of a change of administration. Lastly, the Cheyenne and Arapaho Tribes questioned the "right of the government to take away from the Indians [U.S. citizens since 1924] their lands [allotments] entrusted to them [by allotment in 1887]."[64] Obviously the Cheyenne and Arapaho Tribes gave careful and thoughtful consideration to the proposed legislation. They came to the hearings prepared to give their input and were expecting answers to their concerns before they would consider endorsing the bill.

Open Indian opposition to the Wheeler-Howard Bill appears limited in both the House and Senate hearings. Most opposition, expressed in resolutions from various tribal groups, was presented to the committees and included as attachments to the minutes. One main exception to this pattern was the opposition of the vocal Joseph Bruner. The committee minutes contain a body of correspondence from Bruner to individuals such as John Collier, Senators Thomas and Wheeler, and Representative Will Rogers. Bruner conducted an ongoing attack against Collier and most of his Indian New Deal proposals. In a letter to Collier, Bruner expounded, "Without consulting them you had a bill prepared and then undertook to choke it down their throats and make them like it." He further stated that the Indian congress in Muskogee had been "thoroughly packed" by Collier. Finally, Bruner vented against landless Indians by saying, "I challenge the Commissioner to point to one word in the Collier bill which says any Oklahoma Indian tribe will be given 1 foot of land if the bill in its present form is enacted into law." Bruner concluded by saying, "The Indian who has squandered his land or money is no more to be pitied than any other sucker."[65]

Collier made great efforts to respond thoroughly to Bruner's caustic accusations, and in a methodical and unemotional manner. Many of Collier's responses are included in the minutes. However, on occasion even Collier could not contain his frustration with Bruner and lashed out. Writing a response to one of Bruner's letters, Collier concluded by saying, "You are an interesting human and social type, Mr. Bruner. . . . you have Indian blood and yet some inward compulsion makes you frenziedly active to prevent Indians from receiving the help and protection which they need and for which they are petitioning. Why?" Bruner, attempting to have the last word in this verbal sparring match, responded to Collier, stating, "You are also an interesting human and social type Mr. Commissioner. . . . You never were in Oklahoma in your life, you said, until you came here to tell us in picked assemblies what we want. You have not redeemed any of your promises to us. Why?"[66] Wisely, Collier let the issue drop. As mentioned earlier, Bruner and the American Indian Federation, based in eastern Oklahoma, conducted ongoing state and national campaigns opposing both Collier and the Indian New Deal.

From the testimony and resolutions introduced by American Indians during both the House and Senate committee hearings on Wheeler-Howard, several conclusions can be drawn. Although Indians had no input during the drafting of the original version of the bill, they certainly had input during the congressional hearings and Indian congresses. Tribal groups from all around the nation gave testimony and furnished resolutions. Several amendments proposed by various Indian groups made both during the congresses and the hearings were acted upon. It is also apparent that many concerned Indians focused on immediate bread-and-butter issues such as land,

THE INDIAN NEW DEAL 75

credit, and education. Very few supported John Collier's long-range ideals for transforming Indian policy. They focused on bettering the destitute circumstances in which they found themselves living. There appeared no general consensus among Indians for or against the bill, a fact readily apparent among Oklahoma Indians, who themselves were divided. Some traditional groups opposed the measure for specific reasons while other more progressive groups also opposed it for their own reasons. Particular circumstances seemed to dictate a group's support or opposition. Regardless, many took advantage of the opportunity to express their viewpoints.

The Oklahoma congressional delegation, led by Senator Thomas, strongly opposed the Wheeler-Howard Bill.[67] Thomas felt that with Oklahoma Indians well on the road to assimilation, the reimposition of the reservation system would only set them back. He specifically criticized Title IV as an "effort to repudiate the judiciary of my state." Senator Thomas said of the bill, "It is not meeting with general favor among our Indian citizens. . . . It is not suited to Oklahoma, and will not pass Congress." He declared that "there isn't a chance for its passage in my judgment," and he added that he had not been consulted about the bill during its formulation.[68]

Congressman W. W. Hastings, a mixed-blood Cherokee, represented part of eastern Oklahoma and remained a vigorous opponent of the Wheeler-Howard Bill. He feared local control being replaced with direction from uninterested agency bureaucrats in Washington. Hastings objected to provisions in Title IV allowing Indian courts to handle probate cases, thereby wresting that authority from county courts and placing it hands of "the Secretary of the Interior."[69] As a result of such a wide span of opinions, the Wheeler-Howard Bill faced a long and problem-strewn path as it made its way through the legislative process. From the end of Senate hearings on the bill on May 28, 1934, until July 18, when it was enacted, Senator Thomas worked behind the scene proposing amendments to the bill. He responded not only to his constituents' opposition but also to his own objections. One amendment excluded most Oklahoma Indians from sections in the bill containing procedures for establishing new reservations, Indian corporations, and tribal governments. Another Thomas amendment allowed the Office of Indian Affairs to purchase land for Oklahoma Indians on an individual as well as a tribal basis. Senator Thomas reiterated, "My state is different from the other Indian states. . . . Our Indian reservations have heretofore been allotted, and there are left in Oklahoma no great Indian reservations."[70] Finally, Senator Thomas believed, "Under the amendments passed in the bill, the Oklahoma Indians get all the benefits of the legislation and are not required to suffer any of the objectionable features."[71] On June 12, Senator Thomas and Congressman Hastings moved to have Oklahoma Indians exempted from several "objectionable" features of the bill, including the provisions for self-government and incorporation as well as the section that extended restrictions on Indian allotments indefinitely.

Their motive for opposing the extension of restrictions stemmed from the fact that state tax revenue would not be realized. Senator Thomas justified his actions by stating, "At this time, without conferring with the Indians of Oklahoma, I am unwilling to agree that they shall come under [those] provisions so I have exempted them. During the summer, if the bill shall pass now, I will confer with the several tribes in my State. If those Indian tribes desire to come under the provision[s], then I may come back at the next session and move to amend [the bill]. I make that statement in fairness to the Indians of my State."[72] Thomas's words reflect an assumption that clearly silences Indians' voice.

Many Oklahoma Indians continued to lobby for protection under Wheeler-Howard, soon to be signed into law as the Indian Reorganization Act. Jasper Saunkeah, council chairman for the Kiowa tribe, felt, "Our only chance is to procure an extension of the restrictions so we may have governmental supervision until such time as our people become capable of handling their property wisely, and conducting business for themselves."[73] Saunkeah feared the impact of the withdrawal of the government's trust protection over Oklahoma Indians scheduled for 1936 and strongly supported the bill. He believed many Indians would quickly lose what little of their original holdings they now possessed without it.

The Wheeler-Howard Bill became law on June 18, 1934, with Collier's original proposal cut from forty-eight to five pages. Now known as the Indian Reorganization Act (IRA), this act specifically excluded Oklahoma Indians from six sections of the act, including section 16, acknowledging the right of tribes to organize *constitutional* governments, and section 17, permitting tribal incorporation under charters issued by the secretary of the interior. Several provisions of the law did include Oklahoma Indians. These were provisions for an annual $2 million appropriation for land purchases, exemptions from many civil service requirements necessary for jobs within the Office of Indian Affairs, and participation in an annual fund of $250,000 for vocational training and college scholarships.[74]

In theory, it would appear that Oklahoma Indians received financial benefits from the IRA while being excluded from being able to establish reservations and form tribal governments or tribal corporations. In practice, however, the IRA did little for Oklahoma Indians. They did not qualify for access to the $10 million revolving fund for economic and agricultural development tied to provisions in the act that provided for establishing tribal governments and tribal incorporation. This exemption blocked Oklahoma Indians' access to capital for improvements required by the Indian Bureau before funding land purchases for individual Indians.[75]

In the end, no clear victor emerged. The assimilationists suffered crippling blows. Allotment was dead, with the dream of moving Native Americans into the mainstream of American society severely questioned and found wanting. Newly planted visions of Indian home rule and self-determination beckoned, but the new tribal alternative had not yet fully gestated. Assimilationists proved a formidable foe. Collier, cornered, compromised several of his ideals in order to realize partial success. Gone was his plan for a Court of Indian Affairs. Important goals such as self-government and incorporation as well as proposals for adding to the tribal land base were watered down. Wheeler-Howard moved through the give-and-take of the legislative process, altered and pared to the point where it was hard to recognize the finished bill from the original draft. Nonetheless, it was passed and became a milestone in Indian law. Despite the failure of efforts by many interests to bring the Indian New Deal to Oklahoma Indians, the struggle would continue.

CHAPTER 4

Oklahoma's Newer New Deal

Franklin Roosevelt's signature was barely dry on the Indian Reorganization Act before John Collier blanketed Oklahoma with a series of six articles widely published by newspapers across the state. Collier, a skilled and frequent user of the media, presented the Indian Bureau in a favorable light. Entitled "Present Status of Oklahoma Indians," the series surveyed the condition of the state's Indians and elaborated on the efforts being made by the federal government to aid them in areas such as landholdings, agricultural extension work, education, and medical care. In an interview, Collier expressed his hope that "every tribe would accept the Indian New Deal" and pledged that he would "seek to extend its terms to Oklahoma Indians in the next Congress."[1] Senator Thomas had managed to exempt Oklahoma Indians from most provisions of the Indian Reorganization Act just prior to its enactment in June of 1934, claiming he wanted to gain an understanding of their condition in order to develop a legislative proposal that benefited them. Meanwhile, Collier had not given up hope. If he could build a strong body of support among the Five Tribes, perhaps the Oklahoma congressional delegation would reconsider and place the state's Indians fully under the umbrella of the IRA. Such efforts in Oklahoma aided Collier's efforts to broaden Indian support for the IRA nationwide.

True to his word, in early September 1934 Thomas announced a schedule of planned visits to all the Indian agencies in Oklahoma. On September 22, Thomas telegrammed Commissioner Collier inviting him "or a representative of your office to be present at each meeting." Thomas included a schedule of seven meetings in late October, and he extended invitations to all Indian business committees and "Indians generally." Collier wired back to Thomas, "Delighted you are holding these conferences. Believe superintendents would be best representatives of office. If possible shall join you myself."[2] The conferences were designed to gauge Indian support and collect Indian recommendations for the IRA. Thomas wanted to determine if the IRA was right for Oklahoma Indians or if it needed to be amended. Collier believed Oklahoma Indians ought to be fully a part of the IRA.

On October 1, shortly before he left for Oklahoma, Collier spoke at the opening of the Indian Exposition in Atlanta, Georgia. Collier directed some of his remarks toward Oklahoma and its Indians. He charged, "Oklahoma Indians are suffering cruel and devastating wrongs, [and] this subject will become a political battleground in the next Congress." Collier also claimed, "Oklahoma interests were strong enough to persuade Congress to exclude the Oklahoma Indians from the protections and benefits of President Roosevelt's legislation [the IRA]." Finally, Collier took direct aim at the situation in eastern Oklahoma by stating that the IRA, if it had not included exemptions for Oklahoma, "would have done away with the avaricious local guardians who fatten upon [Oklahoma] Indians."[3] The commissioner used this national forum to bring media attention to judicial and legal interests in eastern Oklahoma. These groups had successfully lobbied the Oklahoma congressional delegation, especially Senator Thomas, to have the original bill emasculated at the end of the legislative process, exempting Oklahoma Indians from most of its provisions.

Surely Collier must have realized the degree of ire he would raise in Oklahoma from these remarks, although he may have believed that they would strengthen his efforts to bring the state's Indians under the umbrella of the IRA. Using opportunities such as the Indian Exposition to bring national exposure to the gross exploitation of Oklahoma Indians might garner public support. In 1923, Collier had engineered a publicity campaign that helped to defeat the Bursom Bill. He used that tactic again in 1934 to draw national attention to Oklahoma. However, Thomas was livid, taking many of Collier's remarks as a direct affront, and lashed out at Collier. Thomas defended his opposition to the IRA, stating, "The legislation was designed to primarily perpetuate the Indian Bureau and I am against that."[4] Once again, Thomas prepared to spar with Collier during the upcoming Oklahoma Indian congresses.

For several days, newspapers across the state grilled Collier. The *Tulsa Tribune* stated, "There is not a community in Oklahoma where it would be impossible to find white citizens willing to serve on a jury for the trial and conviction of any 'avaricious local guardian' whom Commissioner Collier or his assistants might name to the prosecutors."[5] The *Muskogee Daily Phoenix* wondered "why Collier assumed that Georgians would be interested in problems of Oklahoma Indians" and caustically added, "The visionary commissioner evidently doesn't know the difference between members of the Five Tribes and the 'reservation Indians' he pets and pampers in Arizona, New Mexico, and California."[6] Throughout the struggle to enact Indian New Deal legislation, the Oklahoma press, especially in the eastern half of the state, never criticized President Roosevelt, but they unrelentingly attacked Collier. He represented an outside threat from Washington who jeopardized the relationship between white Oklahomans and Oklahoma Indians, which for almost fifty years had entailed plunder of Indian land and resources. The press served as the mouthpiece of those who benefited from the plunder.

Both Thomas and Collier attended the first of several Indian conferences, held in Muskogee on October 15, 1934, using it partially as a forum for directing verbal barbs toward one another. Over two thousand Indians representing the Five Tribes attended the daylong meeting. Thomas opened the session with lengthy remarks. He told the Indians that he had exempted them from six provisions of the IRA in June because the original proposal had been too bulky; moreover, he did not feel it was right for Oklahoma Indians, and he wanted time to confer with them. He told the Indians that the purpose of the meeting was to "advise you what this bill proposes for you, withholds for you and to see your reaction."[7] Throughout this meeting, Thomas directed his remarks to the "progressive" groups, usually mixed-bloods, who were more in favor of assimilation. Also, he continually emphasized his belief that the IRA was "all right for reservation Indians, but it is no good for the Indians in Oklahoma who have land and property."[8]

On October 18, at the Pawnee Agency, Thomas declared, "The Indian problem in Oklahoma is the allotment problem and the Indian problem in the West is the reservation problem." Thomas repeatedly stressed to the Indians, "Every line of this bill [the IRA] is seeking to get the Indians off of their allotments now and back onto a reservation." He demonstrated a misunderstanding of the legislation by stressing at all the meetings that in order for Indians to "form a corporation, they must surrender their homes and move on a reservation." Thomas cajoled the Indians in attendance, saying, "If you want to go back seventy-five years, petition me to come under this bill."[9] While Thomas said he believed that Collier had "the best interests of the Indians at heart," he reiterated several times his belief that Collier was not knowledgeable about the state, saying, "[Collier] knows much more about Indians of Arizona, New Mexico and the far West than he knows about the Indians of Oklahoma." Thomas made clear his view of the relationship of Collier and the Indian Bureau with Congress, stating, "The Congress makes the policies under which the Indian Office operates, so the all-important branch of the federal service is the Congress of the United States."[10]

Collier took a more defensive posture. Early in his remarks he conceded that "the Wheeler-Howard law needs to be changed, so it more accurately fits the needs of the Five Tribes." Collier argued that "we [the Indian Bureau] would not care whether the Oklahoma situation was met by fixing up the Wheeler-Howard Act a little bit, or by introducing a new act."[11] Knowing that he was in Senator Thomas's political backyard, he proceeded guardedly. He wanted the support of the Oklahoma Indians but knew he needed the support of Thomas too. He also realized that he might not be able to position Oklahoma Indians completely under the umbrella of the IRA, but a partial victory through concession and compromise was more palatable than total defeat. Collier had already agreed with Thomas to modify sections 2 and 4 of the IRA, dealing with heirship policies and the prohibition of removing restrictions on Indian allotments.[12] Collier also admitted that the meaning of the word "reservation" in the IRA needed clarification. Many, including Thomas and various Oklahoma Indians, saw Oklahoma reservations comprising tribal lands with individual allotments often checkerboarded with private white landholdings. Thomas doggedly held to the belief that individual Indian allotments could easily be returned to tribal reservation lands under the IRA.

One representative from each of the Five Tribes was permitted to make a comment. William A. Durant spoke for the Choctaws. Addressing the full-bloods, Durant argued that "they [the full-bloods] have been limited in bringing their consensus of opinion to all our law making."[13] He underscored the importance of factions within the tribe working together. In addition to making a call for unity, Durant implied a responsibility on the part of the mixed-bloods to protect full-bloods from being taken advantage of because of their lack of understanding of the IRA.[14] Historian Erik Zissu contends that mixed-bloods tended to "exhibit a strong sense of responsibility to their fellow tribesmen [full-bloods]. . . . [and] acted to lessen the dislocation of their fellow tribesmen. Operating through the Indian Bureau, they recognized an obligation to those tribal members less prepared for the challenges of life in Oklahoma."[15]

Joseph W. Hayes of the Chickasaws spoke of the need to look at Oklahoma Indians not from the context of reservations but more accurately from the sense of an "Indian community." Hayes spoke of Oklahoma Indians organizing into communities such as "a county or other [political] sub-division."[16] His comments focused on an important issue that plagued the process surrounding enactment and implementation of the IRA and the OIWA. There existed an ongoing conflict among tribal groups, "progressives" and "traditionals," bureau administrators, members of Congress, legal experts, and even anthropologists as to how best blend Native American political processes with those of white society into a functioning system that would promote and protect the interests of all. This conflict of interests and perspectives proved difficult to bridge.

A perusal of the minutes of the congresses reveals clearly the differences in thought. The Seven Clan Society Christians, a Cherokee full-blood organization boasting 297 members, directed a resolution to Senator Thomas. In it they asked for his assistance "in forming a reservation or colony where we can hold our lands in common and where we can have a home as we understand the Wheeler-Howard bill [IRA] to give us that right."[17] John Smith, a full-blood Cherokee, stated that "we hear the voice of the Divine through these gentlemen—Senator Thomas and Commissioner Collier," and "[i]f they can get it right, like we want it, we as Cherokees are willing to approve the bill."[18] Apparently Smith was unaware of the disparate viewpoints of Thomas and Collier. Several Indian attendees expressed almost blind support for Collier and his Indian New Deal.

The Seminoles made a short statement: "If we are asked to place our approval upon any legislative program now in the making or to be made in the future, we give notice now that we must have a voice in the initiating of such program and a part in its administration."[19] The Seminoles remained the only tribal group in Oklahoma that expressed a desire to play a part in both the formulation and administration of federal laws affecting them.

At the meeting in Miami, Oklahoma, on October 16, Thomas continued his attacks on Collier and the Indian Bureau. He chastised Collier for his lack of understanding of Oklahoma, saying, "[I]f Mr. Collier will [avail himself of] the opportunity . . . of learning your problems, your mode of living, your wishes, your aspirations, then he and I when we get back to Washington will have no trouble in working out the problems for the Oklahoma Indians." Thomas slammed the Indian Bureau, saying, "the Indian Office will always be opposed to repealing that law [the IRA], because they have a conviction that the government can advise and supervise you Indians better than you can do it yourselves."[20]

Thomas outlined his vision of the chain of command for federal administration of Indian affairs, with Collier and the Indian Bureau subservient to Congress. In all the congresses statewide, Thomas encouraged the Indians to follow a precise order of communicating to Congress their needs and wishes. Each Indian business committee was to communicate its desires to the Indian agent, who, in turn, would forward them to the commissioner, and from there they would go to the secretary of the interior and finally to the Indian Affairs Committees in both houses of Congress. Action would be taken by Congress and then communicated back through the chain of command. Thomas also demonstrated a paternalistic and deeply assimilationist attitude. "There is no reason why Indians can't be the same as everyone else," he believed.[21]

In all the congresses, Thomas encouraged the Indians to carefully consider the IRA, both as individuals and within business committees. He entreated all Indians in attendance to write to him in Washington with their viewpoints, questions, and proposals. At this time, both Thomas and Collier focused on amending the IRA to make it acceptable to Oklahoma Indians.

Collier rebutted most of Thomas's accusations. He dismissed Thomas's contention that the IRA was a means of returning the Indians to reservations, stating that "the use of the word reservation in this bill doesn't mean any idea of putting the Indians back on tribal land or on closed reservations." He admitted that the word "reservation" as used in the IRA was confusing and needed to be redefined to mean "neighborhood, community, or something of that kind."[22] Collier also conceded that section 2 of the IRA, which extended the trust period on allotted lands indefinitely, needed to be amended so that Oklahoman Indians would be able to sell and transfer land. Collier was concerned about the rising costs to the Indian Bureau to administer many heirship lands that had been divided to the extent that they were too small to be productively utilized.

The meeting in Miami on October 16 opened, as the others had, with comments and questions from Indian attendees. The Quapaws, who had allotted themselves in the 1890s, expressed concern about section 4 of the IRA, which outlined organization and incorporation. In a resolution they explained, "This corporation business is so new [that we] don't know what it is and what it will lead to."[23] The Quapaws wanted more time to study and discuss the IRA. By the end of the meeting, Thomas and Collier agreed that Oklahoma Indians did need legislation specifically tailored for their circumstances.

Referring to the verbal sparring that had gone on after Collier's caustic remarks about Oklahoma and Oklahoma Indians, Collier opened his remarks at the October 18, 1934, Pawnee held in Pawhuska by stating, "Some of you have been reading in the newspapers . . . that each of us [Collier and Thomas] had a knife and were getting ready to cut the throat of the other one, that we came down here for a big fight."²⁴ Collier assured the Indians that this would not be the case. He and Thomas now reassured Indian attendees that they were in agreement and were working together in the best interests of the Indians. Though their relationship remained guarded, Collier and Thomas forged a fragile alliance that remained intact through enactment of the Oklahoma Indian Welfare Act.

Toward the end of the Pawnee meeting on October 18, Indian attendees had again been given the opportunity to express their views or to ask questions. Several, such as Owen Tah, a Tonkawa, expressed the idea that there was still "much confusion among the Indians about this bill." Henry Chapman of the Pawnees expressed the feeling of many Indian attendees that more time was needed to look at and discuss various aspects of the IRA before they would be ready to decide whether to support or oppose the bill. The Kaws remained opposed to extension of the IRA to Oklahoma Indians, while the Pawnee business council, named the Welfare Association of the Pawnee Tribe, requested "admittance in the Wheeler-Howard Act." Henry Roberts, a Ponca, indirectly chastised Senator Thomas for believing that only Indians on recognized reservations could incorporate under the IRA, by stating, "Anybody with common sense would know that was the import of the bill when drafted.²⁵ Louis McDonald, a member of the Ponca business committee, referred to factionalization among the Poncas over the IRA, noting that many Poncas had verbally attacked committee members and disrupted meetings. McDonald referred to a rift developing between traditional full-bloods and mixed-bloods. This sort of division was clearly evident among many Oklahoma tribal groups as they considered the IRA.

Collier returned to Washington to handle urgent matters, replaced in Oklahoma by A. C. Monahan, the assistant commissioner of Indian affairs. The next meeting was held in Concho, in central Oklahoma, on October 22. Thomas, in his opening remarks to the Cheyennes and Arapahos, repeated a favorite phrase, "What is good for the white folks is good for you [Indians] and what is good for you is good for the white folks." Thomas repeated his contention that the IRA applied more to reservation Indians in the western states than to Oklahoma Indians, who, Thomas argued, "in almost every respect, are the same as white people." Thomas seemed convinced that Oklahoma Indians were far ahead of other Native Americans with respect to assimilation. He maintained his belief that Indians in eastern Oklahoma and their interests and challenges had little in common with the western tribes he often referred to as "reservation Indians." Thomas also attempted to assure Indian attendees, saying, "You have no enemies in Washington. They are all your friends." In justifying his work to exempt Oklahoma Indians from key provisions of the IRA, Thomas argued, "I do not think the Indians on this reservation [Cheyenne and Arapaho Agency] would be interested in trying to form a charter to go into business of some kind. . . . I know that you are not interested in the continuation of boarding schools."[26]

Thomas appeared interested in learning the desires and needs of Oklahoma Indians, but this genuine concern was blunted by a deeply ingrained paternalistic, assimilationist attitude toward them. His legacy seems to reveal a political motivation channeled by white interests. Thomas often displayed a mocking attitude toward the Indians. During the last meeting with Oklahoma Indians, held the next day, October 23, at the Anadarko Agency in the Kiowa Reservation, he spoke of Alaska Indians falling under the provisions of the IRA. He told the Indian attendees "you have some new relatives. . . . So now when you want to go and see your new relatives you can go to Alaska for some fun on the ice, chasing polar bears and getting a lot of walrus meat."[27] The Indian reaction to this type of statement is unfortunately off the record.

Chief Whiteshirt of the Arapahos discussed factions within his tribe. He argued that the older full-bloods "retained their original allotments because they are more mature" and because they knew "that the land was the only source of livelihood which they could depend on." The mixed-bloods, on the other hand, "were released [from restrictions on their allotments], sold their land; consequently, many of them have big families with no lands or no money to support their families."[28] Whiteshirt's testimony reflects a variation on a common predicament shared by most Oklahoma Indians. Those who had been able to hold on to their allotments were hesitant to see the state come under the IRA. Many shared a common misconception that they would lose their land as it was transferred back to communal tribal holdings. Provisions in the IRA, which seemingly rewarded those Indians who had "lost" their land holdings, upset many Indian landholders. Senator Thomas seemed to share this misconception.

Comanches, Kiowas, and Apaches attended the meeting at the Anadarko Agency. Thomas and Monahan also attended this meeting, and they occupied the bulk of the meeting, along with Congressman Jed Johnson, explaining the IRA and giving their viewpoints of it. Late in the afternoon the meeting opened up to statements and questions from the Indian attendees.

Robert Dunlap, a Caddo representative, voiced the opinion that the IRA might be all right for Indians from other areas of the nation who lived on reservations, but as far as Oklahoma Indians were concerned, "We have a government here. We are under Federal and State laws."[29] Delos Lone Wolf, a Kiowa and plaintiff in the *Lone Wolf v. Hitchcock* Supreme Court case of 1903, strongly protested Oklahoma adopting the IRA or any amended version. Lone Wolf felt that it was "60 years too late now that we have got the place where we are recognized as citizens of Oklahoma and the United States."[30] *Lone Wolf v. Hitchcock* had established the right of Congress to abrogate Indian treaties or policies over thirty years before Lone Wolf expressed fears about the bill, even if it was amended to everyone's liking: "We cannot tell what Congress will do. If we suggest some changes they might throw us in the community feature of it and we do not want any of that."[31] Lone Wolf's statement expressed the distrust of the federal government's Indian policy held by many Oklahoma Indians. After a long history of broken treaties and policy that consistently promoted white expansion at the cost of the Indians, many found it hard to believe that the IRA would be anything more than business as usual, regardless of how attractively it was packaged and presented to them.

Albert Attocknie, speaking for the Comanches, expressed concern over losing educational benefits from boarding schools such as Riverside and Fort Sill, fearing they would be closed under the IRA. Describing Indians, Attocknie said, "We are just like little children . . . we do not know what is good for us. . . . Maintaining boarding schools is the best way to solve the Indian problem."[32] Attocknie's expression of inferiority and helplessness echoes the remarks of some other Indians.

Anthropologist Loretta Fowler speaks of "subordinated peoples in colonial and neocolonial situations . . . [who] face actual as well as symbolic dominance and their tendency to ideologies that rationalize their position and may come to be unconsciously accepted."[33] Remarks by Attocknie and some other Indian attendees of these congresses substantiates Fowler's perceptions. As soon as Attocknie stopped speaking, though, he was confronted by James Ottipoby, a Kiowa, who was critical of Attocknie's words and asked, "Will you kindly tell us where you stand?" Attocknie referred to division within the tribal council and then commenced a personal attack on Ottipoby. Thomas interrupted and quickly put an end to the bickering: "Mr. Monahan and I are not interested in your fights among yourselves." John Loco, a Fort Sill Apache who had been captured with Geronimo in 1886, expressed his opposition to the IRA, believing it was a big step backward for Indians. Loco gave an interesting opinion, stating, "I don't know why the government wants to bring us up like white people and then when we come up like white people, they don't like it."[34]

The conferences of October 1934 lacked substantive input from Indians, input that might have helped Thomas or the Indian Bureau to tailor beneficial legislation. The highly structured nature of the meetings and the presentations by government officials (especially Thomas) left little time for Indian voices to be heard. Further, the pace of the meetings was rushed to fit into one day. Perhaps a day and a half or two days might have proven more effective. In contrast, the congresses held by Collier in March that year, prior to enactment of the IRA, seemed to have been structured so more time was spent answering concerns of individuals and tribal groups as well as gathering recommendations for amendments and changes to the bill.

Newspapers across the state followed these meetings. Protecting the white status quo, they generally took a negative stance toward Collier and the IRA. The *Muskogee Daily Phoenix* defended Oklahoma, saying "our business, industry, courts and law making bodies . . . have done everything for the Indian that Mr. Collier now would completely destroy with his fanciful scheme for socializing the

Indian."[35] In a front-page story, the *Daily Phoenix* disclosed that an unnamed agency employee had reported on the meeting in Muskogee on October 18: "We all feel Collier has put his head in a noose and given it a good yank."[36] The *Oklahoma City Times* reiterated the assimilationist viewpoints of many white Oklahomans: "[I]n the long run, they must become Americans in the modern sense."[37] The *Tulsa Daily World* claimed that the Indian Bureau "persistently ignores the fact that in Oklahoma the Indian is a citizen; that the tendency . . . up to now has been away from the reservation and dependence to citizenship and independence.[38] The *Okemah Semi-Weekly Herald* penned an editorial saying, "Mr. Collier should give a sympathetic ear to Mr. Thomas in the interest of common justice." The *Shawnee Morning News* confirmed reports that Thomas and Collier had reached agreement on several fundamental points that had previously divided them on legislation for Oklahoma Indians.[39] The press in eastern Oklahoma continued to fulfill its role as mouthpiece for white opposition to the Indian New Deal, focusing on Collier as representing the dominant and paternalistic relationship Oklahoma whites wished to preserve with Indians.

Shortly after his return to Washington, Collier took great pains to compliment Senator Thomas, while at the same time denouncing "the newspaper frenzy" in Oklahoma, the press attacks on him and the IRA. In his judgment, "The misrepresentations do not come from the platform, or from the floor where the Indians are listening and talking back. They come from outside the meetings."[40] Here again Collier often referred to "Oklahoma interests strong enough to persuade Congress to exclude the Oklahoma Indians from the protection and benefits of President Roosevelt's legislation."[41] Collier would often refer in a general manner to "Oklahoma interests" who opposed the IRA and OIWA, without naming specific groups or individuals such as Congressmen Jack Nichols and Wesley Disney, who represented eastern districts of the state and had provided strong opposition throughout the legislative process to the IRA (as they would to the OIWA).

On November 5, Collier issued a five-page paper recapping concerns expressed by Oklahoma Indians regarding various provisions in the IRA. Again he answered a number of questions asked frequently and by many Indians during the Thomas conferences. The bulk of them pertained to land issues, such as government land purchases for the Indians and the jurisdiction of Indian probate matters. These concerned both individuals and business committees. In several statements scattered throughout the paper, Collier assured the Indians, "Practically nothing in the act is compulsory." Stressing the bureau's attempts to garner Indian input for amending the act, Collier further remarked that "it is the first time [for] any important legislation affecting Indians in which the decision of acceptance or rejection is left entirely with the Indians to decide by popular vote."[42] Many Indian groups left the conferences leaning more toward acceptance of the IRA than before they came, but Collier also knew that many had lingering doubts and concerns. All across Oklahoma, Indian groups spent the late fall and winter months of 1934–1935 discussing and debating the merits of the IRA as they felt it would affect their tribal groups.

In the November elections in 1934, Elmer Thomas and Will Rogers were reelected by comfortable margins. In January, the two assumed the chairmanships of the Indian Affairs Committees in the Senate and the House., and worked together to draft a bill they felt would give Oklahoma Indians the benefits of the Indian Reorganization Act while at the same time accommodating the uniqueness of the people and their situation. Thomas clung to the belief that Oklahoma Indians were further along the road to assimilation than tribal groups elsewhere. During the new congresses he and Collier had held in Oklahoma in October 1935, Thomas's thinking had shifted toward support for Collier and the Indian New Deal. During this time, Collier wisely remained in the background as the Oklahoma congressional delegation drafted the Thomas-Rogers Bill.

On February 27, 1936, Thomas and Rogers formally introduced their proposal to Congress. Just a few days before, Rogers discussed their proposal before the annual convention of the Oklahoma Education Association in Tulsa. There he touted the proposal as "Oklahoma's Newer New Deal" for the state's Indians.[43] Jimmie Rogers, a full-blood Creek, remarked, "We not only want a New Deal, but we also could use a square deal."[44] "The bill is the result of conferences between the Indian Bureau and the Oklahoma delegation in

Congress," Thomas said.[45] In order to secure its passage, the Thomas-Rogers Bill underwent an arduous eighteen-month struggle.

The original draft of the bill was seven pages long. Section 2 addressed the issue of restrictions. It attempted to introduce the concept of blood quantum in determining whether or not Oklahoma Indians would have their landholdings restricted (held in trust, exempted from taxes, and managed by the secretary of the interior for twenty-five years).

Simply put, blood quantum divided Indians into two groups based on their ethnic heritage, specifically their percentage of "Indian blood." Those with 50 percent or more Indian lineage belonged to the first group. Land and property of "first-degree" Indians would continue to be held in trust by the secretary of the interior, with the president authorized to extended restrictions indefinitely. With the second group, those with less than 50 percent Indian lineage, removal of restrictions applied. A procedure was established for a competency commission to meet every four years and review the situation of each Indian in second-degree status to determine if the individual was capable of managing his or her affairs. If so, restrictions could be removed and a patent in fee issued. Land could then be sold without restrictions.

This concept of blood quantum was absent from both the Dawes Act of 1887 and the IRA of 1934. The Dawes Act authorized the secretary of the interior to decide on the competency of Indian landholders to legally manage their property. The IRA only alluded to the term in its section 19, in defining the term "Indian" as "all persons of one-half or more Indian Blood." While Indian Territory was exempted from the Dawes Act, non-Indians nonetheless incorporated the ideas of competency and restrictions into their ideology, underscoring their perspective of and interaction with Oklahoma Indians. Blood quantum became a measuring tool used by the federal government to "control access to economic resources," while non-Indians used it as "a justification for economic exploitation" of Indian land and resources, writes anthropologist and Cherokee tribal member Circe Sturm.[46]

Blood quantum as a tool to measure competency quickly became a can of worms in the legislative process and it was dropped from the bill before its enactment. Blood quantum continues to remain a hotly debated issue in Indian affairs.

The proposed bill also allowed for land purchases by the secretary of the interior. These land purchases could be for additions to tribal holdings and therefore communal in nature, and for individual Indians as well. Held in trust by the secretary, the purchased lands would be exempted from Oklahoma jurisdiction and taxes. These provisions became the subject of intense debate during congressional hearings.

Section 8, considered by Collier to be of utmost importance, also proved to be one of the most controversial portions of the proposed legislation. This section also incorporated the concept of blood quantum. Applying specifically to the Osages and the Five Tribes, section 8 transferred jurisdiction over land, property, and probate matters for restricted Indians of the first degree from the Oklahoma county courts to the secretary of the interior. It also prohibited the appointment of legal guardians for any Osage or Five Tribe member of the first degree. This section, if enacted, would have wreaked havoc with the legal profession in eastern Oklahoma—and those engaging in graft there—and the response there, immediate and intense, endured through the legislative process. Non-Indian oil, timber, coal, and land speculators used financial resources and exerted much effort against these proposals, which, if enacted, would stymie their efforts to acquire control over restricted Indians' land and its resources. Sections 2 and 8 were battlefields throughout the legislative process, and both sections would be dropped before the bill was passed and enacted.

Section 12 of Thomas-Rogers acknowledged the right of Oklahoma Indians to organize. This section outlined procedures for establishing constitutionally based tribal governments, similar to provisions contained in the IRA. Sections 13 and 14 authorized the creation of an Oklahoma Indian Credit Corporation with an annual appropriation of $2 million. These loans were to be made available to chartered cooperatives and associations, or to individuals. Finally, section 17 removed the exemption to all benefits to the IRA imposed by Senator Thomas. This allowed Oklahoma Indians access to the $10 million revolving credit fund for Indian chartered corporations.

The Indian Bureau, along with Senator Thomas and Representative Rogers, made a substantial effort to distribute copies of the proposed bill to individual Indians as well as tribal business committees. Several tribal groups quickly passed resolutions supporting or condemning the bill. The Choctaw-Chickasaw Protective League sponsored a meeting to discuss the bill. Over two thousand Indians attended the daylong session held in Ardmore in mid-March and unanimously "passed a resolution requesting the Oklahoma [congressional] delegation to support and urge its immediate passage."[47]

The Arapahos opposed the bill, as did the business committees for the Pawnees, Poncas, Kaws, Otoes, and Tonkawas. In a joint resolution, the latter five expressed the sentiment that "our Indian people do not feel that they are capable of handling such a large undertaking."[48] Other groups expressed similar thoughts, feeling that many of their people lacked "business ability in handling their own individual matters."[49] James Kahdot, chief of the Pottawatomies, expressed support for the bill yet revealed a deep division within the tribe: the business committee opposed Thomas-Rogers while the majority of tribal members favored its passage.

As with efforts to secure passage of the Wheeler-Howard Bill the previous spring, most white opposition to the bill came from eastern Oklahoma. L. R. Heflin of Fairfax complained that Thomas-Rogers deprived the state of Oklahoma of much-needed tax revenue. With the federal government purchasing land, thereby increasing tax-exempt tribal holdings, Heflin argued that counties affected "would have no schools at all."[50] Other whites also decried the loss of Oklahoma tax revenue. A major factor in Thomas's original opposition to the Wheeler-Howard Bill was this very issue. However, Collier demonstrated that the impact would be minimal to any specific area, as these land purchases would be spread out across Oklahoma. Thomas eliminated this objection from his own entrenched thinking, rationalizing that a small, short-term loss in any state tax revenue would be more than offset by the taxes that self-sufficient Oklahoma Indians paid.

The legal community in eastern Oklahoma strongly objected to the Thomas-Rogers Bill. Several county bar associations, including those of Pittsburg, Caddo, and Osage, adopted formal resolutions signed by their memberships condemning the proposed legislation. The Wagoner Chamber of Commerce described the bill as a "direct assault on the judiciary of Oklahoma."[51] James I. Howard, a Pawhuska attorney, told Thomas, "I am writing as a friend . . . in order that I may tell you just what the situation is down here. . . . that you will lose nine out of every ten friends that you have in this county."[52] Osage County judge L. F. Roberts, in a letter marked "personal," chastised Thomas: "Your friends and citizens of Osage County are amazed at your introduction of the present pending Indian bill. . . . We trust that you will . . . see to it that the bill in its present form is killed."[53] Thomas responded to Judge Roberts, arguing that the proposal affected only a small portion of Oklahoma's overall population. Roberts replied to Thomas in a terse note, saying, "I desire to call your attention the fact that the population of Oklahoma is 2,396,040 people and it is not necessary in order to protect 150,000 people to injure more than two million.[54] The legal community remained adamantly opposed to section 8 of the proposal, which transferred control of most land issues, including probate matters, from Oklahoma county courts to the secretary of the interior.

Several Oklahoma Indians wrote to Thomas giving their perspective on the bill—and on the Oklahoma legal profession. J. W. B. Nichols, Choctaw, stated "They [lawyers] think this bill if passed will deprive some of them of grafting what little the Indians have left."[55] In a letter signed by "An Osage Indian," the writer spoke of the "many" attorneys in the small town of Pawhuska where most of their practice "is being guardian, attorney or handling suits filed against or between Indians." The writer counseled Thomas, "Of course under these circumstances you will understand that the Bar would be against taking any Indian business out of the county court where you can get an order of court for most anything under the sun, including unreasonably large Attorney fees."[56] In a letter to J. E. Sixkiller of Stillwell, Thomas showed his understanding of the legal profession's stance on the bill: "The opposition to [it] comes entirely from persons who have been living off of the Indians all these years."[57]

On April 5, 1935, both houses of the Oklahoma state legislature passed resolutions condemning the proposed bill. Members in both houses conducted verbal assaults on John Collier. State senator Al Nichols, brother of Congressman Jack Nichols, declared on the senate floor, "He [Collier] looks like one of those Egyptian mummies and all he knows about Indian affairs is what he found out by reading James Fennimore Cooper's books." Senator Claude Briggs likewise declared that "all Collier knows about Indian affairs is something he read in a book," while Senator Henry Johnston decried the commissioner's "innocent ignorance" of Indian affairs.[58] It is worthwhile to note that all of these critics hailed from eastern Oklahoma.

Samplings of Oklahoma newspapers just prior to the commencement of hearings for Thomas-Rogers exuded a great deal of opposition. The *Muskogee Daily Phoenix* editorialized about "the danger to Oklahoma's tax situation" with passage of the bill and concluded that the bill was "a distinct disappointment."[59] The *Tulsa Daily World* referred to the bill as "a back-door attempt at the thing which was attempted a year or so ago" and warned its readers that "the plan of the Thomas Bill is to take away a considerable portion of state sovereignty."[60] The *Okmulgee Daily Times* heralded a familiar theme that the bill, "if enacted into law, would turn back the hands of time many decades and would again make Oklahoma Indians wards of the government as though they were mere children."[61] Finally, the *Okemah Daily Leader*, in an editorial entitled "Dangerous Indian Legislation," took an assimilationist stance and announced that the bill "tends to undo all the careful work that has been done for forty years in training the Indian for citizenship."[62]

Once again, Joseph Bruner, full-blood Creek from Sapulpa and president of the American Indian Federation, led the organized Indian opposition. Bruner denounced Commissioner Collier and again argued that the Indian New Deal and specifically Thomas-Rogers were a step backward for all Native Americans. Bruner claimed to speak for forty Oklahoma tribal groups. The Osages responded to Bruner's claim in a council meeting called by Chief Fred Lookout. Lookout exclaimed, "We members of the tribal council of the Osage are angry because a Washington newspaper [interviewing Bruner] said that the Osages are one of the forty tribes demanding the elimination of 'Collier and Collierism.'" John J. Matthews, Osage, a noted native historian and spokesman for the Osage tribal council angrily denounced Bruner, saying, "No one has the right to speak for the Osage Indians but the tribal council and the Chief or their accredited representatives."[63] At least with the Osages, Bruner's methods backfired in his attempts to garner Indian opposition to Thomas-Rogers.

Because of Bruner's sustained vocal attacks, both Thomas and Rogers delayed committee hearings for their proposal. Rogers stated, "I am waiting for all the Oklahoma Indians to thoroughly digest provisions of the bill and for some of the present heat to die down before taking any further action."[64] Hearings on Thomas-Rogers finally began in the Senate in early April of 1935: the Committee on Indian Affairs conducted hearings from April 8 to April 11. The initial meeting consisted of all members of the committee. Since the proposed bill applied only to Oklahoma Indians, Thomas quickly relegated the remaining meetings to a subcommittee consisting of himself, Senator Lynn Frazier of North Dakota, and Senator Vic Donahey of Ohio.

During these hearings, a number of Oklahoma Indians representing various tribal groups testified. Many brought resolutions from tribal committees to be read into the record. Most favored the proposal, but some suggested amendments. Roly Canard, a Creek chief, announced that the Creeks supported the bill. When asked about any opposition, Canard said that the only opposition he was aware of was from white lawyers who were bitterly opposed to section 8 of the proposal, which transferred jurisdiction on probate matters from Oklahoma courts to the secretary of the interior.[65]

Several Indian groups opposed any new Indian legislation and sought a return to treaties negotiated a century earlier. Ned Blackfox, a Cherokee from Oaks, reported that a committee of the Cherokee Emigrant Indians decided, "Our wants is a treaty, which was made in December 29 in 1835, and 1836 and 1846. This is our own treaty and we cannot exchange [it] with any other laws."[66] Blackfox was referring to the New Echota Treaty of December 29, 1835. The factionalism generated by the New Echota Treaty affected Cherokee politics and society for generations.[67]

Bruner appeared before the committee on April 11, 1935, and quickly launched into an attack on other Creeks who had testified: "They were selected by manipulations of Collier henchmen through

[the] Muskogee Indian Office." Bruner proceeded into a diatribe on the illegality of Creeks who had testified. Thomas cut him short, saying, "I doubt if the committee will be very much interested in the local politics among the Creek Tribe. If you will get down to the bill as soon as you can, please."[68] Congressional patience with Bruner waned as he repeatedly used committee hearings as an opportunity to criticize individuals and groups associated with Indian affairs other than the American Indian Federation. In particular, Bruner aimed much of his venom at the Indian Bureau and Commissioner Collier.

Grady Lewis, a Choctaw and a tribal attorney, presented some challenging testimony. He announced that the Choctaws strongly endorsed the Thomas-Rogers Bill, subject to incorporation of a few minor amendments, but he also strongly condemned federal Indian policy in Oklahoma since statehood in 1907. Lewis viewed Oklahoma Indians as "suspended between two evils, the crookedness of the county court, and the incompetency of the Indian Office." He also compared the conditions of the Choctaw decades before statehood with the present, saying, "Our people are bordering on professional paupers and beggars . . . and it is a deplorable condition, when it is considered that those selfsame Indians a hundred years ago maintained their own government and did a fairly good job of it."[69] Lewis expressed the need for many Indians to remain under the guardianship of the federal government, saying, "The Indian is not a good business man, he can not learn the white man's standards of value."[70] A few days later, an Indian newspaper published in Stroud, Oklahoma, the *Tushkahomman*, reported on Lewis's gripping testimony concerning the deplorable situation of Oklahoma Indians and made an urgent plea: "If the Thomas-Rogers Bill does not appeal to you, in Heaven's name draft another which will remedy the intolerable conditions."[71]

G. B. Fulton, tribal attorney for the Osage, testified before the Senate subcommittee in April 1935. He spoke of the opposition to the proposed bill by the Osage County Bar Association and referred Senator Thomas to their resolution condemning it. Thomas pushed to get Fulton's opinion. Finally Fulton testified, "As I understand it the chief objections would be that under the Thomas-Rogers Bill all estates would be administered by the [federal] government . . . which would deprive those attorneys of large and sometimes exorbitant fees."[72] This bold statement verified the deplorable practices by some probate lawyers in eastern Oklahoma and the threat they felt by the proposed bill.

The Senate hearings ended on April 11, 1935. However, the debate over Thomas-Rogers continued unabated in Oklahoma. The *Tushkahomman* wrote, "[O]pposition to the enactment of this bill is coming from individuals and groups of people who are working for their selfish interests and not for the welfare of the Indians," singling out "certain units of the Bar Association in the state."[73] County judge W. H. Blackbird wired Senator Thomas, stating that the bill "will practically destroy the jurisdiction of county courts in Indian matters and will take away . . . the administration of big estates and result in Indian funds being taken out of the state."[74] Mrs. W. V. Krier, Creek, wrote Thomas expressing her support for the bill. In response to mainly white interests who claimed the bill would take the Indians back fifty years, Mrs. Krier decried, "I'm sure the majority of Indians would gladly go back to the days before allotment." She also believed that Indians needed protection from the federal government—"[a]nd we need to be in a position to exercise some authority about the handling of our affairs."[75] Milford Growingham, a Shawnee from Avery, expressed his opposition to the bill based on the oft-held mistrust of the Indians toward the federal government. Growingham, claiming to speak for "lots of Indians around Shawnee," said, "They say and tell us there is something behind all this dealing. Many still can't understand it clearly. They hate to lose all the land they have."[76] The Indian Rights Association strongly favored the Thomas-Rogers Bill and described the situation in Oklahoma by using a statement that Senator Wheeler, cosponsor of the IRA, had made in 1929 during a Senate subcommittee meeting: "There are only two classes of people in Oklahoma, the Indians and those who live off the Indians."[77]

On April 22, 1935, the House Committee on Indian Affairs, chaired by Representative Rogers, began hearings on Thomas-Rogers. These proved much more argumentative and contentious than the Senate hearings. Oklahoma congressman Jack Nichols, though not a committee member, was allowed to participate in questioning witnesses.

Congressman Nichols was the brother and law partner of Oklahoma state senator Al Nichols, who had given such an eloquent castigation of John Collier on the Oklahoma senate floor in early April. Nichols had asked Chairman Rogers to be allowed to sit in on the hearings, claiming, "I have more Indians in my congressional district than any other Congressman."[78] Nichols's legal background served him well as he skillfully worked witnesses in attempting to extract testimony favorable to his viewpoints on the bill. Nichols represented non-Indian interests from eastern Oklahoma, many of them lawyers, judges, and guardians who had profited from legal dealings involving the sale of Indian allotments and probate matters. This group remained adamantly opposed to sections within the bill that proposed changing the manner in which restrictions were applied or removed. They especially opposed section 8, which took jurisdiction over these matters out of the hands of local Oklahoma courts and rested them with the secretary of the interior. Nichols led opposition to the bill during the House hearings and proved instrumental in having objectionable sections amended or removed. Because Thomas-Rogers affected only Indians in Oklahoma, most members of Congress showed little interest in the proceedings and followed the lead of the Oklahoma members. By this time, many in Congress viewed Indians "as a particularly western problem in much the same way that African Americans were viewed as a 'southern' responsibility," writes historian Frederick Hoxie.[79] Many legislators left it all up to the Oklahoma delegation and would vote whichever way they sided.

With the biased attention of Congressman Nichols devoted to almost every person testifying, contention prevailed at the hearings. The first two Indian witnesses were Roly Canard of the Creeks and Grady Lewis representing the Choctaws. Nichols attempted to get them both to agree to the gist of a question: "Is it your opinion that a man—that the Secretary of the Interior—1,500 miles away from the Indians of Oklahoma, more likely a man who is not even a lawyer . . . is in better shape to determine the heirs of a decedent in Oklahoma than are the county courts of Oklahoma?"[80] Throughout these hearings, Nichols doggedly contended, "There is not an emergency in Oklahoma calling for legislation that would take away from the courts of Oklahoma their jurisdiction over these matters [probate]."[81] Threatened loss of control by the state's county courts over Indian probate matters remained the critical issue for opposing white interests in eastern Oklahoma.

On April 29, 1935, Lawrence E. Lindley testified, representing the Indian Rights Association. The IRA offered strong support for the bill with the exception of provisions that established the degrees of blood quantum as a determining factor over the issue of removing restrictions. Lindley testified that the bill "carries these provisions (namely, for competency commissions and the rapid removal of restrictions of Indians of less than one-half degree Indian blood) that past experience has shown are most effective ways of separating Indians from their land."[82] Others giving testimony criticized these provisions. Many felt they represented a continuation of governmental policies that had effectively contributed to the loss of Indian land to non-Indians.

Alice Lee Jemison, Joseph Bruner's secretary and a former member of the Board of Indian Commissioners, dissolved by Collier in 1933, read a statement from Bruner. In it Bruner characterized Thomas-Rogers as "a wandering, ramifying, communistic scheme" and voiced his complete opposition to it. He concluded, "I am opposed to the so called 'Thomas-Rogers Bill' for Oklahoma Indians; mainly it bristles with Collier and Collierism."[83]

Congressman Disney, who represented Osage County, also testified before the House committee. Disney exerted strong opposition to the bill throughout the legislative process. In his testimony he stated, "The [state] legislature passed a resolution against this bill. . . . Nineteen bar associations passed resolutions against it. Any numbers of chambers of commerce have passed resolutions against it. Public sentiment in eastern Oklahoma is solidly against it."[84] More importantly, Disney based his opposition on the views of former Oklahoma congressman William Hastings. Hastings, now retired from Congress, had strongly opposed the IRA for Oklahoma Indians and expressed opposition to certain provisions in the Thomas-Rogers Bill. Disney claimed that because Collier and Thomas had never lived in eastern Oklahoma, "They are not entitled to have their judgment balanced against that of Mr. Hastings as to this bill, [and] as to eastern Oklahoma."[85] Disney continued to oppose sections of the bill and in conjunction with Congressman Nichols effectively forced a major restructuring of it. Disney would later conclude, "I see lots of good coming from killing the bill and no harm."[86]

Collier opened the hearings with a lengthy explanation of the specifics of Thomas-Rogers, then answered numerous specific questions concerning its mechanics. As mentioned, he had been in attendance at most of the hearings, offering explanations and clarifying technical questions raised from the audience. During later questioning by Representative Usher Burdick of North Dakota, Collier discussed the widespread Indian support for the proposed change in jurisdiction for probate matters contained in the bill. He noted that "before the Senate committee came representatives of tribe after tribe of Oklahoma Indians, 28 of them in all, to testify that they were satisfied that their affairs were being expeditiously, economically, and justly handled under the probate system of the Interior Department."[87] During most of the House hearings, legislators with entrenched assimilationist thinking opposed reform proposals as they contended with Collier's administrators and bureaucrats.

Outside of the instances listed above, few Indian voices were heard during the House hearings. Many Indians had testified during the Senate hearings in early April, but most could not afford to stay in Washington during the weeks between hearings or afford a second trip back to the capital from Oklahoma. Opposition congressmen, especially Nichols and Disney, spent most of their time expressing their views and occasionally grilling witnesses supportive of the proposal. A great deal of blame for past failures of federal Indian policy fell upon the Indian Bureau. Finally, Collier served as a convenient target for attacks, and the opposition characterized his proposals as a step back in time for Oklahoma Indians.

On May 9, Secretary of the Interior Harold Ickes appeared before the House committee and offered a strong endorsement of Thomas-Rogers, saying, "The bill before your committee reverses the heartless policy established by Congress in 1908." Ickes claimed, "The Oklahoma Indians themselves are unanimously in favor of this measure," and he took a swipe at the opposition to the bill when he testified that "the opposition seems to be confined to . . . a fraction of the legal profession, who have directly profited through the mass of frivolous, wholly unnecessary Oklahoma Indian litigation. . . . We are asking that they [Oklahoma Indians] be protected from the rapacity of a small group of unscrupulous lawyers."[88]

At the last session of the hearings, on May 15, Congressman Nichols made a lengthy formal rebuttal of much of Ickes's testimony. Nichols refuted Ickes's claim that the majority of Oklahoma Indians supported Thomas-Rogers, claiming, "I have in my files letters from dozens and dozens of Indians telling me of the opposition to this bill by the Indians in its present form." In closing, Nichols characterized the bill as an attempt by Ickes "to bring under the control of the Secretary of the Interior . . . those six tribes [the Osages and the Five Tribes] over which he does not now enjoy complete and full control."[89]

As the House hearings drew to a close, it was evident that the bill in its present form would not pass without significant amending. In spite of the widespread support among Oklahoma Indians as measured by their testimony in both the Senate and House hearings and the numerous resolutions sent to Congress by tribal councils, the combined efforts of an organized and vociferous opposition led by Congressmen Nichols and Disney, utilizing the support and reputation of former Oklahoma congressman Hastings, proved overwhelming. On May 10, 1935, the Thomas-Rogers Bill was tabled over strong objections from Chairman Rogers. The original version of the bill was dead.[90]

In late June of 1935, Senator Thomas began working with Collier to draft a new version of the bill. On July 29, Thomas introduced it to the Senate, drastically streamlined in order to please opponents and secure passage. Gone was the blood quantum designation. Gone was section 8 that transferred jurisdiction over probate matters from Oklahoma county courts to the secretary of the interior. Scrapped was the proposal for competency commissions to determine restriction issues. Instead, the bill eased procedures for allowing the secretary to remove restrictions. In short, "the amended bill returned the Indians to state court jurisdiction and liberalized the provisions for declaring Indians competent which would speed the lifting of restrictions . . . . The welfare, economic, and organizational aspects of the original bill remained," wrote respected historian Muriel Wright, a Choctaw.[91] This new version passed the Senate in mid-August and moved over to the House for consideration. Nichols and Disney objected to the new version too, however, and kept the bill from consideration for the remainder of the session.

In November of 1935, Assistant Commissioner of Indian Affairs William Zimmerman spent a week in Oklahoma touring the Indian agencies with Congressman Rogers. Touted as a fact-finding mission "to determine sentiment of Oklahoma Indians on the Thomas-Rogers bill now pending before the House of Representatives," considerable effort was expended in urging individuals and business committees to let Oklahoma congressmen know of their support for the bill. Both Zimmerman and Rogers exuded optimism, Rogers predicting that the revised bill would pass "in some form during the next session of Congress."[92]

In April of 1936, the House Committee on Indian Affairs held hearings on the revised version of the Thomas-Rogers Bill. These hearings dragged on into June as Congressman Disney led vociferous ongoing opposition, though he was not a member of the committee. He requested an amendment exempting Osages from the bill and justified the proposal by stating, "The Osage Nation . . . is so different and independent from the rest of the state that I think it would be a serious mistake to put Osage county in this bill." On June 11, Disney motioned to have Osage County exempted. Once this was approved by the committee, Disney announced he would support the bill. Exercising its voice, the Osage tribal council sent a telegram to the committee "requesting that the Osages not be exempted from the bill."[93] Obviously, Disney did not listen to his Indian constituency on this measure but to white business and legal interests. The remaining two days of hearings covered minor points within the bill. These were agreeably ironed out and Thomas-Rogers was favorably reported out of committee on June 15. The next day, the House passed the bill. The Senate passed the House version on June 18, and on June 26, 1936, President Roosevelt signed Thomas-Rogers—now the Oklahoma Indian Welfare Act—into law.

John Collier, commissioner of Indian affairs (1933–1945). Courtesy of National Archives and Records Administration, College Park, Md. (Records of the Bureau of Indian Affairs, RG 75; unnumbered photograph, 75N, folder C, box 40)

A. C. Monohan, regional coordinator of field services, Office of Indian Affairs, State of Oklahoma. Courtesy of National Archives and Records Administration, College Park, Md. (Records of the Bureau of Indian Affairs, RG 75; unnumbered photograph, 75N, folder P, box 40)

William Zimmerman, Assistant Commissioner of Indian Affairs (1933–1950). Courtesy of National Archives and Records Administration, College Park, Md. (Records of the Bureau of Indian Affairs, RG 75; unnumbered photograph, folder C, box 40)

William Durant, Choctaw tribal lawyer and chief. Courtesy of National Archives and Records Administration, College Park, Md. (Records of the Bureau of Indian Affairs, RG75; photograph no. 4, 75N, box 10)

A. M. Landman (*left*), superintendent of the Muskogee Agency, and Roly Canard (*right*), Creek principal chief. Courtesy of National Archives and Records Administration, College Park, Md. (Records of the Bureau of Indian Affairs, RG 75; photograph no. 27, 75N, box 10)

John Collier and his dog Beastie in Zion National Park, September 14, 1943. Courtesy of National Archives and Records Administration, College Park, Md. (Records of the Bureau of Indian Affairs, RG 75; photograph no. 57, 75N, box 40)

Delos Lone Wolf presides at a tribal meeting of Kiowa, Comanche, and Apache Indians held at the auditorium of the Riverside Indian School, Anadarko, Oklahoma, 1940. Courtesy of National Archives and Records Administration, College Park, Md. (Records of the Bureau of Indian Affairs, RG 75; photograph no. 43, 75N, box 17)

Theodore Haas, chief counsel, Bureau of Indian Affairs, 1947. Courtesy of National Archives and Records Administration, College Park, Md. (Records of the Bureau of Indian Affairs, RG 75; unnumbered photograph, 75N, folder P, box 40)

Commissioner John Collier (*right*) with M. L. Hannifan (*left*), farm agent, and J. E. White (*center*), credit agent and extension supervisor, reviewing a turkey farm financed in part by credit under the OIWA, August 1943. Courtesy of National Archives and Records Administration, College Park, Md. (Records of the Bureau of Indian Affairs, RG 75; photograph No. 8, 75N, box 17)

Watching Phillips-Skelly No. 1 gushing at the rate of 1,800 barrels per day, located on the Osage Reservation, on April 5, 1923. Oil leasing of this well brought the Osage tribe $1,245,000. Courtesy of National Archives and Records Administration, College Park, Md. (Records of the Bureau of Indian Affairs, RG 75; photograph no. 13, 75N, box 20)

Oklahoma congressmen Wilburn Cartwright (*left*) and Will Rogers (*standing*) with Oklahoma senator Elmer Thomas (*right*) served as architects for the Indian New Deal in Oklahoma. Courtesy of Carl Albert Center Congressional Archives, University of Oklahoma.

"Backward March Commands John Collier," *Tulsa Tribune*, October 18, 1934.

Indian agricultural laborer's house in McIntosh County, Oklahoma, 1937. Courtesy of National Archives and Records Administration, College Park, Md. (Records of the Bureau of Indian Affairs, RG 75; photograph no. 19, 75N, box 17)

CHAPTER 5

Revival

On the evening of June 27, 1936, Senator Thomas sent a telegram to his friend John Hugh Chambers of Tulsa, saying, "Oklahoma General Welfare Bill passed both Houses before Congress adjourned and was signed by the President yesterday. It will become effective immediately."[1] Thomas, like others closely involved with the passage of the Oklahoma Indian Welfare Act, expected rapid implementation of its terms and programs. Commissioner Collier claimed that the OIWA would allow Oklahoma Indians "to put an end to the wastage of their assets, which has resulted in the loss of more than nine-tenths of their lands and . . . reduced more than 50,000 of their number to landlessness and abject poverty."[2] From enactment in June 1936 until the early 1950s, when federal Indian policy turned a sharp corner and entered the termination era, implementation of the OIWA focused on land purchases, credit, and the reestablishment of tribal governments.

It became apparent soon after enactment that application of the OIWA meant various things to the groups involved. As the burden of the Great Depression wore on, the conflict between focus on relief and focus on reform became quite evident in Oklahoma Indian affairs. Government leaders including Collier and Thomas seemed to concentrate more on long-range reforms, with measures designed to foster fundamental changes in Indian culture and lifestyle and their relationship to the dominant white culture. On the other hand, many

Oklahoma Indians focused on relief measures. For them, day-to-day life remained a formidable struggle. In 1936, many Oklahoma Indians hoped that the OIWA would resolve immediate concerns regarding food, shelter, clothing, medical care, and schooling for their children.

Subsistence agriculture represented the economic lifestyle of many Oklahoma Indians, and Indians in the western half of the state suffered from the effects of the persistent drought during the 1930s, the Dust Bowl. In 1934, agricultural extension workers reported that many western Oklahoma Indians "were unable to get a garden and they are now suffering from the lack of food as well as water and feed for their livestock."[3] In 1935, destitute and starving members of the Five Tribes received 198,000 pounds of canned goat meat from the Southwest, along with 27,000 pounds of canned beef and 17,093 head of "relief" cattle distributed by the federal government.[4] In 1936 another extension report stated, "The Cheyenne and Arapaho Central Farm Chapter . . . voted to discontinue their [annual agricultural] fair this fall due to the fact that they would have nothing to exhibit." The report continued, "At the Ben Buffalow place, the dust was so bad that dust from 6 to 18 inches filled his yard and the floors of the house were covered until you could not tell whether there were rugs on the floor or not."[5] Many Oklahoma Indians looked to the OIWA as an immediate answer to their problems, especially through the loan programs established under provisions in the act.

During the late 1930s, as the Indian Bureau struggled to activate programs under the OIWA, economic depression and drought continued to devastate Indians throughout the state. Alfred Harper from Wewoka, Oklahoma, wrote Senator Thomas in the fall of 1936, "I have six children in the public schools . . . that I shall have to take out for lack of clothing."[6] Angie Whitthorne, Chickasaw, requested governmental funds and wrote, "We Indians are in great need and many are almost starving."[7] The Oklahoma congressional delegation continued to receive a flood of letters from destitute and often starving Indians requesting help from the federal government. Thomas wired President Roosevelt, declaring that "[state and local] relief agents refuse to extend benefits to Indians stating that they should look to [the] Indian office for relief." Thomas requested a "liberal allotment of funds be made direct to the Indian Bureau for use in relieving distress among our Indians wards."[8]

Local political pressure to aid Oklahoma Indians targeted Thomas since he had been a chief architect of the OIWA. Immediately following the 1936 elections, E. H. Labelle, the chairman of the Indian Division of the Oklahoma Democratic Party Central Committee, wrote Thomas and counseled, "You know Elmer these Indians are not to be forgotten after the way they came to the front for the national ticket in the last election. . . . So let's see if we can get some thing done as soon as we can before it gets too cold."[9] Labelle was referring to immediate relief measures such as work, food, and even cash payments to help Indians through the coming winter. The Oklahoma congressional delegation, led by Thomas, pressured the White House and departments within the executive branch, as well as private charities such as the Red Cross, for immediate assistance. The army provided boots and a variety of out-of-date clothing to Oklahoma Indians. Additionally, government food commodities such as canned meat, milk, coffee, butter, and cheese were made available. These actions mitigated the dire situation of many Oklahoma Indians over the winter months of 1936 and 1937, but certainly did not eliminate them.[10]

Immediately following enactment of the OIWA, a great deal of correspondence from Oklahoma Indians flooded the offices of Oklahoma congressmen and bureau officials. Many letters were from individual Indians requesting information or loan applications for all manner of purposes, and these demonstrated a wide variety of misunderstanding concerning OIWA programs. For example, J. L. Nadeu, a Chickasaw from Lexington, Oklahoma, wanted to purchase a home. William Zimmerman, assistant commissioner of Indian affairs, responded via Thomas, "At the present time no rules or regulations have been issued by the Secretary of the Interior for the loaning of funds under this act [OIWA] to the Indians of Oklahoma."[11] The bureau expended a great deal of effort responding to these inquiries. The act had been designed to address issues such as land acquisition, supplying credit for economic undertakings, tribal incorporation for business pursuits, and the reestablishment of tribal governments. The Indian Bureau could only inform Oklahoma Indians that loans under the OIWA had to meet requirements for short-term investments for primarily agricultural endeavors by individuals or small incorporated groups. It was obvious that Indians needed to be educated on the programs and benefits of the OIWA. It also became evident that the bureau needed time to organize and establish procedures for awarding and administering loans as well as administering matters related to land purchases, educational benefits, and tribal reorganization. This type of ongoing bureaucratic wrangling served to delay implementation of the act. Congress had passed the legislation, but implementation moved slowly as the bureau developed an understanding of the act's programs, policies, and procedures, and placed administrators.

In August of 1936, just a month after enactment of the OIWA, the solicitor of the Interior Department filed a court case to obtain a ruling on the "type of organization required of borrowing tribesmen." The bureau had to work through differences between the IRA and the OIWA in order that funding procedures related to the two acts could blend. While both acts applied to Oklahoma Indians, the OIWA provided loans for individuals, cooperatives, and credit associations formed by ten or more Indians.[12] However, funds channeled from the revolving loan fund established under the IRA had to be initially directed through incorporated tribes, which in turn could make loans to individual Indians or incorporated groups.[13] A. C. Monahan, superintendent of the Five Tribes, reported, "If tribal incorporation is demanded, a delay of a year or more is likely before the money actually reaches the Indians. If the simpler organization into groups is sufficient, the money will begin to flow within a few weeks." The case clarified the issue by allowing eligible individuals or associations to receive loans directly from the government without those funds passing through the hands of incorporated tribes. Unfortunately, Monahan's prediction of quickly distributing loans proved wrong. The first loans under the IRA/OIWA did not occur until mid-1937, almost a year from enactment of the OIWA.[14] The wheels of bureaucracy turned slowly.

To compound matters, the first appropriations represented only a fraction of Congress's originally authorized amounts for both bills. Under the IRA, the total amount authorized was $12.5 million per year, including $250,000 for Indian organization, $2 million for land purchases, and $10 million for the revolving credit fund, along with $250,000 for educational loans. However, the amount actually appropriated only totaled $3,825,000, with $150,000 allocated for Indian organization, $1 million for land purchases (Oklahoma Indians would share $350,000), $2.5 million for the revolving credit fund, and $175,000 for educational loans.[15] Continued underfunding of Indian New Deal programs inhibited their effectiveness and long-range impact.

As early as February 1935, Commissioner Collier warned of an impending "attack against the authorized appropriations for implementing the Wheeler-Howard Act," conducted by "important cattle interests, timber interests, oil interests, and other substantial corporate and regional interests antagonized by those features of the Act which safeguard Indian property, and which give the tribes some measure of control over their own property." Collier feared, "Some intervention by the President will be necessary if the new program for Indians . . . is not to be crippled, or possibly even killed."[16] Many in Congress understood little of the plight of Native Americans. Outside of sparsely populated western states, few congressmen included Indians in their constituencies. They tended to follow the lead of legislators from western states, such as Oklahoma, with significant Indian populations, but the political bent of many western legislators was often steeped in assimilation ideology, and they typically yielded to pressure from ranchers, miners, timber industry barons, and ranchers. Collier's warnings suggest a conspiracy of private interests attempting to exert their influence. The experience of Oklahoma Indians discussed in earlier chapters seems to bear this out.

Meager appropriations meant limited ability to implement the IRA and OIWA as they were designed. Congress granted no increases in funding for administrative expenses of the Indian Bureau. This meant that "existing personnel [would] continue to carry the heavy administrative responsibility without much hope of increasing local staffs," Collier wrote.[17] Indian activist and respected anthropologist D'Arcy McNickle, a Flathead tribal member who worked as an administrative assistant in the bureau in the thirties and forties, claims, "Congress was never fully committed to the ideas embodied in the Indian Reorganization Act."[18]

Congress was not alone in its tepid support. The Bureau of the Budget and even Collier himself shared some of the blame. With respect to land purchases in Oklahoma, Collier requested only half of the congressionally authorized $2 million in 1936 and again in 1937. During 1938, the Bureau of the Budget slashed a request for the full $2 million annual appropriation to $500,000.[19] By that year only $1.1 million had been placed into the revolving loan fund. By 1940, only $4 million for land purchases nationwide had been appropriated. Inadequate funding of both the IRA and the OIWA severely constrained their effectiveness in Oklahoma.

By 1936, when the OIWA was enacted, the political headiness of the first two hundred days of Roosevelt's first term had all but evaporated. The "changing political climate of the late 1930s," characterized by growing opposition from a congressional coalition of Republicans and conservative Democrats, coupled with the severe recession of 1937 and backlash from FDR's court-packing scheme, served to dampen the "active phase of the New Deal," including programs under the Indian New Deal, notes historian Alan Brinkley in his book *The End of Reform*.[20]

The recession of 1937 contributed to the withering of New Deal programs, including the IRA and the OIWA, during the late 1930s and into the early 1940s, a period of uncertainty and confusion as to the stability of the economy. Brinkley argues that during this economic slowdown, many New Dealers "repudiated some of the impulses . . . prominent in the early New Deal." According to Brinkley, these "impulses" included moving away from promoting "government sponsored social welfare programs."[21] As industrial production slowed, unemployment once again soared, and the markets declined sharply during 1937 and into 1938. Many in government questioned the ability of the New Deal to lead the country out of depression.

Roosevelt was emboldened by his overwhelming margin of victory in his election to a second term in 1936. Sensing a sustaining vote from the American people for his New Deal programs, FDR moved to reign in a conservative court responsible for decisions that had declared unconstitutional important pillars of his agenda, including the Railroad Retirement Act, the Agricultural Adjustment Act, and the National Industrial Recovery Act. Roosevelt proposed expanding the federal court and imposing mandatory retirement ages. These changes would give him opportunities to appoint justices with thinking more in line with his objectives.

In response to FDR's attempts to alter the federal court structure, many conservative Democrats and Republicans joined in a coalition to oppose much of his domestic agenda. Montana senator Burton K. Wheeler became a leader in this group. Although he had cosponsored the proposal that had become the Indian Reorganization Act, the Wheeler-Howard Bill, shortly after its introduction he had opposed both Collier and the bill. Having never read it before its introduction, Wheeler spoke against the idea of a constitutional government replacing tribal councils. During 1937, Wheeler strongly denounced FDR's court-packing scheme, saying "it is a sham and a fake liberal proposal. . . . It merely places upon the Supreme Court six political hacks."[22] Wheeler's opposition to Collier and the Indian New Deal extended into the 1940s. By 1943, Wheeler had joined with Elmer Thomas and other western senators in calling for repeal of the IRA and the removal of Collier as Indian commissioner.[23] "Like other western progressives, [Wheeler] represented an older hostility to centralized power," writes American historian James T. Patterson.[24]

The inexperience on the part of many Oklahoma Indians in dealing with the Office of Indian Affairs contributed to the difficulty of implementing the IRA and the OIWA. Many harbored negative memories of dealing with the Indian Bureau. Full-bloods and "traditionals" often eschewed contact with white society, choosing to practice subsistence agriculture in isolated rural areas. Some Indians became disheartened with the delay and red tape they experienced in attempting to obtain loans under the OIWA. W. M. Blackhawk from Stillwater complained that "the Indian bill of Oklahoma is not worth the paper and time in which it [has] taken the US senate to wright [sic] it out, there is not one dog gon thing in the bill in whitch will benefit the Oklahoma Indian what so ever. . . . the Indian bill of Oklahoma should be thrown in the fire . . . and burnt, it's a disgrace and no good."[25]

For many, the credit division of the Indian Bureau seemed to move very slowly. On April 23, 1937, Raymond H. Kemp wrote to Senator Thomas requesting his assistance. Kemp reported, "Some two or three months ago we Indians organized a credit association . . . to the present we have had no reply from our application."[26] Assistant Commissioner Zimmerman responded to an inquiry from Thomas stating that the Johnston County Credit Association's application "was under consideration, but with over forty applications [and] with our limited staff it is impossible to act on the same as quickly as we would like."[27] John McCracken asked what was holding up approval for the Nowata County Indian Credit Association. Zimmerman responded, "The bylaws which were to be submitted for approval have not yet been received by this office."[28] Reduced staffing at the bureau contributed still another ongoing obstacle in the path of OIWA implementation.

Haskell Paul, an attorney representing the Chickasaws, wrote to Thomas asking for his help in determining the status of the application for the Garvin County Credit Association. He also asked a number of questions: "How long do you think it will likely be? . . . what degree of blood will be eligible? Is any one at present, authorized to solicit applications for these loans?"[29] Not only were Indians and legal professionals like Paul unclear about the OIWA, so was Thomas and so was the agency charged with responsibility administering it. Additionally, competing viewpoints within and between the legislative and executive branches compounded the difficult situation. During the legislative process, little foresight had been given to funding and mechanisms to implement the law. This shortsightedness on the part of Congress and the Indian Bureau delayed implementation of the OIWA.

In October of 1937, Collier spoke to Oklahoma Indians at two meetings held to determine Indian concerns regarding implementation of the OIWA. Besides land purchases, the topic that generated the most Indian concern was credit. Collier fielded a wide variety of questions on different aspects of the credit programs. Many asked about the limited congressional appropriations for the various programs under the IRA and OIWA, especially low funding for credit programs. Collier explained that many in Congress were leery of extending credit to Native Americans based on their low levels of repayment on $9 million worth of loans over the preceding fifteen years, the so-called industrial reimbursable loans. He affirmed that only $3 million had been repaid. Collier continued by describing a wait-and-see attitude of Congress. If repayment levels on loans made under the IRA and the OIWA were initially high, then Congress would be more likely to increase appropriations to these programs. He put the solution for limited appropriations squarely on the Indians who would participate in the credit programs. He referred to the small appropriation as a "demonstration" and said, "It is enough to use in proving to Congress and to . . . the President that Indians can take loans, make productive use of loans, and pay them back, and then there will be no trouble in getting more money, in any reasonable amount."[30] Collier may have been attempting to explain why appropriations were so low in an effort to motivate Oklahoma Indians toward greater fiscal responsibility.

It was evident that a number of challenges prevented prompt and full implementation of the OIWA. Many Oklahoma Indians were concerned with the immediate challenges of day-to-day life. Depression and drought in the 1930s hit Oklahoma Indians extremely hard. Many simply did not understand the legislative substance of the IRA and the OIWA. Legal and administrative hurdles in channeling IRA funds into OIWA programs had to be cleared. Most in Congress had little interest in Indian affairs or appropriations to fund Indian programs. Staffing shortages in the Indian Bureau spelled delays in the approval of charters for credit associations and loan programs. Additionally, as noted before, many in the bureau were career administrators steeped in assimilationism. Much of the IRA and the OIWA represented a radical departure from objectives many had spent their careers attempting to achieve, contributing to a somewhat uncooperative attitude.

Ben Dwight, an Indian Bureau field agent at the Muskogee office, discussed implementation of the OIWA in an article in the bureau's *Indians at Work* in June 1937. Explaining the workings of the act, Dwight called for a new mind-set on the part of Oklahoma Indians. He counseled, "The program is . . . not a mere relief measure; it is not an emergency plan. . . . [I]t is a permanent long-time program, which will extend over a number of years, even generations. . . . The individual must think in terms of a permanent program rather than about one merely meeting present emergencies." In discussing credit programs, Dwight said that Indians "must accept and assume a large measure of responsibility for sound credit operations," echoing the counsel of Commissioner Collier.[31]

In October 1937, daylong meetings held in Shawnee and Muskogee explored many of the issues surrounding implementation of the IRA and the OIWA. Attending these meetings were Senator Thomas, Congressman Rogers, Collier, and Oklahoma Indian agents—the bureau's superintendents. Over five hundred Oklahoma Indians, representing nineteen tribal groups from the western half of the state, attended the first meeting, held in Shawnee on October 13.

Thomas, chair of the Senate Committee on Indian Affairs, conducted the meetings and introduced them by declaring each "a meeting to try and understand the wishes of the Indian citizens."[32] Thomas organized the meetings in a similar fashion to the Indian congresses he had organized three years earlier, in October 1934, after he had exempted Oklahoma Indians from the IRA enacted in June that year. In his opening statement, Thomas flattered Indian attendees, saying, "We want to know what you want, and then we want to know what you don't want.... If you citizens don't get what you want, it will be largely because you have not advised your member[s] of the House and Senate."[33] Thomas seemed to offer a clear invitation for Indian participation. The senator was then followed on the agenda by attending Oklahoma congressmen, including Lyle Boren, Wesley Disney, William Hastings, and Will Rogers. Legislators and bureaucrats maintained a polite but patronizing tone toward Indian attendees at these meetings. Permission to make a short statement or ask questions fell to a representative from each tribe. Most questions focused on specific aspects of the major programs offered by the IRA and the OIWA, regarding land purchases, credit, and tribal organization. Some voiced concerns over appropriations for the acts and the slow progress in implementing their programs.

At the Muskogee meeting, on October 14, Commissioner Collier made a revealing statement as he encouraged Oklahoma Indians to organize tribal governments. Collier spoke of how, during the allotment period, tribal governments "were dissolved by Congress.... Indians couldn't be good Indians unless they were unorganized Indians." Now the federal government was attempting to "extend to the Indian the white man's opportunity to organize and operate through organization[al] principles."[34] Many Indians complained that Collier was "superimposing white political organization on tribal structures," writes historian Alison Bernstein.[35] Additionally Senator Thomas preached that tribal organizations "give official sanction to [tribal] activities, where heretofore it has been wholly unofficial.[36] Between that time and the enactment of the OIWA in 1936, many Oklahoma tribal groups had established business committees or problem committees charged with dealing with a specific issue. Legally, these types of ad hoc Indian governmental bodies were not officially recognized by the federal government, even though the bureau would work with them to implement and administer programs. Ben Dwight explained, "Up to this time these organizations have existed by courtesy, we will say, of the bureau. . . . They had no legal recognized standing."[37] Bureau officials promoted the idea that tribes organizing under the IRA and the OIWA could now be legally sanctioned by the federal government. An integral part of acts, the reinstitution of tribal government marked a major shift in federal Indian policy.

The tribal organization program of the IRA and the OIWA remains its brightest legacy. It came at a time of transformation for many Oklahoma Indians. As life in mass American society became more commercial, urban, and technological, these accelerating forces filtered down to Indian life as well. This began during the 1920s and intensified during the 1940s with World War II. Tribal organization provided the mechanism that allowed Indian tribes to begin to take control of their own destiny. Just because a tribe did not organize under the IRA and the OIWA did not mean they remained untouched by the transformation. Eventually, almost every tribe organized in some manner for political and economic advancement.

Several Indian representatives expressed confusion over funding for land purchases. They believed that loans from Indian credit associations financed land purchases. Commissioner Collier explained that money from credit associations was to be lent to groups or individuals for mainly agricultural enterprises. "The credit money is not the money for buying land."[38] Both the IRA and the OIWA established funded programs separate from other programs for land purchases. However, as mentioned earlier, Congress appropriated only $4 million for land purchases under both the IRA and the OIWA, and out of that amount only $350,000 was earmarked for land purchases in Oklahoma. Collier mused that this was a very small amount measured against the need and that at that rate the bureau "will be making very slow progress toward the revesting of homeless [Oklahoma] Indians with land."[39] Over the next forty-two years, from 1934 to 1976, Congress appropriated just under $6 million for land purchases nationwide. Of that amount, $4 million was appropriated in the first five years of the IRA. After 1951, requests for land purchases under the OIWA ceased. With the funds appropriated nationwide, 595,157 acres were actually acquired nationwide by 1976.[40]

With respect to Oklahoma, under the IRA and OIWA tribal land bases increased by less than thirty-six thousand acres at a cost of just over $510,000. Most of this was added between 1935 and 1946 and lay in eastern Oklahoma. Evenly distributed among the Five Tribes, 30,703 acres were suitable mostly for grazing, not agriculture. No additional land purchases by the Interior Department using federal funds took place in Oklahoma after 1946.[41] The inability of the Collier administration to significantly increase the land base of Oklahoma tribes was one factor limiting the success of other objectives of the OIWA since so much of the act revolved around land.

One of the foremost objectives of the IRA and the OIWA was to reverse the damage inflicted on Indian landholdings by the allotment policy. The first two sections of the OIWA dealt with Indian land issues. Section 1 outlined the procedures to be used by the secretary of the interior in acquiring land for Oklahoma tribal units. Section 2 gave the secretary preference in purchasing any restricted Indian land that might be put up for sale.[42] Allotment in the Oklahoma Territory began in 1887 with passage of the General Allotment Act but was delayed in Indian Territory where it commenced with passage of the Curtis Act in 1898. By 1933, tribal landholdings in Oklahoma plummeted from 15 million acres to 1.5 million acres, a loss of 90 percent, and by 1933 the vast majority of Oklahoma Indians were landless. The unavailability of land for such a large percentage of Indians living in a subsistence agriculture society was a recipe for the economic and social disaster outlined earlier. Over the history of the

IRA and the OIWA, the effort to restore the Indian land base met with only minimal success. Because of that, landless Oklahoma Indians were unable to benefit from various programs of the OIWA, especially financing for agricultural projects designed to develop income and thereby raise participants' standard of living and independence.

Collier firmly believed that increasing the Indian land base should be at the core of any program designed to help the Indians. He shunned the idea of assimilating Native Americans into white society. His ideas embraced the "objective of self-sufficiency based on land. . . . [Indians] self-supporting without competing, on the one hand, with white industrial labor or, on the other hand, with white commercial agriculture."[43] Native Americans would become part of mass American society, Collier thought, though separate from the dominant white majority, thereby preserving their tribal culture and heritage.

Issues other than the lack of sufficient appropriations would also influence the limited success of agricultural programs of the IRA and the OIWA. As mentioned above, requests from Native Americans for land purchases decreased significantly during the late 1930s and 1940s. Some attribute this drop to a transformation in Oklahoma agriculture during the 1940s. Angie Debo claimed in 1950, "Mechanization and large scale operations have displaced the small farmer, both Indian and white. . . . Since about 1940, it has become impossible to rehabilitate an Indian family starting with nothing. This is a circumstance beyond the control of the Indian service."[44] As in the rest of the nation, technology transformed Oklahoma agriculture. This allowed for increased production while at the same time reducing production costs. Agricultural operations grew in acreage, and farming became more capital-intensive. These changes sounded the death knell for many small Oklahoma farmers, both white and Indian. During this period, many Oklahoma Indians moved from subsistence agriculture to unskilled wage labor, leaving rural areas for nearby towns or urban areas throughout the state. During the war years, many moved throughout the West and worked for defense contractors. The relocation program of the postwar years also created an emigration of hundreds of Oklahoma Indians moving from depressed remote agricultural areas to urban areas such as Oklahoma

City, Tulsa, Muskogee, and Lawton. This migration even extended beyond Oklahoma to cities such as Denver, Chicago, Dallas, Phoenix, and Los Angeles. With the advantage of hindsight, scholars such as Alison Bernstein and Angie Debo questioned the efficacy of land acquisition as a major plank in the Indian New Deal.[45]

The rapid transformation of American society in the first half of the twentieth century from an agricultural and rural footing to urban industrialism affected Native Americans in many ways. The emphasis on land acquisition for agricultural pursuits seemed to move Indians in the opposite direction from the flow of mass society, thereby guaranteeing continued dependence on governmental assistance as they struggled with subsistence. Bernstein argued, "Indian land could not provide a basis for economic survival for most tribes [due to] overexploitation of soil, range, and timber. A majority of Indians lacked the capital to acquire the seed, fertilizer, equipment, and livestock needed to revitalize their land-based economy."[46] This described the situation of many Oklahoma Indians during this time. The small minority who tenaciously held on to allotments were often isolated on their small plots of 80–160 acres, surrounded by white neighbors. As Angie Debo corroborated, many full-blood members of the Five Tribes lived a hand-to-mouth existence, often squatting on inaccessible plots in the hill country of eastern Oklahoma, with little desire to change. Many intentionally chose that lifestyle in order to remove themselves from contact with whites and to maintain their cultural heritage. On the other hand, it can be argued that the transfer from subsistence agriculture to wage labor and from a rural to an urban setting would bring more and more Oklahoma Indians under the influence of the non-Indian economy and culture. While there has been some scholarly study on the impact of these types of influences on Indian economic and political structures, culture, and lifestyle, much more work needs to be done to broaden our understanding.[47]

Reinstituting tribal governments utilizing constitutionalism was certainly a central feature of the IRA and the OIWA. Tribal organization has proven the most lasting and influential aspect of the IRA and the OIWA, if also sometimes the most controversial. The architects of the IRA and the OIWA considered tribal organization second in importance only to resolving the Indian land issue. John Collier considered the philosophy underscoring Indian self-rule as "consonant with American realities and American values and ideals."[48] As discussed earlier, the severe restriction of Oklahoma tribal governments began in 1898 with passage of the Curtis Act and continued after 1907, with Oklahoma statehood, up to the Indian New Deal of the 1930s. The OIWA helped Oklahoma tribal groups reverse that situation by reinstituting tribal governments with constitutions. Though not all Oklahoma tribes would organize under the OIWA, this legislation would prove an influence on all.

The OIWA devoted only a short paragraph to tribal organization. It simply stated, "Any recognized tribe or band of Indians residing in Oklahoma shall have the right to organize for its common welfare and adopt a constitution and bylaws" subject to approval by the secretary of the interior.[49] Like the IRA, the OIWA allowed a tribe to incorporate as a recognized corporate body, with approval by "a majority vote of the adult members of the organization voting."[50] Finally, only organized Oklahoma tribes were allowed to participate in the revolving credit fund established under the IRA.

"Reestablishment" of tribal government is somewhat of a misnomer. Though believed to have been formally dissolved in the years before statehood, tribal governments continued to function, albeit in reduced scope and often from the shadows. Angie Debo argued that with the dissolution of tribal governments, "it was apparent from the beginning that there was certain unfinished business requiring the signature of tribal officers. . . . [involving] the disposal of tribal lands, representing various lingering tribal interests, and [a] liaison relationship" with the federal government.[51] By the time tribal organization became possible under the IRA and the OIWA in the latter 1930s, most Oklahoma tribes maintained some form of functioning government. The Cherokee, Choctaw, Seminole, and Creek Nations had a principal chief, while the Chickasaws had a governor appointed by the president of the United States. Most tribes maintained some form of tribal council or business committee. In 1909, the Creek principal chief under direction of local bureau officials failed to call the Creek legislative council into session. Disgruntled council members and other tribal leaders "met in a rump session, which they termed the 'Creek Convention.' The Creeks refused to abandon their tribal government and political life."[52] They continued to meet regularly until 1934 when Commissioner Collier allowed them to hold elections, resulting in the election of Roly Canard as principal chief. He was subsequently appointed by the president, which gave "legal sanction" to his election by the Creek people.[53] The incubating idea of majority rule challenged the traditional idea of consensus decision-making within some tribal groups. The IRA and the OIWA did not establish or reestablish tribal governments among Oklahoma Indians. This legislation helped to end a kind of "bureaucratic imperialism" evident in the attitude and actions of the Indian Bureau over many decades, which manifested itself as "deliberate attempts to frustrate, debilitate, and generally prevent [the proper] functioning of tribal governments."[54] This important legislation opened a door, allowing self-determination a significant step along the evolutionary process already underway.

Tribal organization under the IRA and the OIWA required two procedures. First, a tribal constitution was written and ratified. This constitution designated the powers and duties of the tribal government. After the tribal constitution was in place, the tribe could then, if desired, apply for a corporate charter. A charter defined the right of the tribal government to exercise the powers of a corporation. Under the OIWA, an Oklahoma tribe could "organize for its common welfare and to adopt a constitution and bylaws, under such rules and regulations *as the Secretary of the Interior may prescribe.*"[55] The secretary also issued the charter for incorporation, which placed the corporation under the laws of the state of Oklahoma and allowed the tribe to participate in the revolving credit fund established under the IRA and the OIWA. A major criticism by many tribal groups concerned the required approval of the secretary of the interior for the establishment of tribal constitutions. The American Indian Policy Review Commission argued that this requirement "exemplifies the paternalism and lack of trust" in a bureau-controlled relationship "which will not recognize the fact that Indian nations are capable of governing themselves."[56] While the idea of tribal groups organizing for home rule or self-rule represented a major change in direction for federal Indian policy, the paternalistic attitude continued.

The majority of Oklahoma tribal groups did not organize under the IRA or the OIWA. Eighteen Oklahoma tribes, mostly from the western part of the state, accounting for 13,241 members, organized under the IRA and OIWA by 1950. Of that group, thirteen also established charters of incorporation. Outside of three Creek tribal towns and the Keetoowah Band of the Cherokees, comprising a total population of only 1,248, none of the Five Tribes boasting the bulk of Oklahoma's Indian population had organized.[57] Angie Debo explained this rejection, writing that the Five Tribes were "subjected to large scale exploitation that disrupted their economic and cultural life and drove many back into the hills and timber."[58] These groups eschewed white society and its institutions. Historian Kenneth Philp observed, "The Oklahoma Indian Welfare Act did not receive a very favorable reception from the more than 100,000 Indians in Oklahoma."[59] With an estimated Indian population in Oklahoma in 1940 of 120,000, just a little over 10 percent were members of organized tribal units.

Records show that of the Five Tribes, only the Creeks organized under the Oklahoma Indian Welfare Act and their organization was not until 1979. The Cherokees organized under a member-written constitution in 1976, while the Chickasaws operate under a constitution the tribe adopted in 1979. In 1983, the Choctaws updated their original constitution of 1860. Finally, the Seminoles organized under a federally approved constitution in 1969.[60] What accounts for the limited involvement by Oklahoma tribal units in this aspect of the IRA and the OIWA?

Loretta Fowler has focused on the evolution of tribal government before, during, and after enactment of the IRA and the OIWA, and she has been critical of Indian New Deal constitutions. She argues, "Generally these constitutions were written by [Indian Bureau] personnel with little interest in or sympathy for tribal perspectives on political and legal relations. Constitutions and by-laws that suited the Bureau were imposed on the tribes."[61] Fowler believes local political traditions were not considered to any real degree when IRA and OIWA constitutions were formulated. However, records show that in at least two instances in Oklahoma, local traditions of tribal groups were considered and exerted tremendous influence on the organization process.

In the spring of 1937, as the McIntosh County Indian Credit Association was being organized, Indian Bureau officials discovered that "old Tribal Towns of the Creek Confederacy were still in existence, [causing] considerable consternation within the Oklahoma branch of the Indian service," wrote anthropologist Morris Opler. "The talk of ancient social units and customs disturbed them [the Bureau]."[62] A "town" was not a tribe or a band as specified as a basis for organization under the OIWA. However, after much study and legal wrangling, the solicitor of the Department of the Interior decided that a Creek town would "constitute a recognized band."[63] This bridged a hurdle and allowed Creek towns to organize under the IRA and the OIWA. Eventually three Creek towns adopted constitutions and charters of incorporation under the OIWA. It is worth noting that one of these towns, the Alabama-Quassarte Tribal Town, preserved in its constitution "some of the traditional Creek customs . . . such as hereditary town offices and matrilineal membership and modes of adoption," when it organized under the OIWA on January 10, 1939.[64] The other two towns are Thlopthlocco, near Okemah, Oklahoma, organized on December 27, 1928, and Kialegee, in Wetumka, Oklahoma, organized on June 12, 1941.

These customized constitutions fly in the face of premises by scholars such as Fowler and Philp that IRA and OIWA constitutions were cookie cutter in nature and forced on tribal groups by the Indian Bureau. In his study, Opler implies that other Creek towns could have been organized under the OIWA had experts such as Felix Cohen remained in the field to resolve unique and complex situations preventing groups from organizing. Instead, regular bureau employees shunned these situations, feeling "that more than one approach to the problem of organization was just a burden and a harassment."[65]

The Keetoowah or United Keetoowah Band (UKB) maintained a history as a distinct group in the Cherokee tribe dating back hundreds of years. At times, groups within the Cherokee such as the Nighthawks and the Seven Clan Society claimed affiliation with the Keetoowah Society. In September of 1905, the Keetoowah formed a political entity known as the Keetoowah Society, Inc. During the debate promoting passage of the Wheeler-Howard Bill in March 1934, the Keetoowah supported passage while the Cherokee tribe as a whole opposed the bill. Ironically, the Keetoowah were denied the ability to organize under the IRA and OIWA in 1937. Subsequently, it was discovered that while the Five Tribes Act of 1906 restricted the governments of the Five Tribes, the Keetoowah Society was not specifically mentioned, a congressional oversight. This created a legal gray area that took a decade for federal courts to resolve. In August 1946, Congress passed a measure recognizing the Keetoowah and allowing them to organize under the IRA and OIWA. In October 1950, the UKB formally organized under the OIWA as its constitution was ratified by members.[66]

Scholars have attributed the limited involvement by Oklahoma Indians in the tribal organization aspects of the IRA and OIWA to a wide variety of factors. James Olson and Raymond Wilson, authors of *Native Americans in the Twentieth Century*, believe that an important factor Collier underestimated was the "diversity" and "intensity" of dissension within many Oklahoma tribal groups.[67] They contend that Collier's experience with the Navajos and Pueblos during the 1920s was of fairly harmonious and close-knit tribal relations. They argue that he might have applied that model to all tribal groups, but Oklahoma Indians often did not fit that model, many being rife with discord. A case in point involves the Sac and Fox tribe in 1936 and is representative of controversies found within other tribes as well: a battle for control of the business committee by groups within the tribe. A river running through Sac and Fox land divided the tribe into northern and southern groups. A Shawnee Agency member, Manda Starr, wrote to Superintendent Perkins referencing an 1846 treaty whereby "the half breed members . . . promised not to meddle in [tribal] affairs and to sit back and let the full blood[s] handle [tribal affairs]."[68] These divisions sometimes created what seemed to bureau officials like havoc within tribal council and business committee meetings.

In August of 1936, F. E. Perkins, agency superintendent, reported that one meeting had "ended in pandemonium and chaos."[69] The tribal business committee headed by a forceful and domineering chairman, Frank O. Jones, often compounded the situation. Jones was accused of strong-arm tactics and of controlling elections for the business committee. Through the business committee, Jones had dominated Sac and Fox tribal affairs for several years. He viewed the possibility of the tribe organizing under the OIWA as a severe threat to his power and position. Jones fought doggedly but lost the battle when the Sacs and Foxes adopted a tribal constitution in

December of 1937. Kenneth Philp proposes that the IRA and OIWA "frequently intensified existing factionalism. Tribal constitutions led to bitter disputes over who would control newly established tribal governments."[70]

For many full-blood tribal members, organization proposed by the OIWA seemed alien. Often the long-accepted practices of tribal governments differed radically from those that accompanied IRA/OIWA organization. Consensus decision-making characterized the tribal heritage of many groups, but voting and majority rule replaced this under the IRA and OIWA. Introduction to "elections, rules of parliamentary procedure, constitutions, and other features of Western political tradition" forced tribal groups "to undertake a major reorganization of their social, cultural, and political relations," writes sociologist Duane Champagne.[71] Non-Indian forms of government forced upon the Indians caused many to lose touch with their indigenous political heritage. Tribal governments under the IRA/OIWA "appealed primarily to younger and more educated Indians, while others felt the IRA/OIWA "superimposed white political structures on tribal structures," which tended to "disrupt traditional decision-making patterns," Bernstein writes.[72] Those groups within a tribe more involved in Anglo society and economic activities often adjusted to the new governments formed under the IRA/OIWA and consequently often dominated them.

Carter Blue Clark argues that some Oklahoma Indians scorned reorganization under the IRA/OIWA because they felt too much direction and control from the federal government in this process. According to Clark, during the 1930s the bureau imposed tribal constitutions and "arbitrarily set up tribal councils." Clark believes the 1930s unveiled "an intensification of federal manipulation of tribal authority." He specifically points out, "The federal government appointed the principal chiefs for the Five Tribes until 1969, and in effect, appointed the entire tribal government, since the principal chief also appointed the tribal legislature."[73] Fowler concurs: "Constitutions and by-laws that suited the Bureau were imposed on the tribes."[74] Champagne questions the legitimacy accorded some tribal governments by members, claiming "many reservation Indians have not internalized the primacy of political commitments to centralized

IRA governments over other political and cultural allegiances."[75] Philp points out that many Indians did not support the IRA/OIWA because "it simply did not go far enough in the direction of self-rule." Many felt that too much power over tribal affairs was left in the hands of the secretary of the interior, with "all important tribal council decisions" being subject to "administrative review by the secretary."[76] This issue would be at the heart of the struggle for self-determination during the latter half of the twentieth century.

Recognition by the Indian Bureau of the right of groups to organize tribal governments under the IRA and OIWA marked a major shift in Indian policy for Oklahoma Indians. For years officials had refused to recognize tribal governments. Shadow governments continued to operate within a number of tribal groups, but their effectiveness was severely limited. With enactment of the OIWA, the bureau actively encouraged tribal groups to organize, a complete about-face in policy. This forced a generation of tribal members only vaguely familiar with tribal governments onto center stage, and the replacement of practices such as consensus rule with non-Indian practices such as voting and majority rule caused uncertainty in Native Americans. This, coupled with other factors such as distrust of the federal government, the impact of depression and drought, the complex path required for organization, and ongoing paternalistic attitudes of governmental officials, contributed to low participation by Oklahoma Indians in organizing under the IRA/OIWA. However, tribal groups, organized or not, were nudged toward more effective tribal government in order to deal effectively with the challenges and opportunities of the new age ushered in by World War II.

A second major provision of the OIWA was to furnish credit for Oklahoma Indians. Funding would allow Indians to embark on the road toward self-sufficiency, with financing for various agricultural operations and expansion, both individual and tribal. However, funds to administer the OIWA were not available until late August 1937, over a year after its enactment. The bill passed Congress at the end of fiscal year 1935/36 and after appropriations had been approved by Congress for the coming fiscal year. John Collier explained, "We didn't get our first dollar until the 21st of August [1937]. . . . We didn't have money to even print forms."[77] Again, limited funding proved to be an ongoing factor, analogous to the rationing of a limited food or fuel supply.

Collier mentioned that while waiting for appropriations, the Indian Bureau streamlined loan application forms from fourteen pages to four pages and established procedures for local approval for individual loans rather than by the office of the secretary of the interior in Washington. Thomas W. Hunter, Choctaw, a county judge from Hugo, presented a tribal resolution supporting the OIWA but decried the lack of funding to establish functioning credit associations. He stated, "I have talked with a number [credit associations] in eastern Oklahoma. I found them without expenses to operate. . . . in order to work the plan [OIWA] out . . . we must have operating expenses to do it with."[78] Roly Canard, the Creek chief, stated, "I feel that we [the Creeks] are a forgotten people. . . . It has been 16 months since this act [OIWA] was legislated, and [no] . . . actions have ever been presented to us."[79] Charles Grounds, Seminole, expressed the frustration of many Oklahoma Indians when he said, "When you have a drought, clouds will come together. They will darken up. You will hear a lot of thunder. You will see a lot of lighting, but no rain. What we want is some rain."[80]

Under the IRA and OIWA, there were four methods available to extend credit to Oklahoma Indians: direct loans to individuals, loans to organized tribes or bands, loans to cooperatives, and loans for Indian credit associations. Indian Bureau officials decided that credit associations were the preferred method.[81] Section 4 of the OIWA authorized Indian credit associations. Simply stated, ten or more Indians, as determined by tribal rolls, could petition the Interior Department for a charter as a local cooperative association formed for the purposes of credit administration. An extensive and often time-consuming application procedure monitored and approved by the bureau was followed. By 1938, there were twenty-four Indian credit associations operating across Oklahoma.

With congressional appropriations providing only a fraction of the amounts authorized by the IRA and OIWA, the bureau focused on insuring that the limited available credit was directed to where it could do the most good. An administrative bulletin from the Oklahoma credit office counseled field personnel that "credit funds should go largely to those Indians who do not have other sources of credit open to them." Blood quantum was used to determine eligibility for loans. The bureau stated, "We feel that Indians with a greater degree of Indian blood should be favored over those of a lesser degree."[82] In establishing eligibility for programs, the Indian Bureau "defined an Indian as a member of a federally recognized tribe or a descendent . . . and shall include persons of one-half or more Indian blood." Lastly, the bureau strongly counseled field agents "not [to] confuse relief with credit. . . . Broadly speaking, relief clients would not be suitable credit clients."[83]

By late 1937, limited appropriations offered at least a breath of life for several Oklahoma Indian credit associations. On December 13, 1937, Senator Thomas informed the Murray County Indian Credit Association that its request for funding for $15,000 had been approved by the bureau.[84] The Grady County Indian Credit Association was also granted a start-up fund of $15,000 in January of 1938.[85] In the spring of 1938, the Oklahoma County Indian Credit Association was also approved for $15,000.[86] That year similar funding was also allocated for Oklahoma Indian credit in Pontotoc, Washington, Rogers, and Grady Counties, to name a few.

A. C. Monahan, a regional coordinator for the bureau, sent Commissioner Collier a report discussing "principal activities in the Indian Service in the Oklahoma-Kansas area" for the 1937/1938 fiscal year. With respect to credit activities, Monahan reported that loans totaling $683,000 for thirty-five Indian credit associations had been approved. Loans to 107 individuals totaling $56,260 had also been approved. Four economic cooperatives had been chartered and one had received a loan of $2,800. Finally, four tribal corporations had received loans of over $63,000 under the OIWA. These tribal corporations had made thirty-one loans to individuals, totaling a little over $15,000.[87]

While several Indian credit associations were able to begin operations during late 1937 and early 1938, many others in the works were not. In January 1938, the bureau turned down a charter request by the Creeks because "the Creek Indians held a Creek Council in Sapulpa and disapproved the Thomas-Rogers Bill."[88] Compounding the situation in Wagoner County was the issue of several tribal groups living in the same county. Bureau policy allowed the establishment of Indian credit associations on a county basis. Bureau records showed the Creeks exclusively occupied Wagoner County. However, part of the Cherokee Nation was located in Wagoner County as well. This created an issue with respect to the desire of bureau officials to see appropriated funds for credit organizations flow through tribal organizations. With two tribal groups in the same county, a roadblock emerged. In late August, Thomas Halfmoon wrote to Senator Thomas stating that the Washington County Credit Association, duly formed, had applied for $25,000 six months earlier. They had heard nothing from the bureau and were "very anxious to help the needy Delawares in Washington County who are very anxious to get loans for farming and cattle raising."[89]

Richard Colbert, the secretary treasurer of the Pontotoc Indian Credit Association, voiced several concerns shared by many Indian credit associations in Oklahoma. Colbert referenced a complaint by Arthur Talbert, the president of the Love County Indian Credit Association, in a letter to Thomas that complained of "the delay in obtaining loans through the Credit Associations set up under the Thomas-Rogers Act applicable to Oklahoma." Colbert placed blame squarely on the shoulders of the bureau, noting the "technicality, and strict requirements prescribed by the Department, which the borrower must undergo to qualify to obtain a loan."[90]

In addition to limited funds to loan, most of the Indian credit associations in Oklahoma also suffered from the lack of funding for operating expenses. Section 6 of the OIWA allowed for a $2 million appropriation for loans and the expenses of administering loans. Colbert spoke of the need for "a small allowance to aid the officials who are directing the business of the Indian Chartered Organizations."[91] Under the OIWA, credit associations borrowed money at 1 percent interest, and then loaned funds at 3 percent. The difference was intended to cover expenses of the credit associations. However, because of the small volume of loans, the 2 percent margin for expenses often proved totally inadequate. Colbert voiced a common complaint of those who served on the boards of Indian credit associations. Many spent long hours administering various aspects of the credit associations and received no remuneration or even money for expenses such as travel. Colbert explained that "we are unable to function properly when we are forced to undergo double duty for association and our own battle for existence."[92] This situation forced Indians selected to manage credit associations into doing volunteer work. Colbert believed that Congress was to blame for not "simplifying the rules and regulations" and not appropriating sufficient funding for loans and operating expenses. Unfortunately, this issue was never completely resolved.

The Indian Bureau farm extension service came to play an important and multifaceted role in administering credit. As some funding became available in late 1937 and early 1938, bureau officials decided that all loan requests, regardless of their origin, "should clear through the respective district [bureau] offices." In addition, "the farm agent should originate the loan and procure verbal approval" from the district office.[93] Commissioner Collier stressed the idea of decentralizing the extension service and charging local offices and staffs with working closely with local Indians. He believed that "the future of the Indian under the Indian Reorganization Act and the Indian New Deal generally, are deeply involved in the success or failure of area plan[s].[94]

Farm agents served as intermediaries between Indian farmers and bureau officials. Most came from a farming background and possessed some college training in agriculture. They coupled their own experience and education to help Indians in their district. Working closely with Indian farmers, often developing trusting relationships, they would advise farmers in the best use of their land, crop selection, fertilizers, livestock, equipment, canning, 4H work for Indian youth, and marketing. As late as 1947, the bureau was still being counseled to use the extension service. Laura Thompson, a sociologist and Collier's second wife, stated in a study on the IRA, "The research indicates that the work of the various Indian Service divisions in rendering services to Indians is effective . . . at the local community level."[95]

Extension agents serving on the front line helped to implement the credit programs of the OIWA. Many of the Oklahoma Indians who would take advantage of programs were those who found doors to other credit opportunities closed to them. Angie Debo claims that many Oklahoma Indians possessed "economic ineptitude, during this time period."[96] They had little experience with credit, banking, business plans, economic forecasting, marketing, contracts, or accounting procedures. Many were traditional in their lifestyle and lived in remote areas. Farm agents would prove instrumental in educating, training, and guiding Indians along the various steps of the credit cycle. One case study followed a Creek farmer over a ten-year period. He progressed from renting 40 acres to owning 120 acres, using a tractor rather than a mule, and living in a solid new home for his family.[97]

The records of three extension workers operating out of the Shawnee Indian Agency are representative of the work of other agents across the state. In December of 1936, these agents held eight meetings, with 309 in total attendance, to explain loans available under the OIWA. During January of 1937, seven meetings were held to explain loans while two meetings were held to help organize credit associations. The report for March showed that three credit associations had been formed, and one meeting had been held to explain tribal organization. During October 1937, the Shawnee Agency Extension Office held thirteen meetings to explain loan procedures, establish tribal organization committees, and facilitate farm planning for credit applications.[98]

Agents would often work with individuals and cooperatives on a long-term basis to help insure their success. The Lyons Indian Cooperative Association, located near Stilwell, represented one such group. This group of eight Cherokee full-blood families formed a cooperative under the OIWA and received a loan for $2,800 to cover start-up operating expenses through the Adair County Indian Credit Association in 1938. Located in eastern Oklahoma, most of their land was extremely hilly and had been rendered virtually useless by overgrazing and poor timber harvesting practices by previous white lessees, leaving a thin, rocky soil that quickly eroded. This cooperative was guided by Herbert Kinnard, an agricultural extension agent who determined that strawberries would grow in this type of soil and terrain. Kinnard worked closely with these people for the life of the cooperative. In addition to guiding them through the loan application procedures, he also taught them how to prepare the soil and plant berries, "how to pick the berries, how to sort them, [and] how to pack [them] ... even taking the Indians to market with him so as to know how to market their berries, [and] how to keep records and cost accounts."[99] At the end of the first year, the cooperative was able not only to pay the loan off in full, it also distributed an average of $600 to each of its eight member families, a dramatic achievement when it is considered that the average annual income of a Cherokee hill family at that time was $54. At the same time, the average annual income for Indians across the United States was $500, while for whites it was $2,300.[100] This cooperative operated until 1946 when it was disbanded and the members opened their own operations.[101] By 1950, Kinnard estimated that approximately three hundred Indian families were involved in individual strawberry-growing operations around Lyon, Oklahoma. Even with only partial funding, credit provisions of the OIWA helped promote a wide variety of agricultural undertakings by individuals and cooperatives growing cotton, peanuts, and wheat; truck gardening; and raising horses, beef, and dairy cattle. In addition, limited funding was directed toward ancillary farming activities such as basketmaking, sales of canned goods, and arts and crafts, as well as for marketing products, buying equipment, purchasing livestock, and leasing mini-farms to members. However, Angie Debo, who conducted the only survey dealing specifically with the impact of the OIWA on Oklahoma Indians, states that "rehabilitated families constitute only a small percentage of the needy population."[102]

A number of issues would continue to plague the Indian credit program well into the mid-1950s when the Office of Indian Affairs, now officially the Bureau of Indian Affairs, disbanded the last credit associations in Oklahoma. The ongoing problems of limited congressional appropriations and the small percentage of Indians who possessed land remained paramount. Inexperience of many Indians with respect to loan and commercial activities, seemingly endless delays in application processing and other bureau paperwork, the remote location of many Indians, and more immediate need for relief for basic food and shelter needs were perhaps the most common concerns of Oklahoma Indians.

There were other problems. James Kahdot, chief of the Citizen Band of Pottawatomi Indians, expressed the problem of favoritism on the part of members of the Pottawatomi business committee. Kahdot complained that "this Indian Loan Business will never amount to anything with the present setup as those that are not popular with these People [the business committee] can't get no benefits."[103] Albert Attocknie, chairman of the Kiowa-Comanche-Apache Council, discussed at length, in a letter to the commissioner, the factionalism between two tribal groups: "Group No. 1," who might be referred to as "progressives" and "Group No. 2," which Attocknie claimed to represent, the traditionals. Attocknie claimed, "The Credit Associations have made almost no loans to the Group No. 2 Indians because of their incompetency and age, when thousands of dollars of federal funds have been . . . loaned through credit associations almost entirely to the Indians of Group No. 1."[104] This gulf between traditionals and progressives is evident in all programs of the IRA and OIWA.

In the western half of the state, the old Oklahoma Territory, the loan programs under the OIWA were not as popular. There was much less credit activity with western plains tribes than in the east with the Five Tribes. Several credit associations were dissolved in the late 1930s and early 1940s due to lack of demand for their services. The bureau dissolved the North Canadian Indian Credit Association in 1942. In 1945, the Southern Sac and Fox Indian Credit Association was dissolved. During the eight-year life of the latter, it had been approved initially for a loan fund of $10,000, but had loaned out only little over $4,800.

In 1956, Angie Debo interviewed Edward F. Ellison who had served over for twenty years as a land management supervisor with the bureau at both the Anadarko and Concho Agencies. Ellison offered insights in explaining differences between eastern and western Oklahoma Indians. Many of the tribal groups located in western Oklahoma had been moved there from the Great Plains. Often they had little if any agricultural heritage. Compounding the situation, Ellison claimed, was the transformation that took place in western Oklahoma between 1934 and 1940, when farming became increasingly mechanized. At the same time, prices for agricultural commodities, particularly wheat, dropped, while the cost of living went up. Farmers in western Oklahoma responded to this by producing more. Indian farms and ranches based on 80-acre and 120-acre allotments of 1934 gave way to the 160-acre (and larger) farm of the

1940s. Ellison claims, "The Indian people did not have the management ability to cope with the situation."[105] Many would leave farming for wage labor and, as World War II approached, many would find work outside Oklahoma in various defense-related industries throughout the West. The numbers of western Oklahoma Indians involved in agriculture would continue to decline into the 1950s. Ellison claimed in 1950 that there were 648 Cheyennes and Arapahos directly involved in farming. By 1956, that number had declined to "not more than 40."[106] During the 1950s, the price of agricultural land in Oklahoma increased, which served as an incentive for many Indians to sell their landholdings and move either to the nearest town or away from the area entirely.

A shortage of farm extension agents was also a factor inhibiting credit activities. For example, just five agents staffed the area of the Five Tribes. In a letter to Oklahoma congressman Jed Johnson, Commissioner Collier stated, "The main reason for the slowness of credit activities in Grady County is that the farm agent has seven other counties to cover."[107] Extension agents, a critical link in the Indian credit process, would remain in short supply. As the country drew closer to war in the late 1930s and defense appropriations rose, funding for BIA programs, including farm extension programs, was slashed. In the early 1950s, the responsibility for extension agents would be transferred from the federal government to the states. This severed the valuable local link between the bureau and many Indian farmers. The extension of credit to Oklahoma Indians for agricultural undertakings affected only a small percentage of the Indian population. Statistics show that in the Five Tribes area, between the 1937 and 1950, 2,358 loans "had been made in the amount of $1,632,191.89 to 1,566 families," out of an estimated 13,825 families—or just a little over 10 percent of families.[108] Out of these 13,825 families, 70 percent depended in part on agricultural income. This 70 percent could not obtain adequate financing through regular commercial institutions other than revolving credit under the IRA and OIWA.[109] It must be remembered that by 1933, the vast majority of Oklahoma Indians were landless. Credit was available only to individuals or groups of Indians who either still possessed their allotments or held clear title to landholdings. Relaying success stories can be dramatic, but those stories pale in light of the small minority of Oklahoma Indians who benefited from these credit measures. Oklahoma Indians lost 90 percent of tribal landholdings between the 1890s and 1933, or approximately 13.5 million acres. The land purchase program under the OIWA failed to place significant amounts of land back into tribal holdings because of limited appropriations. Fewer than thirty-six thousand acres were purchased and added to tribal land bases under the OIWA. The inability of the IRA and OIWA to significantly increase Indian landholdings, coupled with the overall transformation of Oklahoma farming to mechanization and larger operations, closed the door of opportunity for many Indian farmers.

Much of the thinking underpinning the IRA and OIWA followed from the premise that agriculture would serve as the economic base for Oklahoma Indians. This thinking was flawed from the beginning. Coupled with the need for land was the need to finance agricultural undertakings, but congressional appropriations failed to provide the necessary capital needed to support this in Oklahoma. While some of the state's Indians benefited from the bureau's emphasis on farming, they constituted a dwindling minority. The vast majority of Oklahoma Indians were landless and the Indian New Deal did little to change that. From a political standpoint, few Oklahoma tribal groups organized under the IRA and OIWA. None of the Five Tribes had adopted IRA/OIWA constitutions by the early 1950s. However, the influence of the IRA and OIWA in this area helped to foster awareness on the part of many Oklahoma Indians that tribal government organization provided the means whereby they could more effectively deal with the many challenges confronting them, promote the well-being of their members, and protect their cultural heritage as they entered the postwar age.

Conclusion

When analyzing past events, historians often use a simple binary standard in determining success or failure. This tendency seems to hold true for scholarly efforts focusing on the Oklahoma Indian Welfare Act. Some, such as Senator Thomas and Commissioner Collier, hoped that the OIWA would prove a panacea for the problems facing Oklahoma Indians. Others, such as Joseph Bruner, believed the act set back the cause of Indian reform and also that of Oklahoma Indians. Historians who have studied the IRA and the OIWA seem divided as well. This book concludes that the truth lies somewhere in the middle, in the gray area between total success and failure. The OIWA can be credited with a positive impact on Oklahoma Indians in some areas, but at the same time, in other areas, it fell short of intended objectives.

In evaluating the impact of the OIWA, statistics paint a picture of limited success. A miserly thirty-six thousand acres were added to the Oklahoma tribal land base. Most of that land was determined marginal for agricultural purposes. Only a little over 10 percent of eligible Oklahoma Indians took advantage of OIWA loan programs. By 1950, only eighteen Oklahoma tribes had organized under the OIWA, with just thirteen of these incorporating for tribal economic growth. These groups represented only about 10 percent of the Indian population in Oklahoma. Outside of three Creek towns and the United Keetoowah Band, none of the Five Tribes, representing the majority of Indian population in Oklahoma, organized under the OIWA.

Compounding a discussion of the legacy of the OIWA are factors often difficult to measure or categorize. However, these intangibles must be included in any evaluation. This book examines key ingredients that flavor the story of the Oklahoma Indian Welfare Act. While there may be other influencing factors, the major elements include John Collier, emphasis on Indian land and agriculture, changing demographics, factionalism, a hostile Congress, white interests, the failure to economically revitalize tribes, and ideological battles.

Collier remains the towering figure looming over the Indian New Deal. Arguably the most influential individual in Indian affairs administration during the twentieth century, Collier led the charge for drastic reform in federal Indian policy. As commissioner of Indian affairs, he remained at the forefront through the enactment and implementation phases of both the IRA and the OIWA. The bills were a concerted effort by Collier to employ progressive principles of social engineering to answer Indian needs. He referred to his objectives and policies during the first several years of the New Deal as a "laboratory of ethnic affairs."[1] Accepting the concept of cultural pluralism, he believed that the continued political and economic survival of American Indians depended on the organization and incorporation of tribal groups. Collier proved a controversial figure in Roosevelt's New Deal. He spent much of his time struggling to implement his proposals, often against a Congress and bureaucracy steeped in assimilation and vehemently opposed to his "radical" approach to Indian affairs policy. Congressional opposition by an alliance of conservative Democrats and Republicans led to his stepping down as commissioner of Indian affairs in 1945. After his resignation, Collier almost singlehandedly dictated the record of the Indian New Deal, which remained unchallenged for almost a quarter of a century.

The ideas manifested in both the IRA and the OIWA percolated in the minds of Collier and other reformers during most of the 1920s and the early 1930s. Collier claimed that during the 1920s he had formulated the major planks of the Indian New Deal, which ended allotment and provided for tribal organization, economic development, and cultural preservation. The initial Indian reorganization bill was conceived and birthed within the walls of the Department of the Interior, in the offices of administrators and reformers such as Secretary Ickes, Collier, and solicitors Nathan Margold and Felix Cohen, all non-Indians. Introduced in Congress as the Wheeler-Howard Bill in early 1933, it underwent a substantial makeover as provisions were introduced, debated, amended, or dropped. The clash between Collier and legislators such as Senators Thomas and Wheeler and Representative Disney resulted in a shortened proposal with a much narrower focus than that of the original forty-eight-page omnibus bill. As the bill worked its way through the legislative process, ten Indian congresses were held across the country, including five in Oklahoma. Tribal groups were invited and thousands of Indians attended. The proposed bill was explained to the Indian attendees, discussed, questions answered, and recommendations noted, all in a tightly orchestrated format.

Indians exercised a voice during the legislative process, but the degree to which that voice was audible is questionable. These congresses were designed to garner Indian support for a proposal already formulated by non-Indian administrators and legislators; they allowed little opportunity for substantive input from Indians. It is clear from the minutes of these meetings, as well as those of House and Senate committee hearings held during the legislative process, that other factors also seem to have muffled Indian voices. These factors include a paternalistic attitude edged with racist undertones on the part of white legislators, the lack of Indian experience in promoting their interests within the white political realm, and the focus by many Oklahoma Indians on quick fixes to alleviate their dire economic situation rather than on long-term changes in the course of Indian policy. This same formula would be repeated later with five congresses held for Oklahoma Indians just prior to introduction of the Thomas-Rogers Bill in early 1935.

As demonstrated in this book, Indian focus remained at the tribal level. Creeks spoke for Creeks, Kiowas for Kiowas. Lacking at this time was any meaningful attempt on the part of Oklahoma Indians to organize an intra-tribal, pan-Indian response to federal legislators and administrators. The idea that Indians could reach across tribal lines and work together to achieve common interests was in its infancy during this period. There were organizations such as the Indian Association of Oklahoma and the American Indian Federation, but at this time these had not evolved to the level of sophistication where they had honed operating skills and gained the trust of Indians, at least to the degree that they could produce effective results.

The influential National Congress of American Indians (NCAI) did not organize until 1944. Several Oklahoma Indians led the founding of this pan-tribal organization, including N. B. Johnson, W. W. Short, Dan Mederano, Ben Dwight, J. Hartley Milam, and Ruth Muskrat Bronson.[2]

The IRA and OIWA allowed for individual as well as tribal participation. Additionally and importantly, and unlike previous Indian policy, participation in the OIWA's tribal organization and economic programs was not mandatory: individual Indians and tribes could elect to participate or not. The IRA and OIWA cracked open a door for Indian participation in the formulation and implementation of federal policy and programs directly relating to them. This door would be pushed open further in the following decades and culminate in the self-determination movement of the late 1960s and 1970s. Oklahoma Indians, as previously mentioned, mirrored Indians nationwide with respect to limited involvement in IRA and OIWA programs, including tribal organization and chartering and participation in loan programs. Some point to the low level of involvement by Oklahoma Indians in both loan programs and tribal reorganization as evidence of the failure of the OIWA, but I conclude that low participation might be considered a sign of success. Oklahoma Indians took advantage of choices offered to them by the act and chose not to participate. It is recognized that many individuals and tribal groups based their decision not to participate on the grounds that they had not been consulted as the measure was being formulated. Regardless of the factors influencing Indian participation, the fact remains that for the first time they could make that decision for themselves.

As discussed in this book, the relationship between the federal government and Oklahoma tribal groups has been difficult and at times strained. The relationship has also proven different from that of Indians elsewhere. Contributing factors include relocation to Oklahoma Territory of Indians from afar, the Civil War, Reconstruction treaties, and the rapid loss of Indian land and resources following implementation of the allotment policy in the territory in preparation for statehood during the last decade of the nineteenth century and the first of the twentieth century. These events and circumstances became part of Oklahoma Indian heritage and memory, and they left a bad taste in the mouths of many for federal Indian policy. The records relating to the IRA and OIWA are replete with examples of mistrust and uncertainty on the part of many tribes during the enactment and implementation of the acts.

Many Oklahoma Indians were reticent to embrace another federal proposal, based on a track record of broken promises by the white government coupled with what Indians saw as unfettered support of white expansion and exploitation of their land and resources. Full-bloods often eschewed contact and involvement with whites and their institutions. Some wanted only their plot of land and to be left alone. On the other hand, many younger mixed-bloods had assimilated to a degree, incorporating white social and economic practices. This group strove to better their economic situation by increased landholdings and exploitation of resources such as timber and minerals, along with other economic endeavors. Many of this group opposed the IRA and OIWA because they saw such legislation as a step backward to the reservation era, with tighter governmental regulation of Indian land, a threat to the economic success they struggled to build. Joseph Bruner, the outspoken and informal Creek leader for those with this viewpoint, achieved remarkable success in real estate, insurance, and the oil business in eastern Oklahoma. He viewed Collier's Indian New Deal as a formidable threat and became a vocal critic. Interestingly, Bruner sought to promote his viewpoints and garner Indian support through a pan-Indian organization, the American Indian Federation. However, the caustic nature of his opposition may have diminished this support. Oklahoma Indians supported or opposed the bills for a variety of reasons.

Loretta Fowler, although claiming that IRA and OIWA constitutions were often forced on Oklahoma tribes, believes these tribal governments gave individual members a mechanism to challenge tribal leaders, thereby increasing political involvement by the tribe as a whole. Business councils gained more control over the hiring of agency employees, allocation of tribal funds, and economic development. Through these constitutional governments, tribes gained more access to government funds and control over their resources.³ The reestablishment of tribal governments transformed the political world not just internally but also externally, in the ways members resolved issues with the outside world, most importantly with an enhanced standing in the eyes of federal officials. As mentioned, most tribal government had been curtailed in Oklahoma by the turn of the century. With the introduction of constitutional representative government, Oklahoma Indians had to gain experience and success in channeling political interests and tensions through these new mechanisms in order to sustain them.

Carter Blue Clark believes that the reestablishment of tribal governments and incorporation kindled a "revival of long-dormant tribal self-rule."⁴ Tribal members and groups, whether they supported or opposed the IRA and OIWA, were swept along by powerful currents of change that this legislation helped promote. A transformation of tribal politics began during this time, both internally, in the way tribal members interacted and sought solutions to shared issues and problems, and externally, in the manner the tribes interacted with the outside world, governments, business, and society in general. As Oklahoma Indians and tribal groups took a more proactive stance and began to be heard, they demanded more control over their future. This transformation evolved over time. The IRA and OIWA provided the mechanism for a constitutional representative government, but this first had to be incorporated into the Indian mind-set. These factors and others mark the origins of the self-determination movement that would blossom in the decades of the 1960s and 1970s. Clark is correct that the emerging spirit of tribalism fostered by the Indian New Deal "fed later Indian nationalism that erupted in the militancy of the 1960s."⁵ However, it was only one of several important factors contributing to the transformation.

As with all Americans, World War II also proved a transforming experience for Oklahoma Indians. Many had become disenchanted with "federally managed economic development and tribal self-rule" that seemed unable to improve their economic situation, and approximately 25 percent emigrated from tribal areas during World War II.⁶ Many would find employment in war-related industries scattered throughout the West and sent money back home, an

CONCLUSION

economic shot in the arm for remaining Indians. Almost six thousand Oklahoma Indians would serve in the armed forces during the war.[7] By 1945, many returning Indian veterans "possessed a wider knowledge that made them capable of leading tribes into a new era of assertion of tribal sovereignty and heritage in the postwar period," Clark asserts.[8] Veterans were not satisfied with the status quo. Alison Bernstein quotes historian David Nash—"Before the war the American Indian was America's outsider. . . . Assimilation seemed far fetched"—and argues, "By war's end, Indians were part of the American political process, their economic, social, and cultural status irrevocably altered by the conflict."[9] The nation as a whole was transformed by the Depression, the war, and the war's aftermath. Oklahoma Indians were certainly part of this.

Clark claims that the IRA and OIWA changed the focus of Indian policy, from seeking to achieve assimilation through agriculture, to seeking "assimilation through . . . constitutions and corporate charters."[10] This assertion warrants closer scrutiny. Much of the OIWA was based on Indian land, formally ending the allotment policy in Oklahoma and promoting land purchases to augment tribal land bases and loan programs to foster viable agricultural enterprises. Agricultural and resource development served as the foundation for the IRA and OIWA. John Collier believed that the enhancement of Oklahoma Indians' economic standing through agriculture and ranching would serve to increase their voice politically and socially. This, coupled with protection of Indian cultural heritage, would place them in a stronger position to mingle with white society, while at the same time insuring their cultural survival. Collier viewed tribal organization and charters as modern tools necessary to channel political and economic forces to promote the agricultural success of Oklahoma Indians.

Collier's vision, however, steeped in agriculture and the Indian family farmer, ran counter to the trends in American agriculture becoming evident during implementation of the IRA and OIWA. It is important to remember that the vast majority of Oklahoma Indians were landless. As the Depression gave way to World War II, agriculture was transformed. Prices for agricultural commodities, grains as well as livestock, were in a state of decline from World War I on, and

American farmers responded in two ways: the size of farming operations increased and, coupled with technological improvements, production increased while labor costs decreased. Therefore, agriculture became more capital-intensive. Indian allotments of 80 to 120 acres became increasingly difficult to operate at a profit. Small farms could not compete with larger operations. Some Oklahoma Indians still practiced subsistence agriculture. Some generated a little cash by raising a few acres of cotton or a few head of livestock to sell. Other farmers supplemented their income by producing railroad ties or fence posts, if their land was blessed with timber. During this period, many Oklahoma Indians drifted to agricultural labor on larger nearby farms and ranches often owned by whites—or into wage labor in nearby towns and cities. Agriculture declined as a dominant factor as the country became more industrialized and urban.

An ongoing ideological debate buffeted the enactment and implementation phases of the OIWA. This struggle was also evident with the IRA on a national basis. In examining the IRA, Elmer Rusco, a political scientist, built upon four schools of thought that underpinned federal Indian policy at this time: forced assimilation, administrative reform, the tribal alternative, and termination.[11] The Dawes Act, or Allotment Act of 1887, instituted assimilation as the backbone of federal Indian policy. Native Americans would enter the American mainstream as prosperous self-sufficient farmers. While the tribal lands of Oklahoma Territory Indians were allotted as early as 1887 with the enactment of the Dawes Act, the policy of allotment was introduced to the Five Tribes with the Curtis Act of 1898. By the 1920s, however, some policy makers realized that the allotment policy had proven a tremendous failure. Allotment nationally and especially in Oklahoma had the opposite of its desired objective of assimilating Indians into American society. Instead, Native Americans lost the bulk of their landholdings, with Oklahoma Indians losing 90 percent of their land. Rather than being assimilated, Oklahoma Indians were marginalized even further to the fringes of mass society.

During the 1920s and continuing into the New Deal years, administrative reform came to the forefront. While still grounded in assimilation, many began looking for fixes to correct the failures of the allotment policy. Tinkering and repair would get federal Indian

CONCLUSION

policy back on track toward the goal of assimilation. During most of the 1920s, a small minority of those concerned with Indian policy came to promote the idea that allotment and its destructive impact was beyond repair, that a new direction was needed. The Meriam Report of 1928 seemed to substantiate this realization and bolstered the reformers' efforts. By the late 1920s, John Collier became the clarion for this reform movement. He promoted a school of thought that recognized the federal government's responsibility toward Indians while at the same time respecting the right of Native Americans to maintain their tribal institutions and cultural heritage. Dubbed "the tribal alternative," Collier's vision placed Indians in the white world, but not fully part of the white world.[12] He introduced a radical multicultural approach that recognized the right of Indian societies to exist, seeing that forced assimilation would do away with Indianness. Collier's wing of the reform movement saw Indians assimilating by mixing but not melting into American society, with their Indianness protected.

Alternative schools of thought battled with Collier for the future of Indian affairs administration. Political leaders such as Senators Thomas and Wheeler and Congressman Rogers exemplified the pro-assimilation perspective. For them, Indians should surrender their Indianness, adopt white ways, and blend into American society. Like Collier and reformers such as Secretary of the Interior Harold Ickes, they believed, at least for a while, that agriculture was at the heart of any solution to "the Indian problem." They spun their ideology differently than Collier, envisioning Oklahoma Indians incorporated into white society, though at an undetermined but different social, political, and economic standing than whites. Additionally, they above all practiced political pragmatism. Their base of power rested with their white constituencies and campaign contributors, and most of their proposals were evaluated by exposure to the political winds.

Senator Thomas and Commissioner Collier clearly represent two distinct ideological perspectives. Thomas's thinking in particular remained an unsettled conundrum of assimilation, reform, and termination, the latter especially evident during the war years and after. The two struggled for dominance of their viewpoints. The outcome was a mongrelized compromise, which included elements of both agendas. Even a driven reformer like Collier remained politically savvy enough to realize the necessity of compromise during the legislative process. In the face of withering opposition, he sacrificed his proposal for strengthening the Indian court system in order to save what he believed were the more important features of his proposal.

For the most part, the tribal alternative challenged the status quo of assimilationist policy. Assimilation was strongly rooted in many involved in Indian affairs, including legislators and administrators. Collier and other reformers rallied around the standard of this upstart ideology, and they waged a protracted war against assimilationists. This struggle would be played out on the battlefield of administrative reform, and it continued from the 1930s into the 1950s, when a new school of thought, promoting termination, would mark yet another radical course change for federal Indian affairs policy. Though this book ends as the termination era begins, it is important to touch briefly on its origins.

Termination, though based on an ideal of assimilation, took a radical approach toward realizing that end. Assimilation would be achieved and "the Indian problem" resolved by denying the trust obligation and eliminating federal services to the Indians, thereby forcing Indians into mass American society. The federal government would no longer recognize Indian tribes or its responsibility toward them. Over a period of time, services and programs would be dismantled. Responsibilities not eliminated entirely would be delegated to the states. The federal government would get out of the Indian business.

The idea of termination had been debated, to one degree or another, for several decades. However, the intensity of the debate escalated from the mid 1930s onward as a conservative backlash to FDR's New Deal began to build. A group of disillusioned conservative Democrats and Republicans "repudiated some of the impulses ... prominent in the early New Deal," writes Alan Brinkley. These "impulses" included moving away from promoting "government sponsored social welfare programs."[13] In 1943, Senators Thomas and Wheeler, with others in Congress, launched a concerted attack on the Indian New Deal. Senate Report 310, issued that year, recommended such changes as elimination of "all federal control of law and order as specifically applied to Indians," the "transfer of Indian probate and inheritance matters to the states," the elimination of "all central office control of credit funds," and the elimination of "federal trust over all individual Indian lands."[14] In a supplemental report specifically directed to Oklahoma Indians, Senator Thomas stated that Senate Report 310 "was intended to combat the "back to the reservation plan" of officials and persons in high places." Thomas's group "favor[ed] a policy wherein the Indians may be permitted to select their own tribal councils and that [their] recommendations . . . be given due and proper consideration by both the officials of the [BIA] and by the committees of the Congress."[15] Historian Christopher Riggs examined Report 310, and notes that Thomas, in response to Collier's 1944 Indian Appropriations Bill testimony, stated that Indians ought to be "free" and not tied to what he considered was a dead culture.[16] Riggs blames Senate Report 310 as the source for the congressional termination policy that would become formally institutionalized with the enactment of Public Law 280 in 1953, with disastrous results for many Native Americans.

The overall impact of the OIWA on Oklahoma Indians was mixed. While its short-term tangible results remained limited, the long-term intangible results, though difficult to measure, seem substantial. If one looks at the small percentage of Oklahoma Indians who benefited economically from its loan programs, or the miniscule increase of tribal land bases, or the small numbers of Indians who lived under the umbrella of IRA and OIWA governments, then the impact remains dismal at best. However, if one considers intangibles such as increased participation by members in tribal affairs, an intensified and sustained effort to gain control of tribal resources, enhanced relations with white business leaders and all levels of government, increased cultural pride and self-esteem, and a stronger role in the administration of governmental programs, then the impact takes on new luster. The enactment and implementation of the OIWA helped place Oklahoma Indians on the path toward self-determination, enabling a greater role in determining their own future and preserving their cultural heritage. It is clearly an important chapter in the Indian New Deal.

APPENDIX A

The Indian Reorganization Act

BE IT ENACTED *by the Senate and House of Representatives of the United States of America in Congress assembled,* That hereafter no land of any Indian reservation, created or set apart by treaty or agreement with the Indians, Act of Congress, Executive order, purchase, or otherwise, shall be allotted in severalty to any Indian.

Sec. 2. The existing periods of trust placed upon any Indian lands and any restriction on alienation thereof are hereby extended and continued until otherwise directed by Congress.

Sec. 3. The Secretary of the Interior, if he shall find it to be in the public interest, is hereby authorized to restore to tribal ownership the remaining surplus lands of any Indian reservation heretofore opened, or authorized to be opened, to sale, or any other form of disposal by Presidential proclamation, or by any of the public land laws of the United States; Provided, however, That valid rights or claims of any persons to any lands so withdrawn existing on the date of the withdrawal shall not be affected by this Act: Provided further, That this section shall now apply to lands within any reclamation project heretofore authorized in any Indian reservation: *Provided further,* That this section shall not apply to lands within any reclamation project heretofore authorized in any Indian reservation: *Provided further,* That the order of the Department of the Interior signed, dated, and approved by Honorable Ray Lyman Wilbur, as Secretary of the Interior, on October 28, 1932, temporarily withdrawing lands of the Papago Indian Reservation in Arizona from all forms of mineral entry or claim under the public land mining laws is hereby revoked and rescinded, and the lands of the said Papago Indian Reservation are hereby restored to exploration and location, under the existing mining laws of the United States, in accordance with the express terms and provisions declared and set forth in the Executive orders establishing said Papago Indian Reservation: *Provided further,* That the damages shall be paid to the Papago Tribe for loss of any improvements of any land located for mining in such a sum as may be determined by the Secretary of the Interior but not to exceed the cost of said improvements: *Provided further,* That a yearly rental not to exceed five cents per acre shall be paid to the Papago Indian Tribe: *Provided further,* That in the event that any person or persons, partnership, corporation, or association, desires a mineral patent, according to the mining laws of the United States, he or they shall first deposit in the treasury of the United States to the credit of the Papago Tribe the sum of $1.00 per acre in lieu of annual rental, as hereinbefore provided, to compensate for the loss or occupancy of the lands withdrawn by the requirements of mining operations: *Provided further,* That patentee shall also pay into the Treasury of the United States to the credit of the Papago Tribe damages for the loss of improvements not heretofore said in such a sum as may be determined by the Secretary of the Interior, but not to exceed the cost thereof; the payment of $1.00 per acre for surface use to be refunded to patentee in the event that the patent is not required.

Nothing herein contained shall restrict the granting or use of permits for easements or rights-of-way; or ingress or egress over the lands for all proper and lawful purposes; and nothing contained therein, except as expressly provided, shall be construed as authority by the Secretary of the Interior, or any other person, to issue or promulgate a rule or regulation in conflict with the Executive order of February 1, 1917, creating the Papago Indian Reservation in Arizona or the Act of February 21, 1931 (46 Stat. 1202).

Sec. 4. Except as herein provided, no sale, devise, gift, exchange or other transfer of restricted Indian lands or of shares in the assets of

INDIAN REORGANIZATION ACT

any Indian tribe or corporation organized hereunder, shall be made or approved: *Provided, however,* That such lands or interests may, with the approval of the Secretary of the Interior, be sold, devised, or otherwise transferred to the Indian tribe in which the lands or shares are located or from which the shares were derived or to a successor corporation; and in all instances such lands or interests shall descend or be devised, in accordance with the then existing laws of the State, or Federal laws where applicable, in which said lands are located or in which the subject matter of the corporation is located, to any member of such tribe or of such corporation or any heirs of such member: *Provided further,* That the Secretary of the Interior may authorized voluntary exchanges of lands of equal value and the voluntary exchange of shares of equal value whenever such exchange, in his judgment, is expedient and beneficial for or compatible with the proper consolidation of Indian lands and for the benefit of cooperative organizations.

Sec. 5. The Secretary of the Interior is hereby authorized, in his discretion, to acquire through purchase, relinquishment, gift, exchange, or assignment, any interest in lands, water rights or surface rights to lands, within or without existing reservations, including trust or otherwise restricted allotments whether the allottee be living or deceased, for the purposes of providing lands for Indians.

For the acquisition of such lands, interests in lands, water rights, and surface rights, and for expenses incident to such acquisition, there is hereby authorized to be appropriated, out of any funds in the Treasury not otherwise appropriated, a sum not to exceed $2,000,000 in any one fiscal year: *Provided,* That no part of such funds shall be used to acquire additional land outside of the exterior boundaries of Navajo Indian Reservation for the Navajo Indians in Arizona and New Mexico, in the event that the proposed Navajo boundary extension measures now pending in congress and embodied in the bills (S. 2531 and H.R. 8927) to define the exterior boundaries of the Navajo Indian Reservation in Arizona, and for other purposes, and the bills (S. 2531 and H.R. 8982) to define the exterior boundaries of the Navajo Indian Reservation in New Mexico and for other purposes, or similar legislation, become law.

The unexpended balances of any appropriations made pursuant to this section shall remain available until expended.

Title to any lands or rights acquired pursuant to this Act shall be taken in the name of the United States in trust for the Indian tribe or individual Indian for which the land is acquired, and such lands or rights shall be exempt from State and local taxation.

Sec. 6. The Secretary of the Interior is directed to make rules and regulations for the operation and management of Indian forestry units on the principle of sustained-yield management, to restrict the number of livestock grazed on Indian range units to the estimated carrying capacity of such ranges, and to promulgate such other rules and regulations as may be necessary to protect the range from deterioration, to prevent soil erosion, to assure full utilization of the range, and like purposes.

Sec. 7. The Secretary of the Interior is hereby authorized to proclaim new Indian reservations on lands acquired pursuant to any authority conferred by this Act, or to add such lands to existing reservations: *Provided,* That lands added to existing reservations shall be designated for the exclusive use of Indians entitled by enrollment or by tribal membership to residence at such reservations shall be designated for the exclusive use of Indians entitled by enrollment or by tribal membership to residence at such reservations.

Sec. 8. Nothing contained in this Act shall be construed to relate to Indian holdings of allotments or homesteads upon the public domain outside of the geographic boundaries of any Indian reservation now existing or established hereafter.

Sec. 9. There is hereby authorized to be appropriated, out of any funds in the Treasury not otherwise appropriated, such sums as may be necessary, but not to exceed $250,000 in any fiscal year, to be expended at the order of the Secretary of the Interior, in defraying the expenses of organizing Indian chartered corporations or other organizations created under this Act.

INDIAN REORGANIZATION ACT

Sec. 10. There is hereby authorized to be appropriated, out of any funds in the Treasury not otherwise appropriated, the sum of $10,000,000 to be established as a revolving fund from which the Secretary of the Interior, under such rules and regulations as he may prescribe, may make loans to Indian chartered corporations for the purpose of promoting the economic development of such tribes and of their members, and may defray the expenses of administering such loans. Repayment of amounts loaned under his authorization shall be credited to the revolving fund and shall be available for the purposes for which the fund is established. A report shall be made annually to Congress of transactions under this authorization.

Sec. 11. There is hereby authorized to be appropriated, out of any funds in the United States Treasury not otherwise appropriated, a sum not to exceed $250,000 annually, together with any unexpended balances of previous appropriations made pursuant to this section, for loans to Indians for the payment of tuition and other expenses in recognized vocational and trade schools: *Provided,* That not more than $50,000 of such sum shall be available for loans to Indian students in high schools and colleges. Such loans shall be reimbursable under rules established by the Commissioner of Indian Affairs.

Sec. 12. The Secretary of the Interior is directed to establish standards of health, age, character, experience, knowledge, and ability for Indians, who may be appointed, without regard to civil-service laws, to the various positions maintained, now or hereafter, by the Indian office, in the administrative functions or services affecting any Indian tribe. Such qualified Indians shall hereafter have the preference to appointment to vacancies in any such positions.

Sec. 13. The provisions of this Act shall not apply to any of the Territories, colonies, or insular possessions of the United States, except that sections 9, 10, 11, 12, and 16 shall apply to the Territory of Alaska: *Provided,* That Sections 2, 4, 7, 16, 17, and 18 of this Act shall not apply to the following named Indian tribes, together with members of other tribes affiliated with such named located in the

State of Oklahoma, as follows: Cheyenne, Arapaho, Apache, Comanche, Kiowa, Caddo, Delaware, Wichita, Osage, Kaw, Otoe, Tonkawa, Pawnee, Ponca, Shawnee, Ottawa, Quapaw, Seneca, Wyandotte, Iowa, Sac and Fox, Kickapoo, Pottawatomi, Cherokee, Chickasaw, Choctaw, Creek, and Seminole. Section 4 of this Act shall not apply to the Indians of the Klamath Reservation in Oregon.

Sec. 14. The Secretary of the Interior is hereby directed to continue the allowance of the articles enumerated in section 17 of the Act of March 2, 1889 (25 Stat.L. 891), or their commuted cash value under the Act of June 10, 1886 (29 Stat.L. 334), to all Sioux Indians who would be eligible, but for the provisions of this Act, to receive allotments of lands in severalty under section 19 of the Act of May 29, 1908 (25 (35) Stat.L. 451), or under any prior Act, and who have the prescribed status of the head of a family or single person over the age of eighteen years, and his approval shall be final and conclusive, claims therefore to be paid as formerly from the permanent appropriation made by said section 17 and carried on the books of the Treasury for this purpose. No person shall receive in his own right more than one allowance of the benefits, and application must be made and approved during the lifetime of the allottee or the right shall lapse. Such benefits shall continue to be paid upon such reservation until such time as the lands available therein for allotment at the time of the passage of this Act would have been exhausted by the award to each person receiving such benefits of an allotment of eighty acres of such land.

Sec. 15. Nothing in this Act shall be construed to impair or prejudice any claim or suit of any Indian tribe against the United States. It is hereby declared to be the intent of Congress that no expenditures for the benefit of Indians made out of appropriations authorized by this Act shall be considered as offsets in any suit brought to recover upon any claim of such Indians against the United States.

Sec. 16. Any Indian tribe, or tribes, residing on the same reservation, shall have the right to organize for its common welfare, and may adopt an appropriate constitution and bylaws, which shall become effective when ratified by a majority vote of the adult members of the tribe, or of the adult Indians residing on such reservation, as the case may be, at a special election authorized by the Secretary of the Interior under such rules and regulations as he may prescribe. Such constitution and bylaws when ratified as aforesaid and approved by the Secretary of the Interior shall be revocable by an election open to the same voters and conducted in the same manner as hereinabove provided. Amendments to the constitution and bylaws may be ratified and approved by the Secretary in the same manner as the original constitution and bylaws.

In addition to all powers vested in any Indian tribe or tribal council by existing law, the constitution adopted by said tribe shall also vest in such tribe or its tribal council the following rights and powers: To employ legal counsel, the choice of counsel and fixing of fees to be subject to the approval of the Secretary of the Interior; to prevent the sale, disposition, lease, or encumbrance of tribal lands, interests in lands, or other tribal assets without the consent of the tribe; and to negotiate with the Federal, State, and local Governments. The Secretary of the Interior shall advise such tribe or its tribal council of all appropriation estimates or Federal projects for the benefit of the tribe prior to the submission of such estimates to the Bureau of the Budget and the Congress.

Sec. 17. The Secretary of the Interior may, upon petition by at least one-third of the adult Indians, issue a charter of incorporation to such tribe: *Provided,* That such charter shall not become operative until ratified at a special election by a majority vote of the adult Indians living on the reservation. Such charter may convey to the incorporated tribe the power to purchase, take by gift, or bequest, or otherwise, own, hold, manage, operate, and dispose of property of every description, real and personal, including the power to purchase restricted Indian lands and to issue in exchange therefore interests in corporate property, and such further powers as may be incidental to the conduct of corporate business, not inconsistent with law, but no authority shall be granted to sell, mortgage, or lease for a period exceeding ten years any of the land included in the limits of the reservation. Any charter so issued shall not be revoked or surrendered except by Act of Congress.

Sec. 18. This Act shall not apply to any reservation wherein a majority of the adult Indians, voting at a special election duly called by the Secretary of the Interior, shall vote against its application. It shall be the duty of the Secretary of the Interior, with in one year after the passage and approval of this Act, to call such an election, which election shall be held by secret ballot upon thirty days' notice.

Sec. 19. The term "Indian" as used in this Act shall include all persons of Indian descent who are members of any recognized Indian tribe now under Federal jurisdiction, and all persons who are descendants of such members who were, on June 1, 1934, residing within the present boundaries of any reservation, and shall further include all other persons of one-half or more Indian blood. For the purposes of this Act, Eskimos and other aboriginal peoples of Alaska shall be considered Indians. The term "tribe" wherever used in this Act shall be construed to refer to any Indian tribe, organized band, pueblo, or the Indians residing on one reservation. The words "adult Indians" wherever used in this Act shall be construed to refer to Indians who have attained the age of twenty-one years.

Approved, June 18, 1934.

APPENDIX B

THE THOMAS-ROGERS BILL

(FIRST DRAFT INTRODUCED IN CONGRESS)

A BILL to promote the general welfare of the Indians of the State of Oklahoma and for other purposes.

BE IT ENACTED *by the Senate and House of Representatives of the United States of America in Congress assembled,* That the United States, acting through the Congress, hereby readmits, reacknowledges, and assumes continued responsibility for the guardianship of our Indian citizens and in exercising such guardianship, does hereby pledge such Indian citizens of all tribes that it is and will be the continuing policy of the Government to establish justice for and to promote the general welfare of the Indians of the United States.

Sec. 2. Pursuant to the general policy set forth in section 1 hereof, the Government, acting through the Congress, hereby declares it to be in the best interest and general welfare of the Indians of Oklahoma to provide a plan whereunder all Indians may be accorded all rights, opportunities, and privileges and may eventually assume full responsibility as citizens in the said State and Nation.

Pursuant to such policy the follow specific things to be done are hereby set forth:

(a) The lands, property, and funds of the Indians of the first degree, as herein defined, are to be retained in the custody of the Secretary of the Interior in trust save as provided in this act.

(b) All lands, property, and funds of the Indians of the second degree, as herein defined, are to be by the Secretary of the Interior relieved of all restrictions as rapidly as the best interest of the Indians and the public will permit and justify.

(c) The Government hereby declares its policy to be that the aged, infirm, and incompetent Indians shall have every possible care assistance and protection and that the Indian youth shall have educational facilities and advantages to the end that they may assume their place among the citizenship of the State and Nation.

(d) All claims held by any Indian tribe, group, or band against the Government shall be considered and adjudged and such amounts as may be found to be due any such tribe, group, or band shall be paid and expended as may be provided by law.

(e) Pursuant to the provisions of paragraph (b) of section 2, the Secretary of the Interior, at least once during each four-year period, shall cause to be created a Competency Commission, and such Commission shall make a survey and examination of each adult Indian of the second degree in order to ascertain whether such Indian is qualified and should have his or her restrictions removed on all or any part of any property, real or personal, of such Indian, and in the event the recommendations of such Commission are favorable to the removal of the restrictions in whole or in part, the Secretary of the Interior is authorized to issue patent in fee to such Indians on such lands, property, and funds recommended, and is authorized to remove restrictions from property and funds as may be recommended by such Commission and which property and funds are in the possession and under the jurisdiction of the Secretary of the Interior; *Provided, however,* That the Secretary of the Interior at any time may exercise the authorities specified in section 7 of this Act.

Sec. 3. It is hereby declared to be the policy of Congress to provide adequate educational facilities for the Indian population of the State of Oklahoma as follows:

(a) The present policy of providing funds for the payment of tuition to public State schools for Indian children shall be continued and maintained

(b) All existing Indian boarding schools shall be continued as now operating until otherwise provided by law.

(c) Funds may be made available for the purpose of constructing, equipping, and maintaining school buildings in such sections as may be deemed necessary for carrying out the policy stated and the intent of this section.

(d) The Secretary of the Interior is hereby authorized and directed to make diligent effort to provide adequate education facilities for all Indian children of school age, providing that preferences in the boarding schools shall be given to Indian children without means of support, Indian children retarded because of lack of educational facilities, and orphaned Indian children.

Sec. 4. From time to time, as conditions require, funds shall be provided for maintenance of existing boarding and day schools, hospitals, and sanatoria to provide adequate school and hospitalization facilities for the Indian children of Oklahoma.

Sec. 5. That when used in this Act—the term "Indian of the first degree" shall mean any person whose name appears on the membership rolls of such tribe heretofore or hereafter approved by the Secretary of the Interior as a person having one-half or more of Indian blood.

(a) The Term "Indian of the second degree" shall mean any person whose name is now on or may hereafter be placed on the official rolls of the Indian Office of Oklahoma and who is classified by the Secretary of the Interior as a person having less than one-half or more of Indian blood.

(b) The term "tribe" wherever used in this act, shall be confirmed to mean any Indian tribe, organized band, or group of Indians composed of persons of whatever degree of Indian blood and located in the State of Oklahoma.

Sec. 6. For the purposes of providing lands for Indians in the State of Oklahoma, the Secretary of the Interior is hereby authorized, in his discretion, to acquire through purchase, relinquishment, gift, exchange, or assignment, any interest in lands, water rights or surface rights to lands, within or without existing reservations, including trust or otherwise restricted lands now in Indian ownership, allotted or inherited, whenever said Secretary deems it advisable to permit the present Indian owner or owners to part with the same or their interests therein. In the sale of any restricted Indian land pursuant to the terms of this or any other act of Congress, the Secretary of the Interior shall have a preference right, in his discretion, to purchase the same for or in behalf of any other Indian or Indians by meeting the highest bid otherwise offered therefore. Title to all land so acquired or set aside shall be taken in the name of the United States, in trust for the tribe, band, group, or individual, for whose benefit such land is so acquired, and the Secretary of the Interior is hereby authorized to designate or proclaim the tribe, band, community or group of Indians for whose benefit such land is acquired. Said Secretary is further authorized to prescribe such rules and regulations as he may deem necessary to control the management and operation of such lands for the benefit of the Indians, including assignment of the use of part or parts of such land to individual Indians, the ownership of any improvements placed on such tract so assigned for individual use by or at the expense of the occupant to remain with such occupant and to be devisable and inheritable under such rules and regulations as the Secretary of the Interior my prescribe and not otherwise; *Provided*, That in accepting title to any individually owned restricted Indian land for the benefit of any tribe or group of Indians, the Secretary of the Interior, in consideration for such conveyance, may assign the same land to or for the benefit of the former Indian owner or owners, for such period or periods as the Secretary may deem proper, including a further right or power in such former owner or owners to lease such land to third parties, upon such terms and conditions as the Secretary of the Interior may prescribe: *Provided further*, That nothing herein contained shall be construed as granting or recognizing in any such individual occupant or his or her heirs, any title to any tribal or communally owned lands so occupied, or as giving to the courts of the State of Oklahoma any jurisdiction over any matter affecting the title to, right to use or occupy, or the ownership of any improvements located on any such tribal or communally owned lands; all of which questions are hereby committed to the exclusive jurisdiction of the Secretary of the Interior, and securities belonging to Indians of the Five Civilized Tribes of Oklahoma, shall while held by the Secretary of the Interior, be free from any and all taxes save such charge or charges as may be imposed under section 12 of this act.

Sec. 7. That at any time prior to the expiration of the existing period of trust or other restrictions against alienation of any lands, funds, or the property belonging to any Indians of the State of Oklahoma of one-half or more Indian blood, whether held under a trust, tribal, or other form of patent, deed, or any other instrument containing restrictions against alienation, the President of the United States be, and he is hereby authorized, in his discretion, to extend such trust or other restricted period for such further period or periods as he may deem best; *Provided*, That during such trust or restricted period, or any extension of extensions thereof the Secretary of the Interior, in his discretion, whenever satisfied that the best interest of the Indian owner or owners of such restricted property, and that of his immediate family would best be served thereby, upon application from such Indian owner or owners, may remove the restrictions in whole or in part, in such manner and under such rules and regulations as the said Secretary may prescribe; *Provided further*, That the Secretary of the Interior is hereby authorized in his discretion with or without application from the Indian owner of any such restricted lands, funds, or other property of less than one-half Indian blood, remove the restrictions from all or any part of the lands, funds, or other property belonging to such Indians, and said Secretary of the Interior shall direct the Supervisor or other officer in charge of the several Indian agencies in the State of Oklahoma to make a survey from time to time and report as to the ability of each Indian under their supervision of less than one-half Indian blood deemed qualified to manage his or her own affairs or entitled to have his or her restrictions removed; *Provided further*, That before removing the restrictions from any land belonging to any Indian of less than one-half Indian blood without the consent of such Indian, the Secretary of the Interior shall give at least thirty days' notice in writing to such Indian owner to show cause why such action should not be had; *Provided further*, That in any case wherein a restricted Indian has applied to the Secretary of the Interior for the removal of his or her restrictions on land, property, securities, or funds, and such application has been rejected, an appeal will lie to the Federal court under whose jurisdiction the land is located and if the application is for the removal of restrictions on property, securities, or funds, then the appeal will lie to the Federal court having jurisdiction of the legal residence of the applicant and the decision of the Federal court shall be final and binding upon the Secretary of the Interior. In all cases where appeals are authorized as provided herein, the applicant is entitled to have a certified copy of all papers, including the application and the order of rejection, and such applicant shall pay all necessary expenses in connection with the preparation and certification of such transcript; *And provided further*, That in the event an appeal is taken as authorized herein, and such appeal is denied by any Federal court, then the costs of such appeal shall be assessed and taxed against the applicant.

Sec. 8. That the provisions of sections 1, 2, and 3 of the Act of June 25, 1910 (36 Sat. 855), as amended, be, and the same are hereby, extended to all Indians of the Osage and of the Five Civilized Tribes of Oklahoma who are of one-half or more Indian blood, and hereafter, whenever such an Indian dies possessed of any trust or other restricted land, property, or funds, the Secretary of the Interior shall have exclusive jurisdiction to continue administration of the estate of such Indians, including the determination of the heirs of such decedents, the approval or disapproval of wills by such decedents, the partition of lands, funds, or other restricted property among the heirs of such decedents and the settlement of any claims against the restricted estates of such decedents, when approved by said Secretary; all under such rules and regulations as he may prescribe, and the decision or decisions of the Secretary of the Interior in such matters shall be final and conclusive. In addition to the fees authorized to be collected for probating such estates, as authorized by the Act of January 24, 1923 (42 Stat. 1185), the Secretary of the Interior is hereby authorized and directed to assess and collect an additional fee not to exceed one-fourth of 1 per centum of the appraised value of all such estates in excess of $7,500; *Provided*, That hereafter no guardian shall be appointed by the courts of the State of Oklahoma for any person of one-half or more Indian blood except on petition approved by the Secretary of the Interior.

Sec. 9. That the trust or otherwise restricted property of whatsoever kind or nature belonging to any Indian of the State of Oklahoma of less than one-half Indian blood shall, upon the death of such Indian, be subject to probate in that State, and the Secretary of the Interior is hereby directed to surrender to the proper officer appointed by such court or courts all funds or other property in his hands or subject to his supervision belonging to such Indians, but a copy of all papers filed in the county court shall be served on the superintendent of the agency having jurisdiction over the tribe to which the decedent belonged, and the said superintendent is hereby authorized, whenever the interests of any Indians having any interest in such estate require such action, to appear in the county court for the protection of the interests of such Indian or Indians. The said superintendent, or the Secretary of the Interior, whenever he deems the same necessary, may investigate the conduct of executors or administrators having in charge the estate of any such deceased Indian, and whenever he shall be of the opinion that the estate is in any manner being dissipated or wasted or is being permitted to deteriorate in value by reason of the negligence, carelessness, or incompetency of the person in charge of the estate, the said superintendent or the Secretary of the Interior or his representative shall have power, and it shall be his duty, to report said matter to the county court and take the necessary steps to have such case fully investigated, and also to prosecute any remedy, either civil or criminal, as the exigencies of the case and the preservation and protection of the interests of the estate may require, the costs and expenses of the civil proceedings to be a charge upon the estate of the Indian or upon the executor, administrator, or other person in charge of the executor, administrator, or other person in charge of the estate and his surety, as the county court shall determine. Every bond of the executor, administrator, or other person in charge of the estate of any such deceased Indian shall be subject to the provisions of this section and shall contain therein a reference hereto; *Provided*, That no restricted land shall be sold or alienated under the provisions of this section without the approval of the Secretary of the Interior; *And provided further*, That upon the settlement of such estate, any funds or other property belonging thereto, restricted at the time of the death of the former Indian owner thereof, inherited by or devised to any person of one-half or more Indian blood, and which property was paid over or delivered by the Secretary of the Interior to the administrator or executor of such estate, shall be restricted and shall be returned by such administrator or executor to the Secretary of the Interior, for the benefit of such heir or heirs, devisee or devisees, as provided by law. Wherever any question arises as to the quantum of Indian blood of any Indian subject to the provisions of this Act, for the purpose of determining jurisdiction over the estate of such Indian, or otherwise, the Secretary of the Interior shall determine said quantum of Indian blood and his determination thereof shall be final and conclusive.

Sec. 10. To meet in part the cost to the United States of administering the restricted property of Indians of Oklahoma, including the sale of trust or otherwise restricted lands, oil, gas, and/or other leases covering such lands, the Secretary of the Interior, under such rules and regulations as he may prescribe, is hereby authorized and directed to assess and collect from the Indian owner or owners of such restricted lands, funds, or other property subject to the supervision of said Secretary, and additional charge of not to exceed one-fourth of 1 per centum per annum of the gross amount received during any one year from such lands, whether by way of a sale thereof, or from oil, gas, or other leases covering such lands, or from the investment or other disposition of any restricted funds or other property subject to the jurisdiction of the Secretary of the Interior; *Provided*, That no additional charge herein authorized shall be levied or collected in any case where the annual income accruing to the Indian owner thereof from such source or sources is less than $500. At the end of each and every fiscal year the said Secretary of the Interior is further authorized and directed to collect from the Indian owner or owners of restricted property subject to his supervision or control, of whatsoever kind or nature, a sum not exceeding one-fourth of 1 per centum based on the corpus of the accumulated funds or securities in which such funds may be invested belonging to any restricted Indian and remaining in the hands of or subject to the supervision of said Secretary; *Provided further*, That no additional charge in his behalf shall be levied or collected in any case where the corpus of such accumulated funds or other securities subject to the control of the Secretary of the

Interior at the end of any fiscal year is less than $2,000; *And provided further*, That all amounts collected pursuant to this section shall be covered into a special deposit account at each agency where such administration fees are collected, and shall be available for expenditure, with the approval of the Secretary of the Interior, for relief of needy Indians, industrial assistance and advancement, education, medical attention, and such other purposes as may be necessary for the welfare of the respective tribes or individuals members thereof.

Sec. 11. That the provisions of sections 2, 3, 4, 5, 6, and 7 of the Act of January 27, 1933 (47 Stat. 777), entitled "An Act relative to restrictions applicable to Indians of the Five Civilized Tribes of Oklahoma," be, and the same are hereby, made applicable to all Indians of said State, regardless of tribe or degree of Indian blood, and all such Indians having any restricted lands, funds, or other property shall have the right, at their election, either to create private trusts out of such restricted property, pursuant to the terms of said Act, or allow the same to remain subject to supervision of the Secretary of the Interior, but, in the latter event, the fees, commissions, or other charges authorized by section 10 of this Act shall be assessed and collected by the Secretary of the Interior.

Sec. 12. Any group of Indians residing on any area of tribal land or on land acquired by the United States for the use of Indians, shall have the right to organize for its common welfare and to adopt a constitution and bylaws, under such rules and regulations as the Secretary of the Interior may prescribe. The Secretary of the Interior may issue to any such organized group a charter of incorporation, which shall become operative when ratified by a majority of the adult members of the organization. Such charter may convey to the incorporated group, in addition to any powers which may properly be vested in a body corporate under the laws of the State of Oklahoma, the right to participate in the revolving credit fund and to enjoy any other rights or privileges secured to an organized Indian tribe under the Act of June 18, 1934 (48 Stat. 984).

The Secretary of the Interior may from time to time delegate and convey to a corporation so chartered, subject to any qualifications that may appear necessary or desirable, any or all powers now vested in the Secretary of the Interior or in the Commissioner of Indian Affairs with respect to the management or control of lands, funds, or other property held or enjoyed by the corporation or its members, the administration of services performed by the Interior Department for such corporation or its members, or the regulation of the conduct or affairs of such corporation and its members. Wherever the management and control of its funds shall be vested in an Indian corporation, such funds and control of these funds shall be vested in any Indian corporation, and such funds may be deposited in any national bank within the State of Oklahoma or otherwise invested, utilized, or disbursed in accordance with the terms of the corporate charter.

Sec. 13. Any Indian tribe, group, or band within the State of Oklahoma whether or not the members thereof reside on tribal land, or land acquired by the United States for the use of Indians, shall have the right to organize, to adopt a constitution and bylaws, and to receive a charter of incorporation in the manner prescribed under the preceding section for any Indian groups; and any powers, rights, claims, or property now vested in any such tribe or band shall be recognized and confirmed in the constitution, bylaws, and charter of the incorporated tribe or band.

Sec. 14. The Secretary is authorized and directed to establish an Oklahoma Indian Credit Corporation, hereinafter referred to as the corporation, to issue a charter to such corporation, defining its powers and providing for a board of directors to serve without pay and to consist of seven members, one of whom shall be the Director of Credit of the Indian Credit Administration, and four of whom shall be representative Indians of the State of Oklahoma, and to appoint, at a salary determined by him, a manager for such corporation. In addition to any powers which the Secretary may delegate to such corporation necessary for the proper performance of its functions, such corporation shall be authorized in its charter to purchase stock in and to make loans to Indian cooperative credit, producers, consumers, marketing, and land-management associations and to individual Indians as defined in the act of June 18, 1934 (48 Sat. 984), under rules and regulations prescribed by the Secretary of the Interior; *Provided*, That no loan shall be made to any individual unless the establishment of a cooperative credit association in an area reasonably convenient to such individual has been proved to the satisfaction of the corporation not to be feasible; *And provided further*, That no loan to any individual or association nor purchase of stock shall be made without the approval of the manager of the corporation. For the purposes and expenses of the corporation and cooperative associations organized pursuant to this act there shall be appropriated out of the Treasury of the United States the sum of $2,000,000.

Sec. 15. Any 10 or more Indians as defined in the Act of June 18, 1934 (48 Stat. 984), who reside in convenient proximity to each other may petition the corporation for a charter for a local cooperative association for any one or more of the following purposes: Credit administration, production, marketing, consumers' protection, or land management. Upon approval of the petition by the corporation and by the Secretary, the Secretary shall issue to such persons a charter defining the powers of such cooperative association, the district within which it shall operate, and the conditions of membership, and prescribing the manner of conducting its business. The provisions of the charter shall be based on the State law governing cooperative associations insofar as such law is not superseded by this Act and the regulations of the Secretary made pursuant thereto. All credit associations shall, and any other cooperative association may, possess voting and nonvoting stock with a par value as fixed in the charter. The nonvoting stock shall be purchased by the corporation or otherwise taken by it in exchange for loans made to the cooperative associations in such proportion to the loans made as may be prescribed in the regulations of the *Secretary*. The voting stock shall be used only by members of the cooperative association, and must be purchased by every member thereof to the amount required in the charter of the association; except that every credit association shall require of its members the purchase of stock to the amount of 5 per centum of the face value of his loan. Any member may pay for such stock either by cash supplied by him or through assignment to the association of a part of his patronage dividend or, in the case of credit association, out of the proceeds of loans to him from the credit association. In any stock or nonstock cooperative association no one member shall have more than one vote, and membership therein shall be open to all individuals of one-half or more Indian blood residing within the prescribed district. Any Indian, regardless of his degree of blood, who has relinquished to the Secretary title to land and who has been assigned land by said Secretary pursuant to section 2 of this Act is entitled to become a member of a land-management association. The officers of all cooperative associations must be approved by the corporation, and all books and accounts of such associations shall at all times be open to inspection by the corporation or the Secretary.

Sec. 16. The corporation shall continue until otherwise directed by Act of Congress; and the charters of all cooperative associations organized pursuant to this Act shall not be amended or revoked by the Secretary except after a majority vote of the membership. Said corporation and cooperative associations shall have the right to make contracts, to acquire, hold, and dispose of real and personal property, necessary and incident to the conduct of their business, to prescribe fees and charges, subject to the regulations of the Secretary, for loans and other services, to buy and sell stocks in their own or other associations or corporations; and shall have such other powers necessary and incident to carrying out the powers and duties described in this Act as may be provided by the Secretary in their charters. Said corporation and cooperative associations may sue and be sued in any court of the State of Oklahoma or of the United States having jurisdiction of the cause of action, but a certified copy of all papers filed in any action against a cooperative association in a court of Oklahoma shall be served upon the corporation. Within twenty days after such service or within such extended time as the trial court may permit, the corporation may intervene in such action or the Secretary, upon the request of the corporation, may remove such action to the United States district court to be held in the district where such petition is pending by filing in such actions in the State court a petition for such removal together with the certified copy of the papers served upon the corporation. It shall be the duty of the State court to accept such petition and proceed not further in such action. The said copy shall be entered in the said district court within twenty days after the filing of the petition for removal, and the said district court is hereby given jurisdiction to hear and determine said action.

In addition to the foregoing powers the cooperative associations may, by delegation from the Secretary of the Interior, receive the power to manage, operate, and assign lands purchased or acquired by the Secretary pursuant to section 2 of this Act and to regulate the leasing thereof and the disposition, use, inheritance, and devise of the improvements placed thereon.

Sec. 17. The provisions of this Act are to be considered, held, and construed as supplemental to the rights, privileges, and benefits set forth and provided in the Act of June 18, 1934 (48 Stat. 984); *Provided,* That the Indian tribes and Indian citizens of Oklahoma shall have equal rights, opportunities, and privileges under the provision of the last said mentioned Act when applicable; *And provided further,* That all funds appropriated under the several grants of authority contained in said Act for the purchase of land as provided in section 5 thereof; for the purpose of establishing a revolving fund as provided in section 10 thereof; for the making of loans to Indians as provided in section 11 thereof; are hereby made available for the use under the provisions of this Act, and Oklahoma Indians shall be accorded and allocated a fair and just share of any and all funds hereafter appropriated under the authorization herein set forth.

Sec. 18. For the purpose of carrying out the several provisions of this Act and supplemental to the authorizations contained in the Act of June 18, 1934 (48 Stat. 984), funds are hereby authorized to be appropriated out of any moneys in the Treasury not otherwise appropriated, and all sums appropriated pursuant to this authority shall be expended under the direction and supervision of the Secretary of the Interior: *Provided,* That specific authority is hereby granted to appropriated funds for—

(a) General support and civilization, including education.

(b) For relief of distress and conservation of health.

(c) For industrial assistance and advancement and general administration of Indian property.

(d) For the enlargement, extension, improvement, and repair of the buildings and grounds of existing plants and projects.

(e) For the employment of inspectors, supervisors, superintendents, clerks, field matrons, farmers, physicians, Indian police, and other employees.

(f) For the suppression of traffic in intoxicating liquor and deleterious drugs.

(g) For the purchase of horse-drawn and motor-propelled passenger-carrying vehicles for official use.

Sec. 19. The Secretary of the Interior is hereby authorized to prescribe such rules and regulations as may be necessary to carry out any of the provisions of this Act.

Sec. 20. All Acts or parts of Acts inconsistent herewith are hereby repealed.

Sec. 21. This Act may be cited as the "Oklahoma Indian General Welfare Act of 1936."

The Secretary of the Interior, Washington, February 23, 1935.

Source: Congress, Senate, Committee on Indian Affairs, *To Promote the General Welfare of the Indians of Oklahoma*, 74th Cong., 1st Sess., 9 April 1934, 40.

APPENDIX C

THE OKLAHOMA INDIAN WELFARE ACT

BE IT ENACTED *by the Senate and House of Representatives of the United States of America in Congress assembled*, that the Secretary of the Interior is hereby authorized, in his discretion, to acquire by purchase, relinquishment, gift, exchange, or assignment, any interests in lands, water rights, surface rights to lands, within or without existing Indian reservations, including trust or otherwise restricted lands now in Indian ownership: *Provided*, that such lands shall be agricultural and grazing lands of good character and quality in proportion to the respective needs of the particular Indian or Indians for whom such purchases are made. Title to all lands so acquired shall be taken in the name of the United States, in trust for the tribe, band, group, or individual Indian for whose benefit such land is so acquired, and while the title thereto is held by the United States said lands shall be free from any and all taxes, save that the State of Oklahoma is authorized to levy and collect a gross-production tax, not in excess of the rate applied to production from lands in private ownership, upon all oil and gas produced from said lands, which said tax the Secretary of the Interior is hereby authorized and directed to cause to be paid.

Sec. 2. Whenever any restricted Indian land or interests in land, other than sales or leases of oil, gas, or other mineral therein, are offered for sale, pursuant to the terms of this or any other Act of Congress, the Secretary of the Interior shall have a preference right, in his discretion, to purchase the same for or in behalf of any other Indian or

Indians of the same or any other tribe, at a fair valuation to be fixed by the appraisement satisfactory to the Indian owner or owners, or if offered for sale at auction said Secretary shall have a preference right, in his discretion, to purchase the same for or in behalf of any other Indian or Indians by meeting the highest bid otherwise offered therefor.

Sec. 3. Any recognized tribe or band of Indians residing in Oklahoma shall have the right to organize for its common welfare and to adopt a constitution and bylaws, under such rules and regulations as the Secretary of the Interior may prescribe. The Secretary of the Interior may issue to any such organized group a charter of incorporation, which shall become operative when ratified by a majority vote of the adult members of the organization voting: *Provided however*, that such election shall be void unless the total votes cast be at least 30 per centum of those entitled to vote. Such charter may convey to the incorporated group, in addition to any powers which may properly be vested in a body corporate under the laws of the State of Oklahoma, the right to participate in the revolving credit fund and to enjoy any other rights or privileges secured to an organized Indian tribe under the Act of June 18, 1934 (48 Stat. 984): *Provided*, that the corporate funds of any such chartered group may be deposited in any national bank within the State of Oklahoma or otherwise invested, utilized, or disbursed in accordance with the terms of the corporate charter.

Sec. 4. Any ten or more Indians, as determined by the official tribal rolls, or Indian descendants of such enrolled members, or Indians as defined in the Act of June 18, 1934 (48 Stat. 984), who reside within the State of Oklahoma in convenient proximity to each other may receive from the Secretary of the Interior, a charter as a local cooperative association for any one or more of the following purposes: Credit administration, production, marketing, consumers' protection, or land management. The provisions of this Act, the regulations of the Secretary of the Interior, and the charters of the cooperative associations issued pursuant thereto shall govern the cooperative associations: *Provided*, that in those matters not covered by said Act, regulations, or charters, the laws of the State of Oklahoma, if applicable, shall govern. In any stock or nonstock cooperative association no one member shall have more than one vote, and membership therein shall be open to all Indians residing within the prescribed district.

Sec. 5. The charters of any cooperative association organized pursuant to this Act shall not be amended or revoked by the Secretary except after a majority vote of the membership. Such cooperative associations may sue and be sued in any court of the State of Oklahoma or of the United States having jurisdiction of the cause of action, but a certified copy of all papers filed in any action against a cooperative association in a court of Oklahoma shall be served upon the Secretary of the Interior, or upon an employee duly authorized by him to receive such service. Within thirty days after such service or within such extended time as the trial court may permit, the Secretary of the Interior may intervene in such action or may remove such action to the United States district court to be held in the district where such petition is pending by filing in such action in the State court a petition for such removal, together with the certified copy of the papers served upon the Secretary. It shall then be the duty of the State court to accept such petition and to proceed no further in such action. The said copy shall be entered in the said district court within thirty days after the filing of the petition for removal, and the said district court is hereby given jurisdiction to hear and determine said action.

Sec. 6. The Secretary is authorized to make loans to individual Indians and to associations of corporate groups organized pursuant to this Act. For the making of such loans and for expenses of the cooperative associations organized pursuant to this Act, there shall be appropriated, out of the Treasury of the United States, the sum of $2,000,000.

Sec. 7. All funds appropriated under the several grants of authority contained in the Act of June 18, 1934 (48 Stat. 984), are hereby made available for use under the provisions of this Act, and Oklahoma Indians shall be accorded and allocated a fair and just share of any and all funds hereafter appropriated under the authorization herein set forth: *Provide*d, that any royalties, bonuses, or other revenues derived from mineral deposits underlying lands purchased in Oklahoma under the authority granted by this Act, or by the Act of June 18, 1934, shall be deposited in the Treasury of the United States, and such revenues are hereby made available for expenditure by the Secretary of the Interior for the acquisition of lands and for loans to Indians in Oklahoma as authorized by this Act and by the Act of June 18 1934 (48 Stat. 984).

Sec. 8. This Act shall not relate to or affect Osage County, Oklahoma.

Sec. 9. The Secretary of the Interior is hereby authorized to prescribe such rules and regulations as may be necessary to carry out the provisions of this Act. All Acts or parts of Acts inconsistent herewith are hereby repealed.

Sec. 10. The following provisions of the Indian Reorganization Act of June 18, 1934 (48 Stat. P. 984) as modified, are applicable to Oklahoma, and should be considered in connection with the provisions of the Oklahoma Welfare Act.

Sec. 11. That hereafter no land of any Indian reservation, created or set apart by treaty or agreement with the Indians, Act of Congress, Executive order, purchase, or otherwise, shall be allotted in severalty to any Indian.

Sec. 12. The Secretary of the Interior, if he shall find it to be in the public interest, is hereby authorized to restore to tribal ownership the remaining surplus lands of any Indian reservation heretofore opened, or authorized to be opened, to sale, or any other form of disposal by Presidential proclamation, or by any of the public land laws of the United States; Provided, however, That valid rights or claims of any persons to any lands so withdrawn existing on the date of the withdrawal shall not be affected by this Act.

Sec. 13. The Secretary of the Interior is hereby authorized, in his discretion, to acquire through purchase, relinquishment, gift, exchange, or assignment, any interest in lands, water rights or surface rights to lands, within or without existing reservations, including trust or otherwise restricted allotments whether the allottee be living or deceased, for the purpose of providing lands for Indians.

Sec. 14. For the acquisition of such lands, interests in lands, water rights, and surface rights, and for expenses incident to such acquisition, there is hereby authorized to be appropriated, out of any funds in the Treasury not otherwise appropriated, a sum not to exceed $2,000,000 in any one fiscal year: *Provided,* That no part of such funds shall be used to acquire additional land outside of the exterior boundaries of Navajo Indian Reservation for the Navajo Indians in Arizona and New Mexico, in the event that the proposed Navajo boundary extension measures how pending in congress and embodied in the bills (S. 2531 and H.R. 8927) to define the exterior boundaries of the Navajo Indian Reservation in Arizona, and for other purposes, and the bills (S. 2531 and H.R. 8982) to define the exterior boundaries of the Navajo Indian Reservation in New Mexico and for other purposes, or similar legislation, become law.

Sec. 15. The unexpended balances of any appropriations made pursuant to this section shall remain available until expended.

Sec. 16. Title to any lands or rights acquired pursuant to this Act shall be taken in the name of the United States in trust for the Indian tribe or individual Indian for which the land is acquired, and such lands or rights shall be exempt from State and local taxation.

Sec. 17. The Secretary of the Interior is directed to make rules and regulations for the operation and management of Indian forestry units on the principle of sustained-yield management, to restrict the number of livestock grazed on Indian range units to the estimated carrying capacity of such ranges, and to promulgate such other rules and regulations as may be necessary to protect the range from deterioration, to prevent soil erosion, to assure full utilization of the range, and like purposes.

Sec. 18. Nothing contained in this Act shall be construed to relate to Indian holdings of allotments or homesteads upon the public domain outside of the geographic boundaries of any Indian reservation now existing or established hereafter.

Sec. 19. There is hereby authorized to be appropriated, out of any funds in the Treasury not otherwise appropriated, such sums as may be necessary, but not to exceed $250,000 in any fiscal year, to be expended at the order of the Secretary of the Interior, in defraying the expenses of organizing Indian chartered corporations or other organizations created under this Act.

Sec. 20. There is hereby authorized to be appropriated, out of any funds in the Treasury not otherwise appropriated, the sum of $10,000,000 to be established as a revolving fund from which the Secretary of the Interior, under such rules and regulations as he may prescribe, may make loans to Indian chartered corporations for the purpose of promoting the economic development of such tribes and of their members, and may defray the expenses of administering such loans. Repayment of amounts loaned under this authorization shall be credited to the revolving fund and shall be available for the purposes for which the fund is established. A report shall be made annually to Congress of transactions under this authorization.

Sec. 21. There is hereby authorized to be appropriated, out of any funds in the United States Treasury not otherwise appropriated, a sum not to exceed $250,000 annually, together with any unexpended balances of previous appropriations made pursuant to this section, for loans to Indians for the payment of tuition and other expenses in recognized vocational and trade schools: *Provided*, That not more than $50,000 of such sum shall be available for loans to Indian students in high schools and colleges. Such loans shall be reimbursable under rules established by the Commissioner of Indian Affairs.

Sec. 22. The Secretary of the Interior is directed to establish standards of health, age, character, experience, knowledge, and ability for Indians who maybe appointed, without regard to civil-service laws, to the various positions maintained, now or hereafter, by the Indian office, in the administrations functions or services affecting any Indian tribe. Such qualified Indians shall hereafter have the preference to appointment to vacancies in any such positions.

Sec. 23. Nothing in this Act shall be construed to impair or prejudice any claim or suit of any Indian tribe against the United States. It is hereby declared to be the intent of Congress that no expenditures for the benefit of Indians made out of appropriations authorized by this Act shall be considered as offsets in any suit brought to recover upon any claim of such Indians against the United States.

Approved June 26, 1936.

Source: "The Oklahoma Indian Welfare Act," *United States Statutes at Large*, 49, part 1, 1967–1968 (1936).

APPENDIX D

Oklahoma Tribes Organized under the OIWA by 1950

Agency/ Reservation	Official Name of Organization	Constitution Approved	Charter Ratified	Population
Cheyenne & Arapaho/ Cheyenne-Arapaho	Cheyenne-Arapaho Tribes of Oklahoma	Aug. 24, 1937 Amended Feb. 4, 1942	—	2,949
Five Tribes/Creek	Alabama-Quassarte Tribal Town	Jan. 10, 1939	May 24, 1939	150
Five Tribes/Creek	Kialegge Tribal Town	June 12, 1941	Sept. 17, 1942	250
Five Tribes/Creek	Thlopthlocco Tribal Town	Jan. 10, 1939	Apr. 13, 1939	380
Kiowa/Caddo	Caddo Indian Tribe of Oklahoma	Jan. 17, 1938 Amended Jan 11, 1944	Nov. 15, 1938	1,048
Pawnee/Pawnee	Pawnee Indians of Oklahoma	Jan. 6, 1938	Apr. 28, 1938	1,017
Quapaw/Eastern Shawnee Indians	Eastern Shawnee Tribe of Oklahoma	Dec. 22, 1939	Dec. 12, 1940	299
Quapaw/Miami	Miami Tribe of Oklahoma	Oct. 1939	June 1, 1940	299
Quapaw/Ottawa	Ottawa Tribe of Oklahoma	Nov. 30, 1938	June 2, 1938	438
Quapaw/Peoria	Peoria Tribe of Indians of Oklahoma	Oct. 10, 1939	June 1, 1940	393

Quapaw/Seneca	Seneca-Cayuga Tribe of Oklahoma	May 15, 1937	June 26, 1940	288
Quapaw/Wyandotte	Wyandotte Tribe of Oklahoma	July 24, 1937	Oct. 30, 1937	800
Shawnee/Iowa	Iowa Tribe of Oklahoma	Oct. 23, 1937	Feb. 5, 1938	110
Shawnee/Kickapoo	Kickapoo Tribe of Oklahoma	Sept. 18, 1937	Feb. 5, 1938	269
Shawnee/Potawatomi	Citizen Band of Potawatomi Indians of Oklahoma	Dec. 12, 1938	—	2,920
Shawnee/Sac & Fox	Sac and Fox Tribe of Indians of Oklahoma	Dec. 7, 1938	—	910
Shawnee/Shawnee	Absentee-Shawnee Tribe of Indians	Dec. 5, 1938	—	667
Tonkawa	Tonkawa Tribe of Indians of Oklahoma	Apr. 21, 1938	—	54
Total				13,241

Source: Theodore Haas, *Ten Years of Tribal Government under the IRA* (Washington, D.C.: U.S. Indian Service, 1947), 28.

NOTES

INTRODUCTION

1. Daniel K. Richter, *Facing East from Indian Country: A Native History of Early America* (Cambridge, Mass.: Harvard University Press, 2001), 147.

2. U.S. House of Representatives, Congressional Record, 7 June 1934 (Washington, D.C.: Government Printing Office, 1934), 7807.

3. Carter Blue Clark, "The New Deal for Indians," in *Between Two Worlds: The Survival of Twentieth Century Indians*, ed. Arrell Morgan Gibson, 72–84 (Oklahoma City: Oklahoma Historical Society, 1986).

4. Angie Debo, *And Still the Waters Run: The Betrayal of the Five Civilized Tribes* (Princeton, N.J.: Princeton University Press, 1991), 91.

5. John Collier, *From Every Zenith: A Memoir and Some Essays on Life and Thought* (Denver: Sage Books, 1963), 203.

6. Ibid.

7. E. A. Schwartz, "Red Atlantis Revisited: Community and Culture in the Writings of John Collier," *American Indian Quarterly* 18 (Fall 1994): 5.

8. Clark, "The New Deal for Indians," 80.

9. Donald Parman, "Twentieth-Century Indian History: Achievements, Needs, and Problems," *OAH Magazine of History* 9 (Fall 1994), 11.

10. Richard Greene has been a reliable source for the period extending from statehood to the New Deal years of the 1930s. For the most part, the only Indian voice he knows of is contained in the papers of Douglas Johnston, the long-serving tribal governor, and two or three white lawyers occasionally hired by the tribe. Greene concludes, "There was just no one who kept records for the Chickasaw at this time." Phone conversation with the author, 5 September 2003.

11. Parman, "Twentieth-Century Indian History," 14.

12. Erik M. Zissu, *Blood Matters: The Five Civilized Tribes and the Search for Unity in the Twentieth Century* (New York: Routledge, 2001), 4.

13. William Cronan, *Changes in the Land: Indians, Colonists, and the Ecology of New England* (New York: Hill and Wang, 1983), 165.

CHAPTER 1

1. Vicki Rozema, ed., *Voices from the Trail of Tears* (Winston-Salem, N.C.: John F. Blair, 2003), 147.
2. Ibid.
3. The preferred name now is Five Tribes, which will be utilized through the balance of the book.
4. Wayne Moquin and Charles Van Doren, ed., *Great Documents in American Indian History* (New York: Praeger, 1973), 150. The Creek chief Speckled Snake spoke these words to his people in 1830, attempting to sell them on Andrew Jackson's offer of lands in what became Oklahoma in exchange for their holdings in the Southeast.
5. Rozema, *Voices from the Trail of Tears*, 147.
6. Circe Sturm, *Blood Politics: Race, Culture, and Identity in the Cherokee Nation of Oklahoma* (Berkeley: University of California Press, 2002), 63–68.
7. Ibid., 5.
8. Whit Edwards, *The Prairie Was on Fire* (Oklahoma City: Oklahoma Historical Society, 2001), xv.
9. W. David Baird and Danney Goble, *The Story of Oklahoma* (Norman: University of Oklahoma Press, 1994), 178–79.
10. Jeffrey Burton, *Indian Territory and the United States, 1866–1906* (Norman: University of Oklahoma Press, 1995), 15.
11. Arrell M. Gibson, *Oklahoma: A History of Five Centuries* (Norman, Okla.: Harlow, 1972), 159.
12. "Cherokee Treaty of 1866," in *Treaties and Agreements of the Eastern Oklahoma Indians*, ed. Charles J. Kappler (Washington, D.C.: GPO, 1903), 728.
13. Burton, *Indian Territory and the United States*, xiii.
14. Recent scholarship explores the freedmen in Indian Territory fully. Notable works include David Chang's *The Color of the Land: Race, Nation, and the Politics of Landownership in Oklahoma, 1832–1839* (Chapel Hill: University of North Carolina Press, 2010) and Fay Yarbrough's *Race and the Cherokee Nation: Sovereignty in the Nineteenth Century* (Philadelphia: University of Pennsylvania Press, 2008).
15. Cyrus Harris to the Choctaw Legislature, 2 September 1872, box 1, folder 3, Cyrus Harris Collection, Western History Collections, University of Oklahoma Libraries, Norman.
16. Alvin Rucker, "End of the Redman's Law," *Daily Oklahoman*, 11 November 1928, F6.
17. H. Craig Miner, *The Corporation and the Indian: Tribal Sovereignty and Industrial Civilization in Indian Territory, 1865–1907* (Columbia: University of Missouri Press, 1976), 117.

18. David Rich Lewis offers an excellent examination of this issue in "Reservation Leadership and the Progressive-Traditional Dichotomy: William Wash and the Northern Utes, 1865–1928," *Ethnohistory*, Spring 1991, 124–48.

19. Jim Padgett, interviewed by unknown, May 14, 1937, in Indian and Pioneer Papers Collection, Oklahoma Historical Society, Oklahoma City, vol. 68, p. 212.

20. Edmund McCurtain to the Choctaw, 24 October 1885, Edmund McCurtain Collection, box 45, folder 29, Western History Collections, University of Oklahoma, Norman, Oklahoma.

21. Zissu, *Blood Matters*, 5.

22. Ibid., 66.

23. David La Vere, *Contrary Neighbors: Southern Plains and Removal Indians in Indian Territory* (Norman: University of Oklahoma Press, 2000), 7.

24. Quoted in ibid., 62.

25. Debo, *And Still the Waters Run*, 18–21.

26. Quoted in Francis Paul Prucha, *American Indian Policy in Crisis: Christian Reformers and the Indian, 1865–1900* (Norman: University of Oklahoma Press, 1976), 386.

27. Brad A. Bays, *Townsite Settlement and Dispossession in the Cherokee Nation, 1866–1907* (New York: Garland, 1998) offers an excellent examination of this conflict between Indians and non-Indians as it played out between the Civil War and statehood.

28. Kirke Kickingbird and Lynn Kickingbird, "Oklahoma Indian Jurisdiction: A Myth Unraveled," *American Indian Journal* (Fall 1986), 4.

29. Two studies examine the issue of instilling the concept of private property in the minds of Indians. They are Tom Holm, *The Great Confusion in Indian Affairs: Native Americans and Whites in the Progressive Era* (Austin: University of Texas Press, 2005) and Mary Jane Warde, *George Washington Grayson and the Creek Nation, 1843–1920* (Norman: University of Oklahoma Press, 1999).

30. "The Choctaw Reply," *Cherokee Advocate*, 28 February 1894, 2.

31. "Allotment," *Cherokee Advocate*, 7 February 1894, 2.

32. Ibid.

33. Gibson, *Oklahoma: A History of Five Centuries*, 181–84.

34. Prucha, *American Indian Policy in Crisis*, 898.

35. *Cherokee Advocate*, 21 February 1894, 2.

36. Daniel F. Littlefield, *The Chickasaw Freedmen: A People without a Country*, (Westport, Conn.: Greenwood Press, 1980), 113.

37. Danney Goble, *Progressive Oklahoma: The Making of a New Kind of State* (Norman: University of Oklahoma Press, 1980), 72.

38. "To Dissolve Tribal Relations," *Globe Democrat*, 7 March 1894, 3.

39. F. Browning Pipestem, and William G. Rice, "The Mythology of the Oklahoma Indians: A Survey of the Legal Status of Indian Tribes in Oklahoma," *American Indian Law Review* 6, no. 2 (1978), 317.

40. These seven crimes included murder, kidnapping, manslaughter, incest, arson, assault, and burglary.

41. Felix S. Cohen, *Felix S. Cohen's Handbook of Federal Indian Law* (Albuquerque: University of New Mexico Press, 1976), 431.

42. Rennard Strickland, *Indians of Oklahoma* (Norman: University of Oklahoma Press, 1980), 48–49.

43. Department of Interior, *Commissioner of Indian Affairs Annual Report, 1901*, (Washington, D.C.: Government Printing Office, 1902), 149.

44. Rolly McIntosh, 26 November 1898, box 1, folder 8, Western History Collections, University of Oklahoma, Norman.

45. Rennard Strickland, "Genocide-At-Law: An Historic and Contemporary View of the Native American Experience," *Kansas Law Review* 34 (Summer 1986), 718, 747.

46. *Chelsea (Okla.) Reporter* 31 August 1901, 1.

47. Mrs. Alfred Mitchell Collection, box 3, folder 43, Western History Collections, University of Oklahoma Libraries, Norman.

48. Alex Posey, *Red Fork (Okla.) Derrick*, 24 June 1905, 2.

49. Debo, *And Still the Waters Run*, 55–57.

50. Daniel F. Littlefield and Lonnie E. Underhill, "The Crazy Snake Uprising of 1909: A Red, Black, or White Affair?," *Arizona and the West* 20 (Winter 1978): 307–24.

51. Paul Nesbitt, "Governor Haskell Tells of Two Conventions," *Chronicles of Oklahoma* 14 (June 1936), 198.

52. Prucha, *American Indian Policy in Crisis*, 400.

53. Angie Debo, *The Road to Disappearance* (Norman: University of Oklahoma Press, 1941), 91.

54. Goble, *Progressive Oklahoma*, 78.

55. Senate Report, 59th Cong., 2nd sess., vol. I, 1111.

56. There are numerous scholarly works that explore graft in eastern Oklahoma from the 1890s to the late 1920s when the oil boom sputtered out. In addition to Angie Debo, *The Road to Disappearance*, there are Donald Parman, *Indians in the American West in the Twentieth Century*; Terry P. Wilson, *Underground Reservation*; Tanis C. Thorne, *The World's Richest Indian*, and Danny Goble, *Progressive Oklahoma*.

57. Zissu, *Blood Matters*, 33.

58. Francis Paul Prucha, *The Great Father: The United States Government and the American Indians* (Lincoln: University of Nebraska Press, 1986), 903–904.

59. John H. Moore, "The Enduring Reservations of Oklahoma," in *State and Reservation: New Perspectives on Federal Indian Policy*, ed. George Pierre Castile and Robert L. Bee (Tucson: University of Arizona Press, 1992), 101–102.

60. Goble, *Progressive Oklahoma*, 78.

61. Lewis Meriam, ed., *The Problem of Indian Administration* (Baltimore: Johns Hopkins University Press, 1928), 798.

62. Terry P. Wilson, *The Underground Reservation: Osage Oil* (Lincoln: University of Nebraska Press, 1985), 139.

63. Congress, Senate, Committee on Indian Affairs, Select Committee, *Report of the Select Committee to Investigate Matters Connected With Affairs in the Indian Territory*, 59th Cong., 2d sess. (Washington, D.C: Government Printing Office, 1907), 867.

64. Ibid., 1031.

65. Charles J. Kappler, *Laws Relating to the Five Civilized Tribes in Oklahoma 1890–1914* (Washington, D.C.: Government Printing Office, 1915).

66. S. E. Wallen to Charles H. Burke, 31 December 1923, in M. L. Mott, *A National Blunder* (Washington, D.C.: n.p., 1924), 16.

67. Terry Wilson, *The Underground Reservation*, remains the definitive study on this bleak chapter in Oklahoma Indian history.

68. Alvin Rucker, "'Oil Curse' on Osage Indians?," *Daily Oklahoman*, 6 January 1929, F1.

69. Prucha, *The Great Father*, 903.

CHAPTER 2

1. Quoted in Mott, *A National Blunder*, 42.

2. Ibid., 43–44.

3. Ibid., 2, quoting a statement made by John H. Mosier and C. F. Dyer.

4. Gertrude Bonnin, Charles H. Fabens, and Matthew K. Sniffen, *Oklahoma's Poor Rich Indians: An Orgy of Graft and Exploitation of the Five Civilized Tribes—Legalized Robbery*, (Philadelphia: Office of the Indian Rights Association, 1924), 5.

5. Ibid., 37.

6. Ibid., 7.

7. Ibid.

8. Ibid., 39.

9. Frederick E. Hoxie, *A Final Promise: The Campaign to Assimilate the Indians, 1880–1920* (Lincoln: University of Nebraska Press, 1984), xvii–xxiii. Hoxie presents a convincing argument for a two-step process that comprised the assimilation program. First Indians were to be brought into eventual full participation in American society, through education, introduction to private land ownership, and citizenship. However, as the assimilation program evolved, "by 1920 they had become an American minority group, experiencing life on the fringes of what had come to be regarded as a "white man's" land" (xix).

10. Congress, House, Committee on Indian Affairs, *Hearings Pursuant to H. Res. 348* (Washington, D.C.: Government Printing Office, 1924), 394.

11. Congress, House, Committee on Indian Affairs, *Indian Affairs in Oklahoma Report*, (Washington, D.C.: Government Printing Office, 1925), 8.

12. Ibid., 9.

13. Congress, House, Committee on Indian Affairs, *Hearings Pursuant to H. Res. 348*, 396.

14. Ibid.

15. M. K. Sniffen, *Out of Thine Own Mouth: An Analysis of the House Subcommittee Report Denying and Confirming the Looting of Oklahoma's "Poor Rich Indians"* (Philadelphia: Indian Rights Association, 1925), 5.

16. Ibid., 4.

17. *Tulsa World*, 12 May 1925, 1.

18. *Bartlesville Examiner*, 14 May 1925, 2.

19. *Muskogee News*, 12 May 1925, 2.

20. Benay Blend, "The Indian Rights Association, the Allotment Policy, and the Five Civilized Tribes, 1923–1936," *American Indian Quarterly* 7 (Spring 1983), 71.

21. Debo, *And Still the Waters Run*, 352–53.

22. Peter Iverson, *We Are Still Here: American Indians in the Twentieth Century* (Wheeling, Ill.: Harlan Davidson, 1998), 75.

23. Meriam, et al., *The Problem of Indian Administration* (Washington, D.C.: Institute for Government Research, 1928), 18, 471.

24. Ibid., 94.

25. Ibid., 484.

26. Ibid., 488.

27. Ibid., 94.

28. Congress, Senate, Subcommittee of the Committee on Indian Affairs, *Survey of Conditions of the Indians in the United States*, 71st Cong., 2nd sess., 11 November 1930, 5323.

29. Ibid., 5514.

30. Ibid., 5606.

31. Ibid., 5702.

32. Ibid., 5298.

33. Ibid., 5298–99.

34. Ibid., 5324.

35. Ibid., 5600.

36. Ibid., 5620.

37. Ibid., 5615.

38. Ibid., 5351.

39. Ibid.

40. Ibid., 5297.

41. Ibid., 5518.

42. Ibid., 5348.

43. Ibid., 5385.

44. Ibid., 5308.

45. Ibid., 5332.

46. Ibid., 5502–12.

47. Ibid., 5610.

48. Ibid., 5617.

49. Muriel H. Wright, "The Indian Situation Is Perplexing in Eastern Oklahoma," *American Indian*, May 1927, 6.

50. Ibid., 6–7.

51. Congress, Senate, Committee on Indian Affairs, *Tax-Exempt Indian Lands*, 71st Cong., 2nd sess., 13 February 1933, 8.

52. Vine Deloria, Jr., ed., *The Indian Reorganization Act Congresses and Bills* (Norman: University of Oklahoma Press, 2002), 334.

53. Curt Holtin to Elmer Thomas, 27 November 1931, Elmer Thomas Collection, Carl Albert Center, University of Oklahoma, Norman, Oklahoma, box 4. Hereinafter referred to as Elmer Thomas Collection.

54. *Indiana Republican* (Indianapolis), 16 June 1931, 1.

55. *Daily Oklahoman* (Oklahoma City), 10 January 1931, 3.

56. Ibid., 22 August 1931, 3.

57. Elmer Thomas to Frank Davis, 18 February 1932, Elmer Thomas Collection, box 9.

58. *Harlow's Weekly* (Oklahoma City), 11 November 1932, 11.

59. Frank Mauhuchu to Elmer Thomas, 12 June 1931, Elmer Thomas Collection, box 9.

60. B. T. Quinton, "Oklahoma Tribes, the Great Depression," in *The American Indian Past and Present*, ed. Roger L. Nichols and George R. Adams (Lexington, Mass.: Xerox College Publishing, 1971), 192.

61. Ibid.

62. Ibid.

63. *Harlow's Weekly*, 4 February 1932, 4.

64. *Harlow's Weekly*, 1 April 1933, 10.

65. Congress, Senate, "Condition of the Indians in the United States Speech of Hon. William H. King, Delivered in the Senate February 8, 1933," 8 March 1933, *Senate Documents No. 2147*, 2nd Cong., sess. 2, 26.

66. Ibid.

67. Quoted in Prucha, *The Great White Father*, 17.

68. Elmer Thomas to Daisey E. Richard, 15 April 1933, Elmer Thomas Collection, box 9.

69. Harold L. Ickes, *The Secret Diary of Harold L. Ickes: The First Thousand Days, 1933–1936* (New York: Simon & Schuster, 1954), 19.

70. Quoted in Peter M. Wright, "John Collier and the Oklahoma Indian Welfare Act of 1936," *Chronicles of Oklahoma* 50 (August 1972), 349.

71. Lawrence C. Kelly, *The Assault on Assimilation: John Collier and the Origins of Indian Policy Reform* (Albuquerque: University of New Mexico Press, 1983), 5.

72. Kenneth R. Philp, *John Collier's Crusade for Indian Reform 1920–1954* (Tucson: University of Arizona Press, 1977), 23–25.

73. John Collier, *From Every Zenith: A Memoir and Some Essays on Life and Thought* (Denver: Sage Books, 1963), 124.

74. Ibid., 126.

75. John Collier, "The Red Atlantis," *The Survey* 49 (October 1922), 16.

76. E. A. Schwartz, "Red Atlantis Revisited: Community and Culture in the Writings of John Collier," *American Indian Quarterly* 18, (Fall 1994), 507.

77. Collier, "The Red Atlantis," 19–20.

78. Collier, *From Every Zenith*, 131.

79. Ibid., 216.

80. Ibid., 203.

81. Graham Taylor, *The New Deal and American Indian Tribalism: The Administration of the Indian Reorganization Act, 1934–1945* (Lincoln: University of Nebraska Press, 1980), ix.

82. Randolph C. Downes, "A Crusade for Indian Reform, 1922–1934," in *The American Indian: Past and Present*, ed. Roger L. Nichols and George R. Adams (Lexington, Mass.: Xerox College Publishing, 1971), 230.

CHAPTER 3

1. Statement of John Collier given in Washington, D.C., 21 April 1933, John Collier Papers, University of Oklahoma, Norman, Reel 31.

2. Collier, *From Every Zenith*, 179.

3. Ibid., xxvi.

4. Taylor, *The New Deal and American Indian Tribalism*, 65.

5. Elmer Rusco, *A Fateful Time: The Background and Legislative History of the Indian Reorganization Act* (Reno: University of Nevada Press, 2000), 115.

6. "Editorial," *Nation* 86 (26 April 1933), 459.

7. U.S. Congress, Senate, Hearings on S. 2755, *To Grant Indians Living under Federal Tutelage the Freedom of Organizing for Purposes of Local Self-Government and Economic Enterprise*, 73rd Cong., 2nd Sess., 1934, 338.

8. Ibid., 101.

9. Hoxie, *A Final Promise*, 244.

10. Department of the Interior, Office of Indian Affairs, Order No. 420, "Precluding Further Sales of Indian Allotments, Issuance of Fee Patents, Etc.," Washington, D.C., 12 August 1933.

11. Hoxie, *A Final Promise*, 244.

12. Michael T. Smith, "The Wheeler-Howard Act of 1934: The Indian New Deal," *Journal of the West* 10 (August 1971), 523–24.

13. Collier, *From Every Zenith*, 173.

14. Curtis Berkey, "John Collier and the Indian Reorganization Act," *American Indian Journal* 2 (July 1976), 4.

15. Collier, *From Every Zenith*, 172–73.

16. *Muskogee Daily Phoenix*, 18 November 1933, 4.

17. Quoted in *Daily Oklahoman*, 9 February 1934, 5.

18. Flora Warren Seymour, "Trying It on the Indians," *New Outlook* 43 (May 1934), 22.

19. Ibid.

20. *Daily Oklahoman*, 28 February 1934, 8.

21. Department of the Interior, Memorandum for the Press, 13 February 1934, John Collier Papers, Western History Collection, University of Oklahoma, Norman, Reel 30.

22. Congress, House, Committee on Indian Affairs, *Hearings before the House Committee on Indian Affairs on HR 3645*, 73rd Cong., 2nd sess., 6 March 1934, 1–21.

23. Smith, "The Wheeler-Howard Act of 1934," 526.

24. Department of the Interior, Office of the Solicitor, n.d., John Collier Papers, Western History Collection, University of Oklahoma, Norman, Reel 31. Charles Coughlin was a Roman Catholic priest who had gained a nationwide audience via radio.

25. Vera Connolly, "The End of a Long, Long Trail," *Good Housekeeping*, April 1934, 252. Collier is referring the land redistribution program of Mexican president Lázaro Cárdenas in the 1930s. During that period, the Mexican government distributed 17.9 million hectares of land to 810,000 Indians and peasants. Cárdenas enjoyed an international reputation as a true friend of the Mexican peasant and Indian and this is what Collier was playing on. However, like Collier, Cárdenas faced stiff opposition to many of his reform proposals from well-entrenched, conservative landholding elites. For more on Cárdenas's land redistribution programs, see Ben Fallaw's *Cárdenas Compromised* (Durham, N.C.: Duke University Press, 2001) or Nora Hamilton's *Limits of State Autonomy in Post-Revolutionary Mexico* (Madison: University of Wisconsin Press, 1978).

26. Ibid., 50, 260.

27. Ibid., 260.

28. Kelly, "The Indian Reorganization Act: The Dream and the Reality," 296.

29. *Muskogee Times Democrat*, 17 March 1934, 15.

30. Kelly, "The Indian Reorganization Act: The Dream and the Reality," 296.

31. *Muskogee Times Democrat*, 12 May 1934, 6.

32. *Tulsa Tribune*, 10 March 1934, 5.

33. Ibid.

34. *Bartlesville Examiner*, 12 March 1934, 6.

35. Matthew K. Sniffen, "Stop, Look—and Consider," *Indian Truth*, March 1934, 1.

36. Ibid.

37. Vine Deloria, Jr., and Clifford M. Lytle, *The Nations Within: The Past and Future of American Indian Sovereignty* (New York: Pantheon Books, 1984), 92–93.

38. Department of the Interior, Office of the Interior, Harold Ickes to all employees of the Indian Service, John Collier Papers, Western History Collection, University of Oklahoma, Reel 31.

39. Quoted in Vine Deloria, Jr., ed., *The Indian Reorganization Act: Congresses and Bills* (Norman: University of Oklahoma Press, 2000), 263.

40. Quoted in ibid., 268.

41. Quoted in ibid., 262.

42. Quoted in ibid., 281.

43. Ibid., 272.
44. Ibid., 263.
45. Quoted in ibid., 314.
46. Quoted in ibid., 327.
47. Quoted in ibid., 333.
48. Quoted in ibid., 347.
49. Prucha, *The Great Father*, 322.
50. Ibid., 287, 288, 289, 320.
51. "Analysis of Official Vote of Indian Tribes on Wheeler-Howard Bill," 30 April 1934, Wilburn Cartwright Collection, Carl Albert Center, University of Oklahoma, Norman, Oklahoma, box 5.
52. Deloria and Lytle, *The Nations Within*, 122.
53. There are several recent studies that offer in-depth examination and analysis of the legislative process surrounding enactment of the Indian Reorganization Act. Two recent works are Deloria and Lytle, *The Nations Within*, and Elmer Rusco's 2000 study, *A Fateful Time*. An excellent third study has stood the test of time: Freeman J. Leiper, Jr., "The New Deal for Indians: A Study in Bureau-Committee Relations in the American Government," PhD diss., Princeton University, 1952.
54. U.S. Congress, Senate, Committee on Indian Affairs, *A Bill to Grant to Indians Living under Federal Tutelage the Freedom to Organize for Purposes of Local Self-Government and Economic Enterprise*, 73rd Cong., 2nd sess., 85, 86.
55. U.S. Congress, House, Committee on Indian Affairs, *Readjustment of Indian Affairs*, 73rd Cong., 2nd sess., 13 March 1934, 157–64.
56. Ibid., 159.
57. Ibid., 164.
58. Ibid., 168.
59. Ibid., 235; 17 May 1934, 257.
60. Ibid., 28 May 1934, 352.
61. Ibid., 360.
62. Ibid., 17 May 1934, 299.
63. U.S. Congress, Senate, Committee on Indian Affairs, *A Bill to Grant to Indians Living under Federal Tutelage the Freedom to Organize for Purposes of Local Self-Government and Economic Enterprise*, 73rd Cong., 2nd sess., 28 April 1934, 108.
64. Ibid.
65. Ibid., 19 May 1934, 311. The American Indian Federation (AIF) existed from 1934 to the mid-1940s. It attempted to serve as a voice nationally for American Indians but was comprised of a number of disparate Indian groups across the nation promoting local issues and interests. In the 1940s, the AIF attempted affiliation with the American Bund movement. Laurence M. Hauptman offers an excellent though brief exploration of Joseph Bruner and the AIF in "The American Indian Federation and the Indian New Deal: A Reinterpretation," *Pacific Historical Review* 52 (November 1983), 378–402.

66. U.S. Congress, Senate, Committee on Indian Affairs, *A Bill to Grant to Indians Living under Federal Tutelage the Freedom to Organize for Purposes of Local Self-Government and Economic Enterprise*, 73rd Cong., 2nd sess., 28 May 1934, 318.

67. *Harlow's Weekly*, 28 April 1934, 13.

68. Elmer Thomas to James Duncan, 11 April 1934, Elmer Thomas Collection, box 9.

69. *Harlow's Weekly*, 17 March 1934, 15.

70. U.S. Congress, Senate, *Congressional Record*, 12 June 1934, 11126.

71. "Memorandum on Wheeler-Howard Bill—Dictated by Senator Thomas," June 1934, Thomas Collection, box 13.

72. Ibid.

73. *Harlow's Weekly*, 16 June 1934, 13.

74. "Indian Reorganization Act," *United States Statutes at Large*, 48, part 1, 984–88 (1934).

75. U.S. Congress, *Congressional Record*, 74th Cong., 2nd sess., vol. 135, no. 2 (Washington: Government Printing Office, 1936), 5739.

CHAPTER 4

1. *Harlow's Weekly*, 11 August 1934, 15.

2. John Collier, "Oklahoma Indians and The Wheeler-Howard Act," *Indians at Work* 2 (October 1934), 40.

3. *Daily Oklahoman*, 2 October 1934, 6.

4. *Harlow's Weekly*, 13 October 1934, 10.

5. Quoted in ibid., 11.

6. *Muskogee Daily Phoenix*, 15 October 1934, 6.

7. "Meeting Held at City Hall, Muskogee, Oklahoma, October 15, 1934," 4, Elmer Thomas Collection, box 9.

8. Ibid.

9. "Meeting Called by Senator Elmer Thomas with Commissioner John Collier and the Indians Under the Pawnee Jurisdiction on October 18, 1934," 6, 8, 11, 12, Elmer Thomas Collection, box 9. Hereinafter referred to as "The Pawnee Jurisdiction Meeting."

10. Ibid., 1, 2.

11. Ibid., 17, 38.

12. The law of May 27, 1908, eased the process required to have restrictions on Indian allotments removed, aiding white interests who coveted Indian land. Between 1908 and the early 1930s, millions of acres of Indian land had restrictions removed and quickly found their way into the hands of whites. This law provided the impetus for the "orgy of graft and corruption" that Angie Debo and others have researched.

13. "The Pawnee Jurisdiction Meeting," 45.

14. Ibid., 42–44.
15. Zissu, *Blood Matters*, 5, 7.
16. "The Pawnee Jurisdiction Meeting," 45.
17. Ibid., 51.
18. Ibid., 50.
19. Ibid., 52.
20. "Meeting Held in Miami, Oklahoma, October 16, 1934," 3, 10, Elmer Thomas Collection, box 9.
21. Ibid., 3.
22. Ibid., 19, 23.
23. "The Pawnee Jurisdiction Meeting," 11.
24. Ibid., 13.
25. Ibid., 29, 34, 37.
26. "Cheyenne and Arapaho Agency, Concho, Oklahoma, October 22, 1934," 1, 5, 9, 18, Elmer Thomas Collection, box 9.
27. "Proceedings of meeting held by Senator Elmer Thomas and Mr. A.C. Monahan, Assistant to the Commissioner of Indian Affairs, with the Indians of the Kiowa Reservation, relative to the Wheeler-Howard Law, at Anadarko, Oklahoma on October 23, 1934," 8, Elmer Thomas Collection, box 9. Hereinafter referred to as "The Anadarko Agency."
28. Ibid., 2.
29. "The Anadarko Agency," 19.
30. Quoted in David H. Getches, Charles F. Wilkinson, and Robert A. Williams, Jr., *Cases and Materials on Federal Indian Law*, 4th ed. (St. Paul: West Group, 1998), 175–85.
31. "The Anadarko Agency," 20.
32. Ibid., 22.
33. Loretta Fowler, *Tribal Sovereignty and the Historical Imagination: Cheyenne-Arapaho Politics* (Lincoln: University of Nebraska Press, 2002), xvii.
34. "The Anadarko Agency," 23, 24, 25.
35. Quoted in *Harlow's Weekly*, 20 October 1934, 5.
36. Quoted in ibid., 21.
37. Ibid.
38. Quoted in *Harlow's Weekly*, 27 October 1934, 7.
39. Ibid.
40. *Indians at Work*, 1 November 1934, 4.
41. *Indians at Work*, 15 October 1934, 37–38.
42. Department of the Interior, Office of Indian Affairs, "Facts as to the Wheeler-Howard Act," 6 November 1934, John Collier Papers, University of Oklahoma, Norman, Reel 32.
43. *Tulsa Tribune*, 16 February 1935, 3.
44. *Tushkahomman*, 12 March 1934, 3.
45. *Tushkahomman*, 5 March 1935, 2.

46. Sturm, *Blood Politics*, 48, 78.

47. *Tushkahomman*, 12 March 1935, 1.

48. Joint Resolution of Tribal Business Committees Representing the Pawnee, Ponca, Kaw, Otoe, and Tonkawa Tribes, 17 March 1935, Elmer Thomas Collection, box 22.

49. Ibid.

50. L. R. Heflin to Elmer Thomas, 14 March 1935, Elmer Thomas Collection, box 21.

51. Phil Harris to Elmer Thomas, 24 April 1935, Elmer Thomas Collection, box 21.

52. James I. Howard to Elmer Thomas, 6 April 1935, Elmer Thomas Collection, box 21.

53. L. F. Roberts to Elmer Thomas, 3 April 1935, Elmer Thomas Collection, box 21.

54. L. F. Roberts to Elmer Thomas, 13 April 1935, Elmer Thomas Collection, box 22.

55. J. W. B. Nichols to Elmer Thomas, 16 April 1935, Elmer Thomas Collection, box 22.

56. An Osage Indian to Elmer Thomas, 18 March 1935, Elmer Thomas Collection, box 22.

57. Elmer Thomas to J. B. Sixkiller, 12 April 1935, Elmer Thomas Collection, box 22.

58. *Tulsa Daily World*, 6 April 1935, 1.

59. *Muskogee Daily Phoenix*, 31 March 1934, 14B.

60. *Tulsa Daily World*, 6 April 1935, 6.

61. *Okmulgee Daily Times*, 5 April 1935, 4.

62. *Okemah Daily Leader*, 7 April 1935, 4.

63. *Tushkahomman*, 9 April 1935, 2.

64. *Tushkahomman*, 26 March 1935, 2.

65. Congress, Senate, Committee on Indian Affairs, *To Promote the General Welfare of the Indians of Oklahoma*, 74th Cong., 1st Sess., 9 April 1935, 40.

66. Ned Blackfox to A. M. Landman, 8 April 1935, Elmer Thomas Collection, box 21.

67. Several historians have explored in depth the split within the Cherokee tribe that developed over the New Echota Treaty of 1835. Among the best are Gary E. Moulton, *John Ross, Cherokee Chief* (Athens: University of Georgia Press, 1978) and Theda Perdue, "The Conflict Within: Cherokees and Removal," in William L. Anderson ed., *Cherokee Removal: Before and After* (Athens: University of Georgia Press, 1991).

68. Congress, Senate, Committee on Indian Affairs, *To Promote the General Welfare of the Indians of Oklahoma*, 74th Cong., 1st Sess., 11 April 1935, 106.

69. Ibid., 119.

70. *Daily Oklahoman*, 12 April 1935, 1.

71. *Tushkahomman*, 30 April 1935, 3.

72. Congress, Senate, Committee on Indian Affairs, *To Promote the General Welfare of the Indians of Oklahoma*, 74th Cong., 1st Sess., 9 April 1935, 42.

73. *Tushkahomman*, 16 April 1935, 4.

74. W. H. Blackbird to Elmer Thomas, 1 May 1935, Elmer Thomas Collection, box 21.

75. Mrs. W. V. Krier to Elmer Thomas, 22 April 1935, Elmer Thomas Collection, box 22.

76. Milford Growingham to Elmer Thomas, 25 April 1935, Elmer Thomas Collection, box 21.

77. *Indian Truth*, May 1935, 5.

78. Congress, House, Committee on Indian Affairs, *To Promote the General Welfare of the Indians of Oklahoma*, 74th Cong., 1st Sess., 22 April 1935, 21.

79. Frederick E. Hoxie, *A Final Promise: The Campaign to Assimilate the Indians 1880–1920*, (Lincoln: University of Nebraska Press, 1984), xi.

80. Quoted in Congress, House, Committee on Indian Affairs, *To Promote the General Welfare of the Indians of Oklahoma*, 31.

81. Quoted in ibid., 59.

82. Quoted in ibid., 72.

83. Quoted in ibid., 81–82.

84. Quoted in ibid., 154.

85. Quoted in ibid.

86. Quoted in ibid., 169.

87. Quoted in ibid., 199.

88. Quoted in ibid., 218–22.

89. Quoted in ibid., 236–37, 241.

90. American Indian Defense Association, Inc., "General Bulletin, No. 35," 29 May 1935, Elmer Thomas Collection, box 21.

91. Peter M. Wright, "John Collier and the Oklahoma Indian Welfare Act of 1936," 368.

92. *Tushkahomman*, 26 November 1935, 1.

93. Congress, House, Committee on Indian Affairs, *To Promote the General Welfare of the Indians of Oklahoma*, 74th Cong., 2nd Sess., 1 April 1936, 14, 22.

CHAPTER 5

1. Elmer Thomas to John Hugh Chambers, 27 June 1936, Elmer Thomas Collection, box 21.

2. John Collier, "Oklahoma Indian Welfare Act," *Indians at Work*, 15 July 1936, 15.

3. "Individual Weekly Report for Extension Workers, Aug. 4, 1934, Concho Agency," entry 78, box 2, record group 75, National Archives and Records Administration, Southwest Region (Ft. Worth).

4. Angie Debo Collection, Oklahoma State University, Stillwater, Oklahoma, box 25. Hereinafter referred to as Angie Debo Collection.

5. "Individual Weekly Report for Extension Workers, Aug. 27, 1936, Concho Agency," entry 77, box 71, record group 75, National Archives and Records Administration, Southwest Region (Ft. Worth).

6. Alfred Harper to Elmer Thomas, 9 September 1936, Elmer Thomas Collection, box 10.

7. Angie Whitthorne to Elmer Thomas, 19 September 1936, Elmer Thomas Collection, box 10.

8. Elmer Thomas to Franklin Roosevelt, 22 September 1936, Elmer Thomas Collection, box 10.

9. E. H. Labelle to Elmer Thomas, 20 November 1936, Elmer Thomas Collection, box 10.

10. *Daily Oklahoman*, 14 January 1937, 13.

11. William Zimmerman to Elmer Thomas, 24 August 1936, Elmer Thomas Collection, box 22.

12. Act of June 26, 1936, 49 Stat. 196.

13. Unidentified newspaper clipping, 12 December 1936, Elmer Thomas Collection, box 21.

14. The IRA and the OIWA were closely connected. As discussed earlier, Oklahoma Indians were initially exempted from most provisions of the IRA when it was enacted in June of 1934. However, when the OIWA was enacted two years later, its section 7 refers to the IRA/OIWA when both are implied. In a Senate hearing in Muskogee in October of 1937, Collier stated that "the two acts, the Indian Reorganization Act and the Oklahoma Indian Welfare Act, hang together."

15. *Tushkahoman*, 21 May 1935, 3.

16. John Collier to Harold L. Ickes, 15 February 1935, papers of John Collier, Western History Collection, University of Oklahoma, Reel 15.

17. Ibid.

18. D'Arcy McNickle, "Four Years of Indian Reorganization," *Indians at Work*, December 1938, 11.

19. Lawrence C. Kelly, "The Indian Reorganization Act: The Dream and the Reality," *Pacific Historical Review* 23 (Fall 1975), 308.

20. Alan Brinkley, *The End of Reform: New Deal Liberalism in Recession and War*, (New York: Vintage Books, 1996), 3–4.

21. Ibid., 6–7.

22. Burton K. Wheeler, *Yankee from the West* (New York: Doubleday, 1962), 314.

23. In May 1943, the Senate Indian Affairs Committee, chaired by Thomas, announced its recommendations based on an extensive survey of conditions among Native Americans. Its report, Senate Report 310, demonstrated intense congressional opposition to Collier and the programs of the Indian Bureau. Its recommendations read like a preview of the termination era and include a freeze in hiring for the Indian Bureau, the transfer of bureau functions to various federal agencies (or, in the case of education and probate matters, to the states), all with the long-range goal of eliminating the bureau.

24. James T. Patterson, *Congressional Conservatism and the New Deal: The Growth of the Conservative Coalition in Congress, 1933–1938* (Lexington: University of Kentucky Press, 1967), 116.

25. W. M. Blackhawk to the Senate Appropriations Committee, 12 December 1936, Elmer Thomas Collection, box 55.

26. Raymond H. Kemp to Elmer Thomas, 23 April 1937, Elmer Thomas Collection, box 10.

27. William Zimmerman to Elmer Thomas, 3 June 1937, Elmer Thomas Collection, box 10.

28. William Zimmerman to Elmer Thomas, 17 August 1937, Elmer Thomas Collection, box 10.

29. Haskell Paul to Elmer Thomas, 14 June 1937, Elmer Thomas Collection, box 10.

30. Congress, Senate, Subcommittee of the Committee on Indian Affairs, *Survey of the Conditions of Indians in the United States*, 76th Cong., 1st sess., 1940, 21311.

31. Ben Dwight, "The Oklahoma Indian Welfare Act—What It Can Do; What We Must Do," *Indians at Work*, June 15, 1937, 11, 13.

32. Congress, Senate, Subcommittee of the Committee on Indian Affairs, *Survey of the Conditions of Indians in the United States*, 76th Cong., 1st sess., 1940, 21264.

33. Ibid.

34. Ibid., 21335.

35. Alison R. Bernstein, *American Indians and World War II: Toward a New Era in Indian Affairs* (Norman: University of Oklahoma Press, 1991), 8.

36. Congress, Senate, Subcommittee of the Committee on Indian Affairs, *Survey of the Conditions of the Indians of the United States*, 21283.

37. Ibid.

38. Ibid., 21286.

39. Ibid., 21336.

40. Theodore W. Taylor, *Report on Purchase of Indian Land and Acres of Indian Land in Trust 1934–1975* (Washington, D.C.: American Indian Policy Review Commission, 1976), 5.

41. Ibid., 53.

42. Act of June 26, 1936, 49 Stat. 196.

43. Quoted in Taylor, *Report on Purchase of Indian Land*, 22.

44. Angie Debo, "What Oklahoma Indians Need," *American Indian Quarterly* 4 (Winter 1950), 85.

45. Wilma Mankiller and Michael Wallis, *Mankiller: A Chief and Her People* (New York: St. Martin's Press, 1993), 63–74.

46. Bernstein, *American Indians and World War II*, 15.

47. Morris W. Foster, *Being Comanche: A Social History of an American Indian Community* (Tucson: University of Arizona Press, 1989) remains a classic in this area of inquiry with Oklahoma Indians.

48. Quoted in William H. Kelly, *Indian Affairs and the Indian Reorganization Act: The Twenty Year Record* (Tucson: University of Arizona Press, 1954), 2.

49. Act of June 26, 1936, 49 Stat. 196.

50. Ibid.

51. Angie Debo, "Present Tribal Organization," unpublished, no date, 25, box 25.

52. "Harjo v. Kleppe," in *420 Federal Supplement* (St. Paul: West Publishing, 1977), 1133.

53. Ibid., 1135–36.

54. David H. Getches, Charles F. Wilkinson, and Robert A. Williams, Jr., *Cases and Materials on Federal Indian Law* (St. Paul: West Group, 1998), 189.

55. Act of June 26, 1936, 49 Stat. 196. Italics added for emphasis.

56. American Indian Policy Review Commission, *Report on Tribal Government*, (Washington, D.C., 1977), 336.

57. Theodore Haas, *Ten Years of Tribal Government Under the IRA* (Washington, D.C.: U.S. Indian Service, 1947), 28. This study, one of a small handful compiled to explore the impact of the IRA, continues to be widely cited by scholars exploring the Indian New Deal. Haas's work is an objective statistical study examining the evolution of tribal governments under the IRA and the OIWA. However, it presents an antiseptic picture. Haas shows the forest, but not the trees.

58. Debo, "What Oklahoma Indians Need," 85.

59. Kenneth R. Philp, "Oklahoma Indian Reform in Crisis: John Collier & the Thomas-Rogers Act," in *Hard Times in Oklahoma*, ed. Kenneth E. Hendrickson (Oklahoma City, Oklahoma Historical Society, 1983), 163.

60. Blue Clark, *Indian Tribes of Oklahoma a Guide* (Norman: University of Oklahoma, 2009), 62, 93, 107, 210, 323.

61. Loretta Fowler, "Local-Level Politics and the Struggle for Self-Government," in *The Struggle for Political Autonomy: Papers and Comments from the Second Newberry Library Conference on Themes in American Indian History* (Chicago: Newberry Library, 1989), 130.

62. Morris E. Opler, "The Creek Indians Towns of Oklahoma in 1937," In *Papers in Anthropology*, ed. Harold N. Ottaway (Norman: University of Oklahoma, 1972), 6.

63. Ibid., 96.

64. Ibid., 7.

65. Ibid., 8.

66. Allogan Slagle, *Burning Phoenix* (Tahlequah, Okla.?: A. Slagle, 1993), 3–13.

67. James Olson and Raymond Wilson, *Native Americans in the Twentieth Century* (Urbana: University of Illinois Press, 1986), 122.

68. Manda Starr to F. E. Perkins, 30 August 1937, Shawnee Agency, entry 44, box 1, record group 75, National Archives and Records Administration, Southwest Region (Ft. Worth).

69. F. E. Perkins to John Collier, 2 September 1936, Shawnee Agency; entry 44, box 1, record group 75; National Archives and Records Administration, Southwest Region (Ft. Worth).

70. Kenneth R. Philp, "Termination: A Legacy of the Indian New Deal," *Western Historical Quarterly* 14 (April 1983), 172–73.

71. Duane Champagne, "American Indian Values and the Institutionalization of IRA Governments," in *American Indian Policy and Cultural Values: Conflict and Accommodation*, ed. Jennie R. Joe (Los Angeles: American Indian Studies Center, 1986), 25.

72. Bernstein, *American Indians and World War II*, 8.

73. Carter Blue Clark, "How Bad It Really Was before World War II: Sovereignty," *Oklahoma City University Law Review* 23 (Fall 1998): 187.

74. Fowler, "Local-Level Politics," 130.

75. Champagne, "American Indian Values and the Institutionalization of IRA Governments," 28.

76. Philp, "Termination," 172.

77. Ibid., Congress, Senate, Subcommittee of the Committee on Indian Affairs, *Survey of the Conditions of Indians in the United States*, 76th Cong., 1st sess., Washington, D.C., 1940), 21338.

78. Ibid., 21345.

79. Ibid., 21353.

80. Ibid., 21350.

81. A. C. Monahan to John Collier, 12 January 1937, entry 44, box 4, Indian Credit Associations, record group 75, National Archives and Records Administration, Southwest Region (Ft. Worth).

82. U.S. Department of the Interior, Indian Field Service, "Statement of Policy Affecting Revolving Credit Loans in Oklahoma, 31 January 1938," 1, entry 44, box 4, Indian Credit Associations, record group 75, National Archives and Records Administration, Southwest Region (Ft. Worth).

83. Ibid., 2.

84. Elmer Thomas to Hazel Jack, 13 December 1937, Elmer Thomas Collection, box 10.

85. "Annual Report and Suggestions of the Activities of the Grady County Indian Credit Association, From October 22, 1937 to October 22, 1938," by J. E. Jones, secretary treasurer, Elmer Thomas Collection, box 10.

86. *Daily Oklahoman*, 11 May 1938, 17.

87. A. C. Monahan to John Collier, 1 July 1938, entry 44, box 4, Indian Credit Associations, record group 75, National Archives and Records Administration, Southwest Region (Ft. Worth).

88. Thompson Tucker to Elmer Thomas, 13 January 1938, Elmer Thomas Collection, box 10.

89. Thomas Halfmoon to Elmer Thomas, 17 August 1938, Elmer Thomas Collection, box 10.

90. Richard Colbert to Elmer Thomas, 8 July 1938, Elmer Thomas Collection, box 10.

91. Ibid.

92. Ibid.

93. F. E. Perkins, Superintendent of Five Civilized Tribes, to District Agents, Field Clerks, and Farm Agents, 22 November 1938, entry 573, box 1, Five Tribes Agency, record group 75, National Archives and Records Administration, Southwest Region (Ft. Worth).

94. John Collier, "Decentralization," *Indians at Work*, no date, 22. This issue, printed most likely in 1936, was devoted entirely to the implementation of the IRA and is a valuable resource as to programs, activities, and progress of implementation efforts to that date.

95. Quoted in William H. Kelly, ed., *Indian Affairs and the Indian Reorganization Act*, 33.

96. Angie Debo, "Indian Assimilation", unpublished, no date, 13, Angie Debo Collection, box 25.

97. Debo, "What Oklahoma Indians Need," *American Indian* 4 (Winter 1950), 83–84.

98. Department of the Interior, Office of Indian Affairs, Division of Extension and Industry, "Monthly Report of Extension Workers, Shawnee Indian Agency," December 1936, January 1937, March 1937, and August 1937, entry 73, box 57, Shawnee Indian Agency, record group 75, National Archives and Records Administration, Southwest Region (Ft. Worth).

99. Department of the Interior, Division of Extension and Industry, *Supervisor's Report*, by Ira T. Goddard, May 1941, entry 573, box 1, Five Civilized Tribes Agency, record group 75, National Archives and Records Administration, Southwest Region (Ft. Worth).

100. Bernstein, *American Indians and World War II*, 15.

101. Angie Debo, *The Five Civilized Tribes of Oklahoma* (Philadelphia: Indian Rights Association, 1951), 11–12.

102. Debo, "What Oklahoma Indians Need," 87.

103. James Kahdot to Elmer Thomas, 23 February 1939, entry 44, box 4, Indian Credit Associations, record group 75, National Archives and Records Administration, Southwest Region (Ft. Worth).

104. Albert Attocknie and Felix Kowano to Commissioner of Indian Affairs, 9 May 1949, Toby Morris Collection, Carl Albert Center, University of Oklahoma, Norman, box 9.

105. Quoted in Angie Debo, *Lowdown on Credit—Western Area*, unpublished notes, 30 June 1956, Angie Debo Collection, box 22.

106. Ibid.

107. John Collier to Jed Johnson, 16 May 1939, Five Tribes Agency, entry 573, box 2, record group 75, National Archives and Records Administration, Southwest Region (Ft. Worth).

108. Department of the Interior, *Extension and Credit* (Muskogee, Okla.: Five Tribes Agency, 1988), 42–43, Angie Debo Collection, box 25.

109. Ibid.

CONCLUSION

1. Collier, *From Every Zenith*, 224.

2. Thomas W. Cowger, *The National Congress of American Indians* (Lincoln: University of Nebraska Press, 1999), 40–44.

3. Fowler, "Local Level Politics and the Struggle for Self-Government," 128–31.

4. Clark, "The New Deal for Indians, 80.

5. Ibid.

6. Kenneth Philp, *Termination Revisited: American Indians on the Trail to Self-Determination, 1933–1953* (Lincoln: University of Nebraska Press, 1999), 11.

7. Debo, "Present Tribal Organization," 33.

8. Carter Blue Clark, "How Bad It Really Was before World War II: Sovereignty," 188.

9. Bernstein, *American Indian and World War II*, 15.

10. Clark, "The New Deal for Indians," 80.

11. For purposes of this discussion, Elmer Rusco's definition of ideology, "the structure of ideas, which determine the meanings ascribed to particular events," will be utilized. Rusco, *A Fateful Time*, xiii.

12. Graham D. Taylor, *The New Deal and American Indian Tribalism* (Lincoln: University of Nebraska Press, 1980) offers an in-depth analysis of the evolution of the ideology that underpinned and affected the actions of players involved in the Indian New Deal.

13. Brinkley, *The End of Reform*, 5.

14. Congress, Senate, Committee on Indian Affairs, "Survey of Conditions Among the Indians of the United States," report prepared by Elmer Thomas, 78th Cong., 1st Sess., 1943, 19–21.

15. Congress, Senate, Committee on Indian Affairs, "Survey of Conditions Among the Indians of the United States-Supplemental Report," report prepared by Elmer Thomas, 78th Cong., 2nd Sess., 1944, 1; also see Anthony Godfrey, "Congressional-Indian Politics: Senate Survey of Conditions Among the Indians of the United State," PhD diss., University of Utah, 1985.

16. Christopher Riggs, "American Indians, Economic Development, and Self-Determination in the 1960s," *Pacific Historical Review* 69 (August 2000): 434.

BIBLIOGRAPHY

MANUSCRIPT COLLECTIONS

Carl Albert Congressional Research and Studies Center, University of Oklahoma, Norman
    Elmer Thomas Collection
    Toby Morris Collection
    Wilburn Cartwright Collection
Oklahoma Historical Society, Oklahoma City
    Indian and Pioneer Papers Collection
Oklahoma State University, Stillwater
    Angie Debo Collection
Western History Collections, University of Oklahoma Libraries, Norman
    Cyrus Harris Collection
    Doris Duke Collection
    Edmund McCurtain Collection
    John Collier Papers

GOVERNMENT DOCUMENTS

Court Decision

"Harjo v. Kleppe." In *420 Federal Supplement* (St. Paul: West Publishing, 1977), 1110–47.

Department of the Interior

Bureau of Indian Affairs, Division of Extension and Industry. "Monthly Report of Extension Workers, Shawnee Indian Agency." December 1936; January, March, and August 1937. National Archives and Records Administration, Southwest Region (Ft. Worth), entry 73, box 57, record group 75.

Bureau of Indian Affairs, Division of Extension and Industry. *Supervisor's May 1941 Report*. National Archives and Records Administration, Southwest Region (Ft. Worth), entry 573, box 1, record group 75.

Bureau of Indian Affairs. *Indian Credit Associations*. National Archives and Records Administration, Southwest Region (Ft. Worth), entry 44, box 4, record group 75.

Bureau of Indian Affairs. "Individual Weekly Report for Extension Workers, for Aug 4, 1934, Concho Agency." National Archives and Records Administration, Southwest Region (Ft. Worth), entry 78, box 2, record group 75.

Bureau of Indian Affairs. "Individual Weekly Report for Extension Workers for Aug 27, 1936, Concho Agency." National Archives and Records Administration, Southwest Region (Ft. Worth), entry 77, box 71, record group 75.

Laws

The Indian Reorganization Act. *United States Statutes at Large*, 48, 984, PL 74-355.

The Oklahoma Indian Welfare Act. *United States Statutes at Large*, 49, 1967, PL 74-816.

U.S. Congress

House. Committee on Indian Affairs. *Hearings before the House Committee on Indian Affairs on HR 3645*. 73rd Cong., 2nd Sess., 6 March 1934.

House. Committee on Indian Affairs. *Readjustment of Indian Affairs*. 73rd Cong., 2nd Sess., 13 March 1934.

House. *Congressional Record*. 7 June 1934, 11121-26.

Senate. Committee on Indian Affairs. *Hearings Pursuant to H. Resolution 348*. 68th Cong., 1st Sess., March 1925.

Senate. Committee on Indian Affairs. *Hearings on Senate 2755, to Grant Indians Living under Federal Tutelage the Freedom of Organizing for Purposes of Local Self-Government and Economic Enterprise*. 73rd Cong., 2nd Sess., October 1934.

Senate. Committee on Indian Affairs. *Indian Affairs in Oklahoma*. 68th Cong., 2nd, Sess., October 1925.

Senate. Committee on Indian Affairs. *Survey of the Conditions of the Indians of the United States*. 78th Cong., 1st Sess., 1943.

Senate. Committee on Indian Affairs. *Survey of the Conditions of the Indians of the United States-Supplemental Report*. 78th Cong., 2nd Sess., 1944.

Senate. Committee on Indian Affairs. *Tax-Exempt Indian Lands*. 71st Cong., 2nd Sess., 13 February 1933.

Senate. Committee on Indian Affairs. *To Promote the General Welfare of the Indians of Oklahoma*. 74th Cong., 1st Sess., 9 April 1935.

Senate. "Condition of the Indians in the United States," speech by Senator William H. King, *Senate Document No. 2712*. 72nd Cong., 1st Sess., 8 March 1933.

Senate. Subcommittee of the Committee on Indian Affairs. *Survey of Conditions of the Indians in the United States*. 71st Cong., 2nd Sess., 11 November 1930.

Senate. Subcommittee of the Committee on Indian Affairs. *Survey of Conditions of the Indians in the United States.* 76th Cong., 1st Sess., 1940.

NEWSPAPERS

Bartlesville Examiner. 14 May 1925; 12 March 1934.
Cherokee Advocate. 30 September 1871; 7 February 1894.
Daily Oklahoman. 11 November 1928; 10 January 1931; 28 February 1934; 11 August 1934; 2 October 1934; 12 April 1935; 14 January 1937; 11 May 1938.
Harlow's Weekly, 4 February 1932; 11 November 1932; 1 April 1933; 17 March 1934; 28 April 1934; 16 June 1934; 13, 20, 21, 27 October 1934.
Indiana Republican. 16 June 1931.
Okemah Daily Leader. 7 April 1935.
Okmulgee Daily Times. 5 April 1945.
Muskogee Daily Phoenix. 18 November 1933; 31 March 1934; 15 October 1934.
Muskogee News. 12 May 1925.
Muskogee Times Democrat. 17 March 1934.
Red Fork (Okla.) Derrick. 24 June 1905.
Tulsa Daily World. 12 May 1925; 6 April 1935.
Tulsa Tribune. 10 March 1934; 16 February 1934.
The Tuskahomman. 15 August 1933; 5, 12, 26 March 1934; 9, 30 April 1934; 16 April 1935; 21 May 1935; 26 November 1935.

BOOKS, DISSERTATIONS, AND PUBLISHED GOVERNMENT REPORTS

American Indian Policy Review Commission. *Report on Tribal Government.* Washington, D.C.: American Indian Policy Review Commission, 1977.
Baird, David W., and Danney Goble. *The Story of Oklahoma.* Norman: University of Oklahoma Press, 1994.
Bays, Brad A. *Townsite Settlement and Dispossession in the Cherokee Nation, 1866–1907.* New York: Garland Press, 1988.
Bernstein, Alison R. *American Indians and World War II: Toward a New Era in Indian Affairs.* Norman: University of Oklahoma Press, 1991.
Bonnin, Gertrude, Charles H. Fabens, and Matthew K. Sniffen. *Oklahoma's Poor Rich Indians: An Orgy of Graft and Exploitation of the Five Civilized Tribes—Legalized Robbery.* Philadelphia: Indian Rights Association, 1924.
Brinkley, Alan. *The End of Reform: New Deal Liberalism in Recession and War.* New York: Random House, 1996.
Burton, Jeffrey. *Indian Territory and the United States, 1866–1906.* Norman: University of Oklahoma Press, 1995.
Chang, David A. *The Color of the Land: Race, Nation, and the Politics of Landownership in Oklahoma, 1832–1929.* Chapel Hill. University of North Carolina Press, 2010.

Clark, Blue. *Indian Tribes of Oklahoma: A Guide*. Norman: University of Oklahoma Press, 2009.

Cohen, Felix. *Handbook of Federal Indian Law*. Albuquerque: University of New Mexico Press, 1976.

Collier, John. *From Every Zenith: A Memoir and Some Essays on Life and Thought*. Denver: Sage Books, 1963.

Cowger, Thomas. *The National Congress of American Indians*. Lincoln: University of Nebraska Press, 1999.

Cronan, William. *Changes in the Land: Indians, Colonists, and the Ecology of New England*. New York: Hill and Wang, 1983.

Debo, Angie. *And Still the Waters Run: The Betrayal of the Five Civilized Tribes*. Princeton: Princeton University Press, 1991.

———. *The Five Civilized Tribes of Oklahoma*. Philadelphia: Indian Rights Association, 1951.

———. *A History of the Indians of the United States*. Revised ed. Norman: University of Oklahoma Press, 1983. First published 1970.

———. *The Road to Disappearance*. Norman: University of Oklahoma Press, 1941.

Deloria, Vine, Jr. *The Indian Reorganization Act: Congresses and Bills*. Norman: University of Oklahoma Press, 2002.

Deloria, Vine, Jr., and Clifford Lytle. *The Nations Within: The Past and Future of American Indian Sovereignty*. New York: Pantheon Books, 1984.

Edwards, Whit. *The Prairie Was on Fire*. Oklahoma City: Oklahoma Historical Society, 2001.

Foster, Morris W. *Being Comanche: A Social History of an American Indian Community*. Tucson: University of Arizona Press, 1998.

Fowler, Loretta. *Tribal Sovereignty and the Historical Imagination Cheyenne-Arapaho Politics*. Lincoln: University of Nebraska Press, 2002.

Getches, David H, Charles Wilkinson, and Robert A. Williams, Jr. *Cases and Materials on Federal Indian Law*. 4th ed. St. Paul: West Group, 1998.

Gibson, Arrell M. *Oklahoma: A History of Five Centuries*. Norman: Harlow, 1972.

Goble, Danney. *Progressive Oklahoma: The Making of a New Kind of State*. Norman: University of Oklahoma Press, 1980.

Haas, Theodore. *Ten Years of Tribal Government under the IRA*. Washington, D.C.: U.S. Indian Service, 1947.

Holm, Thomas. *The Great Confusion in Indian Affairs: Whites in the Progressive Era*. Austin: University of Texas Press, 2005.

Hoxie, Frederick E. *A Final Promise: The Campaign to Assimilate the Indian, 1880–1920*. Lincoln: University of Nebraska Press, 1984.

Ickes, Harold L. *The Secret Diary of Harold L. Ickes: The First Thousand Days, 1933–1936*. New York: Simon and Schuster, 1954.

Iverson, Peter. *"We Are Still Here": American Indians in the Twentieth Century*. Wheeling, Ill.: Harlan Davidson, 1998.

Kappler, Charles J. *Laws Relating to the Five Civilized Tribes in Oklahoma, 1890–1914*. Washington, D.C.: Government Printing Office, 1915.

———. *Treaties and Agreements of the Eastern Oklahoma Indians*. Washington, D.C.: Government Printing Office, 1903.

Kelly, Lawrence C. *The Assault on Assimilation: John Collier and the Origins of Indian Policy Reform*. Albuquerque: University of New Mexico Press, 1983.

Kelly, William H., ed. *Indian Affairs and the Indian Reorganization Act: The Twenty-Year Record*. Tucson: University of Arizona Press, 1954.

Leeds, Georgia Rae. *The United Keetoowah Band of Cherokee Indians in Oklahoma*. New York: Peter Lang, 1996.

Mankiller, Wilma, and Michael Wallis. *Mankiller: A Chief and Her People*. New York: St. Martin's Press, 1993.

Meriam, Lewis, et. al. *The Problem of Indian Administration*. Washington, D. C.: Institute for Government Research, 1928.

Miner, H. Craig. *The Corporation and the Indian Tribal Sovereignty and Industrial Civilization in Indian Territory, 1865–1910*. Columbia: University of Missouri Press, 1976.

Moquin, Wayne, and Charles Van Doren, eds. *Great Documents in American Indian History*. New York: Praeger, 1973.

Mott, M. L. *A National Blunder*. Washington, D.C.: 1924.

Moulton, Gary E. *John Ross: Cherokee Chief*. Athens: University of Georgia Press, 1978.

Olson, James and Raymond Wilson. *Native Americans in the Twentieth Century*. Urbana: University of Illinois Press, 1986.

Opler, Morris E. *The Creek Indian Towns of Oklahoma in 1937*. Norman: University of Oklahoma Press, 1937.

Parman, Donald. *Indians in the American West in the Twentieth Century*. Bloomington: University of Indiana Press, 1994.

Patterson, James T. *Congressional Conservatism and the New Deal: The Growth of the Conservative in Congress*. Lexington: University of Kentucky Press, 1967.

Perdue, Theda. *Nations Remembered: An Oral History of the Cherokees, Chickasaws, Choctaws, Creeks, and Seminoles of Oklahoma, 1865–1907*. Norman: University of Oklahoma Press, 1993.

Philp, Kenneth R. *John Collier's Crusade for Indian Reform 1920–1954*. Tucson: University of Arizona Press, 1977.

———. *Termination Revisited: American Indians on the Trail to Self-Determination, 1933–1953*. Lincoln: University of Nebraska Press, 1999.

Prucha, Francis Paul. *American Indian Policy in Crisis: Christian Reformers and the Indian, 1865–1900*. Norman: University of Oklahoma Press, 1976.

———. *The Great Father: The United States Government and the American Indians*. Lincoln: University of Nebraska Press, 1984.

Richter, Daniel K. *Facing East from Indian Country: A Native History of Early America*. Cambridge, Mass.: Harvard University Press, 2001.

Rozema, Vicki. *Voices from the Trail of Tears*. Winston-Salem, N.C.: John F. Blair, 2003.

Rusco, Elmer. *A Fateful Time: The Background and Legislative History of the Indian Reorganization Act*. Reno: University of Nevada Press, 2000.

Slagle, Allogan. *Burning Phoenix*. Tahlequah, Okla.?: A. Slagle, 1993.

Sniffin, Matthew K. *Out of Thine Own Mouth: An Analysis of the House Subcommittee Report Denying and Confirming the Looting of Oklahoma's "Poor Rich Indians."* Philadelphia: Indian Rights Association, 1925.

Strickland, Rennard. *Indians of Oklahoma.* Norman: University of Oklahoma Press, 1980.

Stuart, Paul. *Nations Within a Nation: Historical Statistics of American Indians.* Westport, Conn.: Badger Press, 1987.

Sturm, Circe. *Blood Politics: Race, Culture, and Identity in the Cherokee Nation of Oklahoma.* Berkeley: University of California Press, 2001.

Taylor, Graham D. *The New Deal and American Indian Tribalism: The Administration of the Indian Reorganization Act, 1934–1945.* Lincoln: University of Nebraska Press, 1980.

Taylor, Theodore W. *Report on Purchase of Indian Land and Acres of Indian Land in Trust 1934–1975.* Washington, D.C.: American Indian Policy Review Commission, 1976.

Thorne, Tanis C. *The World's Richest Indian: The Scandal over Jackson Barnett's Oil Fortune.* New York: Oxford University Press, 2003.

Warde, Mary Jane. *George Washington Grayson and the Creek Nation, 1843–1920.* Norman: University of Oklahoma Press, 1999.

Wheeler, Burton K. *Yankee from the West.* New York: Doubleday, 1962.

Wickett, Murray. *Contested Territory: Whites, Native Americans, and African Americans in Oklahoma, 1865–1907.* Baton Rouge: Louisiana State University Press, 2000.

Wilson, Terry P. *The Underground Reservation: Osage Oil.* Lincoln: University of Nebraska Press, 1985.

Wright, Muriel H. *A Guide to the Indian Tribes of Oklahoma.* Norman: University of Oklahoma Press, 1951.

Yarbrough, Fay. *Race and the Cherokee Nation: Sovereignty in the Nineteenth Century.* Philadelphia: University of Pennsylvania Press, 2008.

Zissu, Erik M. *Blood Matters: The Five Civilized Tribes and the Search for Unity in the Twentieth Century.* New York: Routledge, 2001.

ARTICLES AND BOOK CHAPTERS

Benay, Blend. "The Indian Rights Association, the Allotment Policy, and the Five Civilized Tribes, 1923–1936." *American Indian Quarterly* 7 (Spring 1983): 67–80.

Berkey, Curtis. "John Collier and the Indian Reorganization Act." *American Indian Journal* 2 (July 1976): 2–7.

Champagne, Duane. "American Indian Values and the Institutionalization of IRA Governments." In *American Indian Policy and Cultural Values: Conflict and Accommodation,* edited by Jennie R. Joe, 25–31. Los Angeles: American Indian Studies Center, UCLA, 1986.

Clark, Carter Blue. "How Bad It Really Was before World War II: Sovereignty." *Oklahoma University Law Review* 23 (Fall 1998): 175–88.

———. "The New Deal for Indians." In *Between Two Worlds: Survival of Twentieth Century Indians*, edited by Arrell M. Gibson, 72–84. Oklahoma City: Oklahoma Historical Society, 1986.

Collier, John. "Oklahoma Indians and the Wheeler-Howard Act." *Indians at Work* 2 (October 1934): 2–3.

———. "The Red Atlantis." *Survey* 49 (October 1922): 15–20, 63, 65.

Debo, Angie. "What Oklahoma Indians Need," *The American Indian Quarterly* 4 (Winter 1950): 82–88.

Downes, Randolph C. "A Crusade for Indian Reform, 1922–1934." In *The American Indian, Past and Present*, edited by Roger L. Nichols and George R. Adams, 230–42. Lexington, Mass.: Xerox College Publishing, 1971.

Dwight, Ben. "The Oklahoma Indian Welfare Act—What It Can Do; What We Must Do." *Indians at Work* (June 1937): 9–12.

"Editorial." *Nation* 86 (26 April 1933): 459.

Fowler, Loretta. "Local-level Politics and the Struggle for Self-government." In *The Struggle for Political Autonomy, Papers and Comments from the Second Newberry Library Conference on Themes in American Indian History*, 25–32. Chicago: Newberry Library, 1989.

Hauptman, Lawrence M. "The American Indian Federation and the Indian New Deal: A Reinterpretation." *Pacific Historical Review* 52 (November 1983): 378–402.

Johnson, N. B. "The National Congress of American Indians." *Chronicles of Oklahoma* 30 (Summer 1952): 140–48.

Kelly, Lawrence C. "The Indian Reorganization Act: The Dream and the Reality." *Pacific Historical Review* 44 (May 1975): 291–312.

Kickingbird, Kirke, and Lynn Kickingbird. "Oklahoma Indian Jurisdiction: A Myth Unraveled." *American Indian Journal* 4 (Fall 1986): 26–43.

Lewis, David Rich. "Reservation Leadership and the Progressive-Traditional Dichotomy: William Walsh and the Northern Utes, 1865–1928." *Ethnohistory* 38, no. 2 (Spring 1991): 124–48.

Littlefield, Daniel F., Jr., and Lonnie E. Underhill. "The Crazy Snake Uprising of 1909: A Red, Black, or White Affair?" *Arizona and the West* 20 (Winter 1978): 307–24.

Meredith, Howard. "Native Response: Rural Indian People in Oklahoma, 1909–1939." In *Rural Oklahoma*, edited by Donald E. Greed, 74–84. Oklahoma City: Oklahoma Historical Society, 1977.

Monahan, Forrest D., Jr. "Constitutions for the Indians: Trials and Tribulations for the Kiowa, Comanche, and Apache." In *Hard Times in Oklahoma: The Depression Years*, edited by Kenneth E. Hendrickson, 168–85. Oklahoma City: Oklahoma Historical Society, 1983.

Moore, John H. "The Enduring Reservations of Oklahoma." In *State and Reservation: New Perspectives on Federal Indian Policy*, edited by George Pierre Castile and Robert L. Bee, 92–109. Tucson: University of Arizona Press, 1992.

Nesbitt, Paul. "Governor Haskell Tells of Two Conventions." *Chronicles of Oklahoma* 14 (June 1936): 18–217.

Parman, Donald. "Twentieth-Century Indian History: Achievements, Needs, and Problems." *OAH Magazine of History* 9 (Fall 1994): 10–16.

Perdue, Theda. "The Conflict Within: Cherokees and Removal." *Georgia Historical Quarterly* 73, no. 3 (Fall 1989): 467–91.

Philp, Kenneth. "Indian Reform in Crisis: John Collier and the Thomas-Rogers Act." In *Hard Times in Oklahoma: The Depression Years* edited by Kenneth E. Hendrickson, 168–85. Oklahoma City: Oklahoma Historical Society, 1983.

———. "Termination: A Legacy of the Indian New Deal." *Western Historical Quarterly* 14 (April 1983): 165–80.

Pipestem, F. Browning, and William G. Rice. "The Mythology of the Oklahoma Indians: A Survey of the Legal Status of Indian Tribes in Oklahoma," *American Indian Law Review* (1978): 259–358.

Quinton, B. T. "Oklahoma Tribes, The Great Depression." In *The American Indian Past and Present*, edited by Roger L. Nichols and George R. Adams, 179–98. Lexington, Mass.: Xerox College Publishing, 1971.

Riggs, Christopher. "American Indians, Economic Development and Self- Determination in the 1960s." *Pacific Historical Review* 69 (August 2000): 431–63.

Schwartz, E. A. "Red Atlantis Revisited: Community and Culture in the Writings of John Collier." *American Indian Quarterly* 18 (Fall 1994): 507–31.

Seymour, Flora Warren. "Trying It on the Indians." *New Outlook*, May 1934, 39–46.

Smith, Michael T. "The Wheeler-Act of 1934: The Indian New Deal." *Journal of the West* 10 (November 1970): 521–34.

Sniffin, Matthew K. "Stop, Look—and Consider." *Indian Truth* (March 1934): 2–7.

Strickland, Rennard. "Genocide-At-Law." *Kansas Law Review* 34 (Summer 1986): 715–49.

Wright, Muriel H. "The Indian Situation Is Perplexing in Eastern Oklahoma." *American Indian* 5 (May 1927): 3–12.

Wright, Peter M. "John Collier and the Oklahoma Indian Welfare Act of 1936." *Chronicles of Oklahoma* 50 (August 1972): 347–71.

INDEX

Act of March 1, 1895, 23
Act of March 3, 1905, 30
Act of May 27, 1908 ("Crime of 1908"), 29, 34–35
Act of July 4, 1894, 18
Adair County Indian Credit Association, 142–43
Agricultural Adjustment Act, 57, 122–23
Alabama-Quassarte Tribal Town, 134
Alford, Thomas W., 68
Allotment, 21–22, 44, 56–57, 60, 77, 81, 130, 150, 153
American Indian Association, 33
American Indian Defense Association (AIDA), 34, 52, 58
American Indian Federation, 62, 97, 149, 151
American Indian Policy Review Commission, 132
American Red Cross, 46, 119
Anadarko, Okla., conference, 86–88
Anadarko, Okla., congress, 64–65, 70
Apes, William, 3
Appropriations Act of 1897, 24
Appropriations for Indian affairs, 38, 46, 129
Arapaho, Ute, 72
Arkansas state legal codes, 24
Ashurst, Henry, 69

Assimilation, 8, 36, 38, 43, 45, 52, 54, 71, 77, 86, 12, 125, 129, 153–56
Association of Oklahoma Indians, 33
Atkins, J. D., 21
Atoka Agreement (1896), 23
Attocknie, Albert, 87–88, 144
Attwood, Stella, 51

Battiest, Sina, 35
Bedoka, Morris, 64
Blackbird, W. H., 98
Blackfox, Ned, 96
Blackhawk, W. M., 123
Blood quantum, 29, 91–92, 102, 139
Board of Indian Commissioners, 56, 59, 100
Bonnin, Gertrude, 34
Boosterism, 18
Boren, Lyle, 126
Boudinot, Elias, 15
Bronson, Ruth Muskrat, 150
Bruner, Joseph, 62, 73–74, 95–97, 147, 151
Bryan, William Jennings, 45
Buffalow, Ben, 118
Burbank oil field, 31
Burdick, Usher, 101
Bureau of the Budget, 122
Burke, Charles H., 34, 52

Burke Act (1906), 37
Bursom Bill, 51–52, 79
Butrick, Daniel, 12, 15

Canard, Roly, 96, 99, 132, 138
Chambers, John Hugh, 117
Chapman, Henry, 85
Charters for incorporation, 133
Chavez, Dennis, 51
Cherokee Nation v. Southern Kansas RR (1889), 18
Choctaw-Chickasaw Protective League, 93
Civilian Conservation Corps, 57
Civil War, 12, 15–17
Cleveland, Grover, 23
Cloud, Henry Roe, 65
Cobb, Guy, 28
Cohen, Felix S., 24, 57, 62, 67, 70, 149
Colbert, Richard, 140–41
Commercialization, 12
Committee on Indian Affairs (House, Senate), 39–40, 90, 98
Concho, Okla., conference, 85–86
Connolly, Vera, 61
Coolidge, Calvin, 38
Cosmos Club, 58, 63
Cotton culture, 13, 16
Coughlin, Father Charles E., 60
County Bar Associations, 93, 97
Court of Indian Affairs, 60, 69, 77
Court packing scheme, 122–23
Crazy Snake Rebellion, 27
Credit associations, 120
Creek tribal towns, 9, 134. *See also* Alabama-Quassarte Tribal Town; Kialegee Tribal Town; Thlopthlocco Tribal Town
Crozier, Lucy, 49
Curtis Act, 10, 24, 26, 128, 131, 154

Davis, Frank, 47
Dawes, Henry L., 23
Dawes Act, 22, 55, 91, 154. *See also* General Allotment Act of 1887
Dawes Commission, 22, 24, 26, 32

Disney, Wesley, 7, 9, 48, 89, 100–103, 126, 149
Dodge, Mabel, 50
Donahey, Vic, 96
Dunlap, Robert, 87
Durant, William A., 40, 42, 82
Dust Bowl, 40, 118
Dwight, Ben, 42, 125, 127, 156

Eastern Oklahoma opposition, 58–59, 62, 80, 94
Economic cooperatives, 139, 142–43
Ellison, Edward F., 144–45
Ex Parte Crow Dog (1883), 23

Fabens, Charles, H., 35
Fall, Albert B., 51
Farm Extension Service, 141–43, 145
Federal Emergency Relief Administration, 57
Five Tribes Act of 1906, 26, 134
Four Mothers Society, 26
Frazier, Lynn, 96
Freedmen, 18
Friends of the Indians, 21, 35, 45

Garvin County Indian Credit Association, 124
General Allotment Act (1887), 37, 128
General Federation of Women's Clubs, 33–34, 51–55, 58, 60
Government food commodities, 118–19
Grady County Indian Credit Association, 139
Grafting, 28, 35
Great Depression, 11, 38, 40, 43–44, 60, 117, 160
Grounds, Charles, 138
Growingham, Milford, 98
Guardian, 29–30, 35, 39

Haas, Theodore, 9
Hamilton Statehood Bill (1906), 27
Harjo, Chitto (Crazy Snake), 26
Harlin, James, 17
Harper, Alfred, 118

INDEX

Harris, Cyrus, 18
Haskell, Charles, 27
Hastings, William, 36, 48, 75–76, 100–102, 126
Hayes, Joseph, 82
Heflin, L. R., 92
Holtin, Curt, 45
Hoover, Herbert, 38, 45–46
House Concurrent Resolution 108 (HCR 108), 6
Howard, E. B., 48, 59, 67
Howard, James I., 94
Hunter, Thomas W., 138

Ickes, Harold, 49, 56, 63, 100–102, 149, 155
Indian Association of Oklahoma, 149
Indian boarding schools, 87–88
Indian conferences, 80, 88. *See also* Anadarko, Okla., conference; Concho, Okla., conference; Miami, Okla., conference; Muskogee, Okla., conference; Pawnee, Okla., conference
Indian congresses, 8, 64–72. *See also* Anadarko, Okla., congress; Miami, Okla., congress; Muskogee, Okla., congress
Indian education, 41, 55, 87–88
Indian exposition, Atlanta, Ga., 79
Indian health conditions, 41–42
Indian New Deal, 4–5, 8, 10–11, 32–33, 52–53, 56, 68, 73, 77–78, 80, 88, 95, 121–23, 130–31, 141, 147, 151–52, 157
Indian Removal Act, 3, 13, 15
Indian Reorganization Act (IRA), 4, 6, 9, 33, 45, 55, 58, 76, 78, 79, 120–21, 124, 127, 129–36, 141, 145, 147, 159–66. *See also* Wheeler-Howard Bill
Indian Rights Association, 33–34, 36–37, 44, 58, 63, 98, 100
Indian self-determination, 61, 130–31
Indian Territory, 12, 15–21, 26–27, 91, 128
Indian voice, 10, 48, 61, 149

Industrialization, 11
Irvine, A. L., 40

Jackson, Andrew, 3, 13
Jemison, Alice Lee, 100
Johnson, N. B., 150
Johnson County Indian Credit Association, 124
Johnston, D. H., 41
Johnston, Henry, 95
Jones, Frank O., 135–36

Kahdet, James, 93, 143–44
Keetoowah, 26, 133–35, 147
Kemp, Raymond H., 123
Kialegee Tribal Town, 134
King, William H., 48
Kinnard, Herbert, 142–43
Krier, W. V., 98

Labelle, E. H., 119
Landholdings, 29, 32, 43–44, 151
Land purchases, 70, 90, 92, 117, 120–22, 128, 130, 145, 153
Lane-Pomeroy Plan, 17
Lawlessness, 20
Leasing fees, 21
Lewis, Grady, 42, 97, 99
Lindley, Lawrence E., 100
Lindquist, Dr. C. C., 56, 59
Locke, V. M., 40
Loco, James, 88
Lone Wolf, Delos, 87
Lone Wolf v. Hitchcock (1903), 87
Lookout, Fred, 32, 95
Louisiana Purchase, 13
Love County Indian Credit Association, 140
Lyons Indian Cooperative Association, 142

Major Crimes Act (1885), 23–24
Margold, Nathan, 57, 62, 67, 70, 149
Matthews, A. P., 42
Matthews, John J., 95
Mauhuchu, Frank, 47

McCurtain, Edmund, 19, 40
McIntosh, Rolly, 26
McIntosh County Indian Credit Association, 133
McNickle, D'Arcy, 121
Merderano, Dan, 140
Merriam Report, 30, 38–40, 44, 155
Miami, Okla., conference, 83–85
Miami, Okla., congress, 64–66, 72
Milam, J. Hartley, 150
Monohan, A. C., 85, 87, 120, 139
Murray County Indian Credit Association, 139
Muskogee, Okla., conference, 80–81
Muskogee, Okla., congress, 64–65
Muskogee, Okla., meeting, 126–27

Nadeu, J. L., 119
National Association of Indian Affairs, 58
National Congress of American Indians (NCAI), 150
National Indian Confederacy, 62
National Industrial Recovery Act, 122–23
Nichols, Jack, 89, 95–98, 103
North Canadian Indian Credit Association, 144
Nowata County Indian Credit Association, 124

Oil boom, 31
Oklahoma Bar Association, 34
Oklahoma congressional delegation, 36, 44, 75, 78–79, 118–19
Oklahoma County Indian Credit Association, 139
Oklahoma Democratic Party Central Committee (Indian Division), 119
Oklahoma Education Association, 90
Oklahoma Enabling Act (1906), 27
Oklahoma Indian Credit Corporation, 92
Oklahoma Indian Welfare Act (OIWA), 4, 6, 11, 45, 33, 53, 82, 85, 103, 117–45, 147–57, 181–87. *See also* Thomas Rogers Bill

"Oklahoma Poor Rich Indians," 34
Oklahoma probate courts, 29–30, 35–37, 39, 90, 92, 102
Oklahoma state legislature, 94–95
Oklahoma Territory, 19, 27, 154
Organic Act (1890), 23
Osage Reservation, 31

Padgett, Jim, 19
Parker, Gabe, 47
Paul, Haskell, 124
Pawnee, Okla., conference, 81–83, 85
Per capita distributions, 40–41, 44
Perkins, F. E., 135
Permit fees, 20
Plain Indians, 20, 40, 144
Pontotoc Indian Credit Association, 140
Populism, 45
Porter, Pleasant, 24, 30
Posey, Alex, 26–27
Presidential election of 1932, 47–48
Public Law 280, 157
Public Works Administration, 57
Pueblo Indians, 50–51, 62

Railroad Retirement Act, 122–23
Railroads, 18
Ranchers, 21
Reconstruction, 12, 17–18
Reform movement, 21, 33–34, 49–53, 55, 66, 155
Relocation program, 129–30
Restrictions, 30, 35, 38–39, 91, 102
Revolving Credit Fund, 65, 70, 92, 121–22, 132
Rhoades, Charles J., 38
Ridge, John, 15
Ridge, Major, 15
Roberts, Henry, 85
Roberts, L. F., 94
Robertson, Joseph T., 48
Rogers, Jimmie, 90
Roosevelt, Franklin D. (FDR), 3, 47–49, 57, 78, 118, 122, 148, 156
Roosevelt, Theodore, 28
Ross, John, 15
Rowlodge, Jesse, 73

INDEX

Saluskin, James, 72
Saunkeah, Jasper, 64, 76
Scattergood, Joseph, 38
Schwartz, E. A., 8, 50–51
Senate Report 310, 156–57
Short, W. W., 150
Sequoyah Convention, 27
Seven Clan Society, 82, 134
Seymour, Flora Warren, 56, 59
Shawnee, Okla., meeting, 126
Sixkiller, J. E., 94
Slavery, 16–18
Snake band of Creeks, 26
Sniffen, Matthew K., 34, 36, 63
Social engineering, 49
Southern Sac and Fox Indian Credit Association, 144
Stand, Watie, 15
Starr, Manda, 135
Subsistence agriculture, 118, 128, 130

Tah, Owen, 85
Termination, 117, 154–56
Thirteenth Amendment, 17
Thlopthlocco Tribal Town, 134
Thomas-Rogers Bill, 5, 7, 31, 58, 62, 90, 93, 96–97, 101, 103, 139, 149, 167–80; House hearings, 98–102; Senate hearings, 96–98
Thompson, Verne E., 71
Tidwell, William, 42
Timber industry, 21
Trachoma, 41
Trail of Tears, 15
Treaty of New Echota, 13–15, 96
Tribal alternative, 8, 52, 54, 71, 77, 155–56
Tribal constitutions, 132–33, 136, 145, 151

Tribal corporations, 139
Tribal councils, 137
Tribal culture, 21
Tribal factionalism, 13–15, 16, 19–20, 36, 135–36, 144, 148
Tribal governments, 9–10, 20, 44, 70, 75, 92, 117, 119, 127, 130–32, 136–37, 188–90
Tribal landholdings, 21, 24, 32, 128, 146
Tribal membership rolls, 24
Tribal sovereignty, 23–24, 32, 77
Tuberculosis, 41

Unassigned lands, 22
Urbanization, 11
U.S. v. Kagama (1886), 23

Wage labor, 130
Wagoner County Indian Credit Association, 139–40
Wallen, S. E., 31, 34
Washington County Indian Credit Association, 140
Westward expansion, 12, 19
Wheeler, Burton K., 9, 55, 59, 67, 68, 71, 73, 76, 149, 156
Wheeler-Howard Bill, 3, 81, 83, 93, 121, 134; House hearings, 69–75; Senate hearings, 69–75
White Shirt, Chief, 86
Whitthorne, Angie, 118
Work, Hubert, 38
Works Progress Administration, 57
World War II, 11, 20, 127, 145, 152–53
Wright, Muriel, 43, 103

Zimmerman, William, 103, 119, 124

CPSIA information can be obtained at www.ICGtesting.com
Printed in the USA
LVOW12s1220240913

353883LV00004B/7/P